GHOST STRASSE

Away from Main Street, it has a threadbare gloom, an emptiness, and a sullen resistance to the tinctured tidiness of the West. In spite of the modern Western-built cars and the neon lighting, the East remains another country. It is sometimes like looking down a street of ruins, a street where nobody comes any more, a ghost strasse.

GHOST STRASSE

Germany's East Trapped Between Past and Present

SIMON BURNETT

BLACK
ROSE
BOOKS

Montreal/New York/London

CHRONOLOGY

1917—Russian Revolution. Bolsheviks take power. The Bolsheviks subsequently become the Communist Party.

1918—December 30-January 1, 1919: German Communist Party (KPD) founded.

1933—Nazis come to power in Germany.

1939—World War Two begins.

1945—The Big Three (Britain, United States, Soviet Union) meet at Yalta to discuss what to do with Germany after war ends; the Red Army marches into Berlin; Hitler commits suicide in bunker; World War II ends in defeat of Nazi Germany; Berlin divided into British, U.S., and Soviet sectors, with a French sector added later. But Berlin becomes an island inside the Soviet zone of occupation. Potsdam conference, where the Big Three discuss reparations.

1946—April: Social Democrat Party (SPD) in Soviet zone forced into merger with the KPD.

1948—June: German mark introduced in the three Western sectors of Berlin and in Western Germany. Soviets block land, water and rail access to Western sectors of Berlin. Round-the-clock airlift begins to keep the city supplied with essential goods.

1949—The western region of occupied Germany becomes West Germany (the Federal Republic of Germany), part of the political West. The Eastern region (the Soviet zone) becomes East Germany (the German Democratic Republic), part of the Soviet-dominated East Bloc. Soviets end blockade. Airlift ends.

1953—Workers in East Germany revolt in protest against higher production norms. Protests widen to include political demands. Soviet tanks take to streets and revolt ends.

1955—West Germany introduces Hallstein Doctrine, under which it refuses to grant diplomatic recognition to countries that recognize East Germany.

1958—Soviet leader Nikita Krushchev demands that Berlin become a demilitarized "free city." The Western Powers reject the idea.

1961—East Germany builds the Berlin Wall to prevent people heading West because of the much higher standard of living and political freedom. The border with West Germany is also fenced off.

1963—East Germany introduces economic reforms in a desperate, but futile, effort to improve its dismal economic performance.

1974—Willy Brandt, who ended the Hallstein Doctrine and introduced a more conciliatory policy toward East Germany, resigns as West German chancellor after a close aide, Guenter Guillaume, is revealed to be an East German spy.

1989—The Berlin Wall comes down.

1990—First East German free and democratic election is won by a center-right coalition. In October, Germany becomes unified.

GHOST STRASSE

Germany's East Trapped Between Past and Present

SIMON BURNETT

BLACK
ROSE
BOOKS

Montreal/New York/London

Black Rose Books No. JJ347

National Library of Canada Cataloguing in Publication Data

Burnett, Simon

Ghost strasse : Germany's East trapped between past and present / Simon Burnett

Includes bibliographical references and index.

ISBN: 1-55164-291-3 (bound)   ISBN: 1-55164-290-5 (pbk.)

(alternative ISBNs 9781551642918 [bound]   9781551642901 [pbk.])

1. Germany (East)--History. 2. Germany (East)--Politics and government.
3. Germany (East)--Social conditions. 4. Germany--History--Unification, 1990.
5. Germany--History--1990-. I. Title.

DD289.5.B87 2006   943'.1088   C2006-902800-1

Cover Photograph: Barber Shop Corner. The sign shows that a barber shop once occupied this site at the intersection of Stein Strasse and Gormann Strasse in the historic Scheunenviertel district of Eastern Berlin.

The author is grateful to Macmillan Ltd for their kind permission to use an excerpt from *Red Harvest*, by Dashiell Hammett (Chapter 5, page 34).

All photos—except where indicated—including the cover photo, are the property of the author.

BLACK ROSE BOOKS

C.P. 1258	2250 Military Road	99 Wallis Road
Succ. Place du Parc	Tonawanda, NY	London, E9 5LN
Montréal, H2X 4A7	14150	England
Canada	USA	UK

To order books:
In Canada: (phone) 1-800-565-9523 (fax) 1-800-221-9985
email: utpbooks@utpress.utoronto.ca

In United States: (phone) 1-800-283-3572 (fax) 1-651-917-6406

In the UK & Europe: (phone) 44 (0)20 8986-4854 (fax) 44 (0)20 8533-5821
email: order@centralbooks.com

Our Web Site address: http://www.blackrosebooks.net

Printed in Canada

TABLE OF CONTENTS

CHRONOLOGY

1917—Russian Revolution. Bolsheviks take power. The Bolsheviks subsequently become the Communist Party.

1918—December 30-January 1, 1919: German Communist Party (KPD) founded.

1933—Nazis come to power in Germany.

1939—World War Two begins.

1945—The Big Three (Britain, United States, Soviet Union) meet at Yalta to discuss what to do with Germany after war ends; the Red Army marches into Berlin; Hitler commits suicide in bunker; World War II ends in defeat of Nazi Germany; Berlin divided into British, U.S., and Soviet sectors, with a French sector added later. But Berlin becomes an island inside the Soviet zone of occupation. Potsdam conference, where the Big Three discuss reparations.

1946—April: Social Democrat Party (SPD) in Soviet zone forced into merger with the KPD.

1948—June: German mark introduced in the three Western sectors of Berlin and in Western Germany. Soviets block land, water and rail access to Western sectors of Berlin. Round-the-clock airlift begins to keep the city supplied with essential goods.

1949—The western region of occupied Germany becomes West Germany (the Federal Republic of Germany), part of the political West. The Eastern region (the Soviet zone) becomes East Germany (the German Democratic Republic), part of the Soviet-dominated East Bloc. Soviets end blockade. Airlift ends.

1953—Workers in East Germany revolt in protest against higher production norms. Protests widen to include political demands. Soviet tanks take to streets and revolt ends.

1955—West Germany introduces Hallstein Doctrine, under which it refuses to grant diplomatic recognition to countries that recognize East Germany.

1958—Soviet leader Nikita Krushchev demands that Berlin become a demilitarized "free city." The Western Powers reject the idea.

1961—East Germany builds the Berlin Wall to prevent people heading West because of the much higher standard of living and political freedom. The border with West Germany is also fenced off.

1963—East Germany introduces economic reforms in a desperate, but futile, effort to improve its dismal economic performance.

1974—Willy Brandt, who ended the Hallstein Doctrine and introduced a more conciliatory policy toward East Germany, resigns as West German chancellor after a close aide, Guenter Guillaume, is revealed to be an East German spy.

1989—The Berlin Wall comes down.

1990—First East German free and democratic election is won by a center-right coalition. In October, Germany becomes unified.

ACKNOWLEDGMENTS

THE AUTHOR IS GRATEFUL TO THE hundreds of East Germans prepared to speak to a complete stranger who murdered their language. Most of these meetings were casual encounters on trains, on the street, or in bars or restaurants; but many took place only after much time and effort on both sides.

Specifically, the author wants to thank Torsten Ruehrdanz, who not only told me his story but who also helped with some astute political insights and who, on many occasions, chauffeured me round Berlin.

Thanks to Sigrid Ruehrdanz, who always found time to talk about her imprisonment, and to the cheerful Hartmut Ruehrdanz, who was likewise incarcerated.

Thanks to the man who, against the odds, managed to survive imprisonment and torture, Hans-Joachim Helwig-Wilson, who was also kind enough to allow me to use photographs from his extensive collection.

I want to record my appreciation of another survivor against almost impossible odds, Horst Wiener, and of the lady with the combative spirit, Eva-Maria Storbeck.

Always helpful was the resilient and enthusiastic Ursula Popiolek, while Frank Kempe gave me sanctuary in his art atelier from a freezing Munich winter's day and told me how the East German state-sponsored smugglers stole his property.

My thanks are due to Michael Sobotta for retracing the protest marches through Dresden for me, and to his friend, Andreas Schulz, for turning up to talk at short notice.

Thanks to the doctor and former *Volkskammer* deputy, Burkhart Schneeweiss, for his diverse recollections, and to Cold War lawyer Wolfgang Vogel for his constant readiness to help.

Along the way I spoke to many pastors, but I owe special thanks to two: Alfred Scharnweber, of Boizenburg, and Wolfram Haedicke, of Ronneburg, both of whom gave me a lot of their time. Heinz Mueller, in Quedlinburg, spent much time digging into his treasure trove of a memory, while Werner Bley, deacon at the St. Servatius Church in Quedlinburg, was open and helpful.

Florian Havemann was generous with his time both before the 2002 general election, in which he was a candidate for the Party of Democratic Socialism (PDS) "reformed communists," and afterwards. Former Berlin party boss and Politburo member Guenter Schabowski was extremely obliging, while Wolfgang Leonhard told me what it was like to be on the run ahead of a Stasi hit squad. Michael Hinze, the man the Stasi wanted to kidnap, was good enough to find time for a chat. The cheerful Richard Peck explained how a private-enterprise retailer survived under the communists.

I spent an informative evening in a Magdeburg bar listening to Lothar Lienicke and Franz Bludau talking about the life and death of Michael Gartenschlaeger. Lienicke kindly made available his library of photographs.

Rosemarie Gramsch went to much trouble to record her recollections of life in East Germany.

I also must mention the former East German border guard whose name I do not know who spent an afternoon taking me through his one-time patrol area inside the former no-man's-land.

Unfortunately, I was unable to contact a number of people who could have made valuable contributions, while others did not respond to my efforts to reach them, and I had to go ahead without them. I want to record my appreciation of help given by assistants at many libraries and archives, especially those at the Berlin State Library in Breite Strasse.

Not least, thanks to Douglas Sutton and Martin Bensley, who read and gave constructive comments on early versions of the text; and to Alexander Anthony, whose acute judgement helped me improve several chapters.

However, these three do not necessarily agree with all opinions and conclusions in this book.

The end of East Germany was not the death of the socialist idea, declared Egon Krenz, (left), at Lotte Ulbricht's funeral.

Cross purposes. This forest of black crosses, a hard-hitting memorial to the more than 1,000 people killed at the Berlin Wall, didn't fit the image of nice things local politicians wanted tourists to see. It was erected in 2004 and pulled down by court order in 2005.

The face of the East. Gregor Gysi on 2005 campaign poster in Dresden.

Icon watches over by iconoclast. Florian Havemann under the double gaze of communist pioneer Rosa Luxemburg.

November 11, 1989. As Easterners streamed to the West, East German border guards, silhouetted against the sky, keep vigil on top of a now useless Berlin Wall. Behind is the Brandenburg Gate.

Looking into no-man's-land, East Berlin.

Darkening the enemy door. Torsten Ruehrdanz in 1996 in front of the Palast der Republik, once home to the Volkskammer, East Germany's rubber stamp parliament.

Above: Former Stasi officer Walter Thraene tells a television audience how he was kidnapped by Mielke's thugs in Austria.

Right: Jail revisited. Sigrid and Hartmut Ruehrdanz in the exercise cage at Hohenschoenhausen prison, now a museum.

The last shop in town. Heidelberger Strasse, looking towards Elsen Strasse.

Knocking holes in a dogma, November 11, 1989. Guenter Schabowski's announcement two days before that the Berlin Wall was no longer an impediment to travel released all sorts of pent-up forces. This man was one of an army of people that furiously attacked the hated Wall from the Western side.

Construction of the Berlin Wall begins in 1961. A party agitator, one of many sent to the border to harangue Westerners, snarls at Helwig-Wilson, who stands his ground and takes the photograph.

(*Photo: H.-J. Helwig-Wilson*)

Hans-Joachim Helwig-Wilson, former prisoner, back in Hohenschoenhausen jail for a visit in 1996.

View from inside the Bar at the End of the World. Corner of Heidelberger Strasse and Elsen Strasse.

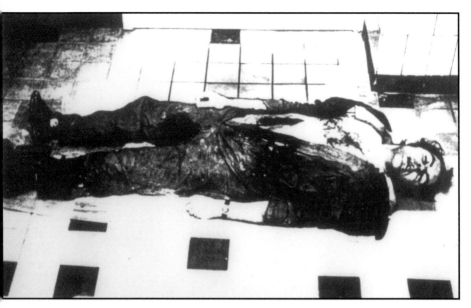

Michael Gartenschlaeger's body in Schwerin, East Germany, the day after the shooting. (*Photos, above, lower right: L. Lienicke*)

Nearly thirty years later, Lothar Lienicke recalls the fatal night.

Gartenschlaeger returns to border post 231 after removing his first SM-70.

East Berlin border guard Conrad Schumann leaps to the West in August 1961. Photographer Peter Leibing was on the spot to take the photo of a lifetime. It appeared on front pages of newspapers around the Western world. (*Photo: Staatsarchiv Hamburg*)

Truncheon blows crunched down on his neck and back and legs...Michael Sobotta remembers the Dresden marches and riots of 1989.

When art dealer Frank Kempe negotiated his way out of East Germany to escape harassment by state-sponsored smugglers, he set up business in these rooms in Munich once occupied by the House of Wittelsbach royal art gallery.

GUENTER'S DROOPING MOUSTACHE, long unkempt hair, and perpetually mournful expression gave him the air of a dog that had just emerged from the sea. I met him in a Hamburg bar in the days when two German states—capitalist West Germany and communist East Germany—were separated by a mined no-man's-land and high walls and fences. He was an East German aged about thirty who had committed some offence—its precise nature never became clear—had been arrested, tried, convicted, sentenced, jailed, and finally expelled to West Germany. Guenter seldom had money, but the crowd at our regular bar was international, optimistic, and generous. He bought beer when he could, and no one minded when he couldn't.

One night, we talked about his court case. Guenter said sadly, "My mother was the judge."

I lent him ten marks that night. It was the last time I saw him. I have no way of verifying his story. If it were true, his mother had probably done him a favor.

Squalls of driving rain drove pedestrians off the Berlin streets one blustery April morning in 1993, three years after the communists were thrown out of power in East Germany. I came down the steps of the Marx-Engels Platz S-Bahn station and stood at the entrance waiting for the rain to stop. Pedestrians scurried in off the street to take shelter. A tall, gray-haired man, coat collar pulled high, peered from beneath an umbrella as he strolled through the wet with the unhurried haste of a bank director. He turned and stood next to me.

I asked after his well-being. All things considered, not bad, he replied. His tone was courteous. But, he said, "coming to terms with the fact that you have made a mistake is difficult for everyone."

"How do people react to you these days?" I wanted to know.

"They talk to me just like you and I are talking," he replied.

He talked about a pending prosecution against him on vote-rigging charges, saying, "They are trying to kick me out of parliament." (A few months later, he was convicted on three counts of electoral fraud dating from 1989.)

The rain stopped, we shook hands, and Hans Modrow, East Germany's last communist head of government, and by now representing the PDS "post communists" in the all-German parliament, walked out of the station, and vanished into the crowd.

INTRODUCTION

GERMAN UNIFICATION WAS EXPECTED to be a triumph of the human spirit, of political resourcefulness, and of economic power. Instead, the process that began in late 1989 when the Berlin Wall came down, has turned into an unending chronicle of division rather than unification, and of economic bust rather than boom. The former communist state of East Germany, now Eastern Germany, is poor. It is wallowing in pessimism. Its unemployment is double the Western rate. The youngest and the most able have left. It is trapped between a sophisticated high-tech region to the west and low-wage countries to the east. It is perceived by Western Germans to be populated by ungrateful, lazy people, many of whom spied for the Stasi.[1]

At the time of unification in 1990, the capitalist state of West Germany made a crucial mistake by stoking the euphoria and saying exactly what a people desperate for change wanted to hear. It promised that no one would be worse off—and never gave the slightest hint that tough times might be ahead. Voices of warning were ignored. The Christian Democrat (CDU) right-of-center West German chancellor who orchestrated unification, Helmut Kohl, spoke of a "blooming landscape," thus conjuring up images of sun-drenched paths meandering through floral gardens toward some misty fairyland. Kohl then stepped back. The "blooming landscape" failed to flower.

Instead, mass unemployment and debt arrived.

Worse. When warning signs emerged that recovery was going badly, they were ignored. Many of the problems have now become insoluble. Kohl's successor as chancellor, Gerhard Schroeder, pledged to make the East a "task for the boss" but, instead, looked the other way.

During the Cold War when West Germans visited their relatives in the walled-off East Germany, they took gifts of chocolate, coffee, bananas and Western cash. The relationship was one of donor and recipient. Westerners were appreciated for the largesse they brought, but only to an extent. Now, a decade and a half after unification, Easterners are still mendicants, and they know it, and they resent it, and they are refusing to doff their hats in gratitude.

The West badly misread the minds of its neighbors. Easterners might not have liked living in a Stalinist state, but it had been their home. They had cheered their athletes to victories on the world stage, and they liked to think that they, as people, treated each other better than those in the capitalist country next door. After the Berlin Wall fell, they saw their culture ripped apart and discarded like an old rag. They were left in no doubt that they were inferior.

Neither at street level nor political level have Westerners really tried to understand Easterners. Not now, not then. Gerd Resag's experience is typical. After ten years in an East German jail, he came to the West in 1971 with other former political prisoners. He recalls Westerners commiserating; "They would say, 'You people have been through a lot. Come and have a beer.' But that was as far as it got. The interest was superficial."[2]

Nothing caused such bad feeling as legislation allowing property abandoned during the Nazi and communist dictatorships to be reclaimed by former owners or their descendants. Opponents of the legislation predicted it would cause trouble. They pushed for financial compensation to be paid, with restitution only in exceptional circumstances. They lost the battle, but they were right. Resentment was stoked as Easterners were forced to look on as both Westerners and foreigners laid claim to residential and commercial property occupied for generations by those forced to remain behind the Iron Curtain. This was not only close to legalized plunder, it was unnecessary. The system was choked by the avalanche of applications for restitution, and investment was delayed or abandoned as ownership of commercial premises remained undecided.[3]

The decrepit state-run Eastern economy has been gutted. But, although a number of snazzy, new high-tech works have been built in the south, they shine like a cluster of lights at the end of a long, dark street. The region remains an economic junkie, hooked on cash transfers from the West.

The costs of unification are staggering. In thirteen years to 2003, a total of €1.250 trillion ($1.50 trillion at the December 2005 exchange rate)[4] was transferred, and no end is in sight. Eastern productivity has stagnated at, proportionally, about seventy percent of the West's.[5] The figure drops to around fifty percent if the handful of big high-tech firms are excluded. If the cash transfers are ignored, Eastern Germany's per-head GDP is below that of Portugal, one of the poorest regions of the European Union.[6] And the money is not even achieving what it was intended to achieve—economic recovery and raising Eastern living standards to Western levels.

A colossal seventy per cent of the transferred cash is spent on social welfare, which means that, instead of being invested in innovation and development, it goes on consumption. Put another way, thirty percent of consumer spending in the East comes from the taxpayer.

The cost of keeping the East afloat is holding back both investment and growth right across Germany at a time when Europe needs a strong German economy.

Helmut Schmidt, a member of the left-of-center Social Democrat party (SPD), and Kohl's predecessor as chancellor, said, "No politician from any party has so far made a genuine attempt to accelerate the recovery process of the Eastern economy."[7]

Many Easterners, mainly young and qualified, see no future and head West. This is not only because of actual lack of opportunity but also because of perceived lack of opportunity. In some areas the exodus even threatens to leave a shortage of skilled workers.[8]

Another factor has entered the equation. The impression that cash continues to be poured into a bottomless pit is creating ill feeling among politicians in deprived Western regions who look at tarted-up Eastern main streets, and showpiece shopping centers, and who point out that they, too, could use some handouts to smarten up their dowdy towns.

But the situation cannot be reduced to economics. When East Germans celebrated the end of their hated state with intoxicated elation, they had no idea that they would wake up with a hangover. Life has quickened and become more complex and fraught with pitfalls. It is as if the driver of a horse-drawn cart bumping over a rural track had suddenly been placed at the wheel of a Porsche flitting through busy city traffic.

The communist system suffocated individual enterprise. People did not learn to use initiative. Now, whenever they face adversity such as unemployment or bankruptcy, they tend to withdraw and mope instead of bouncing back. This lack of resilience itself is crucial.

Under communism, survival depended on guile. People throughout the East Bloc needed to be street wise to survive the shortages, political chicanery, and bureaucratic arbitrariness.

An example of this: before the communist system collapsed, I met three Poles who shared a room little bigger than a telephone cell in a Hamburg apartment house. My vodka-lubricated conversations with Bragin, Czeskaw and Stanislaus consisted of fragments of Polish, German and English spiced with declarations of eternal world peace, many gesticulations, and much thumbing of dictionaries.

The three lived by their wits. They had arrived in Hamburg a few months before me on tourist visas and with little money. They needed to work, but had no work permits. They combed the telephone book until they found a business with a Polish name, in the hope that the employer would be sympathetic toward them. A Mr Kowalsky took them on in his metal-bashing workshop.

Bragin, Czeskaw and Stanislaus, paid in cash and no questions asked, would visit vegetable markets just before closing time and buy, at giveaway prices, fruit that was beginning to rot. They sliced out the bad pieces and preserved the rest in jars. They knew where the cheapest beer and vodka in town could be bought. They pooled their resources and bought a used car. They bought a used truck fitted with a canopy. By the time they were preparing to return to Poland, the car, fully laden with preserved food, German beer, hi-fi sets, and clothing, was inside the truck.

The three were masters of any given situation. When I locked myself out of my room, Bragin held up his hand: "Nix problemo!" He took a wire coat hanger, bent and twisted the hook, fitted it into the keyhole, and the door sprang open.

The morning they left, they were unable to contact the landlady. They wanted their bond money back. Would I give them the cash and claim it from the landlady? Sure, I said, and took their bond receipt and handed over the cash. Afterwards the landlady told me: sorry, no deal. They had left owing a month's rent.[9]

Such resourcefulness helped people in communist countries to ease a drab existence in which there were few avenues upwards. After the fall of communism, the game changed. Street-level shrewdness became merely a survival tactic for the poor. Now there were ladders to climb, careers to be made, money to be earned, wealth to be acquired and, perhaps, flaunted. That most dubious of human properties, status, changed its outlines.

The East of Germany differs from other former East Bloc countries in that it has always measured itself against the West of the country. People in the gray, Stalinist republic were materially better off than anyone else in the East Bloc, but the real yardstick was always next door—the consumer paradise of West Germany. Today, Easterners still measure themselves against the West, and find they are coming up short.

Of course, the end of the dictatorship has brought many positive developments. They include new housing, a cleaner environment as the old factories were closed down, and a catalogue of freedoms—to travel, talk, read, write, and associate freely without running the risk of being spied on by stool pigeons and arrested by the secret police. Wages in the free-market economy were paid in real money as opposed to the non-convertible East marks. But prices rose from low communist levels to soaring capitalist levels. Under the old system, Easterners who did have money had little to spend it on. Personal savings levels were high. Now Easterners can buy anything they want—if they have the cash.

Westerners just don't understand it. Easterners were enslaved by a dictatorship. Now they are materially better off. Now they have "freedom." But both sides are talking past one another. For example, 56 percent of Easterners believe "equality" with the West is more important than "freedom," while only 36 percent say "freedom" is more important. To complicate matters, their respective definitions of "freedom" differ. To Westerners, "freedom" means the right to take self-responsibility and to be able to decide on career or place of abode, whereas Easterners relate "freedom" to relief from social want, poverty, homelessness, and unemployment.[10]

This gets to the heart of one of the biggest misjudgements of unification: in the headlong rush to unification, no one seemed to consider that two different peoples were being brought together. Both spoke the same language, but forty years under a Stalinist dictatorship had instilled different sets of values. What was important to a suburbanite from the manicured outskirts of Munich was not necessarily important to a resident of the smoky, cobblestoned gulches of East Berlin. The Munich suburbanite was basically the same person day and night. The East Berliner was usually—but even then not always[11]—able to talk freely with family members at night, but, during the day would pull on a mask and enter the make-believe world of socialist political conformity, carefully saying the right thing, worrying about the ubiquitous informers, joining in party rent-a-crowds on big occasions, and pretending to be a happy member of a utopian society. He play acted to survive.

The big losers of unification are the former "political prisoners." The term "political" was a euphemism to mean whatever the state intended it to mean. These victims of Stalinist repression who were often tortured in Stasi cells where the conditions were as oppressive as in banana republic dictatorships, have been treated shabbily. Many are financially badly off, in ill health from their prison maltreatment, and, inexplicably, regarded with widespread scepticism, even by doctors. They see their former tormentors, their Stasi jailers, receiving solid pensions as an apparent reward for services to a dictatorship.[12]

Worse, the old order, headed by former Stasi officers, is mounting an offensive to whitewash East German history and gloss over the prison system.

Throughout the East, red tape has become a nightmare. Unification gave West Germany a chance to slim down its bureaucracy. Instead, it transferred the entire jungle of paragraphs to the East. This not only stifles commercial enterprise, it also kills initiative at a personal level. People changing their status from employed to self-employed to unemployed or back again find that the bureaucracy cannot keep up, and they soon find themselves embroiled in a paper war as they try to decode documents written in impenetrable officialese, grit their teeth as they confront abitrary recalcitrance or read computer-compiled letters often phrased in hostile language, and shake their heads as one branch of a public authority seems unable to comprehend what another does.

Minds began to play tricks. Life's certainties in the dark old days had once been frustrating. But as the uncertainties of existence in the new Germany mounted, those frustrations were forgotten. The Stalinist restrictions came to represent security. The past looked better.

Central to all this is the joker in the political pack, The Left Party. Until 2005, it was known as the Party of Democratic Socialism (PDS). The party emerged in 1989 from the wreckage of the SED, the Stalinist party that ruled East Germany with an iron hand for forty years. When the hopes raised by Kohl's "blooming landscape," guaranteed by democracy and free-market economics, were dashed, many Easterners turned to these PDS "post communists" (The terms "post communists," and "ex communists" are convenient shorthand terms but are, in many ways, misnomers).

There is something almost transcendental about the expectations of a large minority of Easteners. This probably comes from the prospects of a utopia held out by communism but which that same communism was hopelessly unable to deliver. When Easterners saw this dismal failure, they pinned their hopes instead on the capitalist glitter brought to them every day on their television sets and which they mistook for their utopia. But capitalism can't deliver, either. And not even most PDS voters believe that party is more capable of dealing with the country's economic problems than other parties.[13] The conclusion is that most of them are not voting for a political party but for a nursemaid. The PDS offers a refuge from the unpredictabilities of life, a wall to wail at, and a means by which Easterners can express their resentment towards Westerners. It drives Western politicians nuts but they cannot ignore it.[14]

In a disturbing trend, resentful Easterners are increasing voting for neo-Nazi parties. This is disastrous for the region's reputation. During the 1990s televised images of Eastern German thugs with close-cropped skulls were beamed round the world as organised confrontations against foreigners erupted in town after town. More than one hundred people have been killed, and many more injured, by neo-Nazis since 1990. A region with so much neo-Nazi influence and skinhead violence frightens off both investors and people. What Asian firm, for example, would set up a factory employing, say, 200 people if a manager were worried about being attacked during a walk in a park? German firms, especially those represented in other countries, also tend to think twice about setting up in the East because of the potential damage to their overseas image.[15]

The roots of this resurgence of Nazism and the simplistic message it offers lie ironically not only in Germany's past but also in the warped reasoning of East Germany's Stalinist education system, which instilled the belief that any problems in the state were the fault of outsiders.

This extremism is a vicious circle drawn by an icily false logic. The lack of job-creating investment keeps the region depressed. In the continuing atmosphere of depression, voters turn to extremist parties of both the right and the left. These parties not only cannot deliver solutions, but actually increase doubts about the wisdom of setting up enterprises and sending people there. Thus the region moves closer to perpetuating its own depression.[16]

This book looks why unification has been such a buffeting, painful process and why Easterners have had such trouble adjusting to a world they once wanted eagerly to be part of. Because the origins of the problems lie as much in the past as in the present, this book delves into the forty years of the East German dictatorship and discusses how the region has become trapped between that past and the present.

NOTES

1. There are no official figures, but it is widely believed that two percent of the population as a whole worked in some way for the Stasi, either as official, full-time staff; spies in the West; or as domestic informers.

2. "You people…," Gerd Resag speaking in *Gegen die Grenze*, a television documentary by Alexander Dittner and Ben Kempas about Michael Gartenschlaeger, (Rundfunk Berlin-Brandenburg, 2004). See Chapter 24—Gartenschlaeger's Private War.

3. See Chapter 2—An Economic Flop.

4. There are different ways of calculating the amounts transferred to the East. The sum of €1.25 trillion ($1.50 trillion at the December 2005 rate) is not official, but it is a widely accepted total. However Manfred Stolpe, transport minister in the Schroeder government, challenges this amount and comes up with his own total of €15 billion ($18 billion) a year between 1990 and 2003, a total of about €210 billion ($252 billion). Klaus Schroeder, of the Berlin Free University, was quoted as telling the *Frankfurter Allgemeine Sonntagszeitung* that "all federal governments have tried to disguise the costs of unification to head off a debate [driven by] envy." When Schroeder put the total transfer figure even higher, at €1.5 trillion [$1.8 trillion], Stolpe responded by saying anyone arriving at any figure other than his own was talking "nonsense," according to a report, "Stolpe kritisiert Studie ueber Einheitskosten—Minister nennt Summe von 1,5 Billionen Euro 'Unsinn,'" *Berliner Zeitung*, September 20, 2004. But Stolpe, as an Easterner, has a political interest in playing down the figure and preventing resentment from growing in the West. The figure of €1.25 trillion has gained wide acceptance such as by *Der Spiegel* of April 5, 2004, in "Tabuzone Ost," which gives the Bundesbank as the source; and the *Economist* of September 18, 2004, in "Eastern Germany—Getting Back Together Is so Hard."

5. Although seventy percent is a commonly extrapolated figure, some observers put productivity even lower. Klaus George, editor-in-chief of *Wirtschaft & Markt*, an economics magazine, writes, "Despite all efforts at reconstruction, the Eastern productivity level has only reached sixty percent of the Western level. Another 3,000 medium-sized works are needed with half a million jobs." (In "Thema Ost: Abgehakt," *Wirtschaft & Markt*, August 2004).

6. Observation by Klaus von Dohnanyi, head of "Gespraechskreis Ost," a government commission set up to examine Eastern Germany's economic problems, in "Tabuzone Ost," *Der Spiegel*, April 5, 2004. Dohnanyi later said that the Social-Democrat-Green coalition government that set up the commission had ignored its recommendations. See "Regelsystem West korrigieren," *Wirtschaft & Markt*, January 2006.

7. "No politician from…," Helmut Schmidt in *Auf dem Weg zur Deutschen Einheit*, (Reinbek bei Hamburg: Rowohlt Verlag, 2005) 196.

8. A shortage of 10,000 skilled workers is projected by the year 2010 alone in the Chemnitz-Zwickau region, according to the Friedrich-Schiller University in Jena, quoted by Klaus George in "Klotz am Bein," *Wirtschaft & Markt*, November 2005.

9. Three years later I received a post card from Czeskaw, posted from a refugee clearing center in Austria. He was hoping to go to Switzerland. He said Bragin, the part-time locksmith, was already in Canada. I have never held the bond episode against the Poles. The landlady might have been lying.

10. Survey by the Allensbach Opinion Polling Institute, published in *Hamburger Abendblatt*, September 18, 2004. Many opinion polls reveal similar trends.

11. See Chapter 18—Fading Heroes.

12. See Chapter 13—Victims Fight to Avoid Oblivion.

13. According to a TNS Infratest survey in August 2005, only five percent of Easterners believe the PDS was the party best able to solve Eastern Germany's economic problems. In the same survey, a total of twenty-nine percent said they intended voting PDS in the general election a few weeks later. See "Das Politische Profil des Ostens," *Der Spiegel*, August 22, 2005.

14. See Chapter 8—The Conjuror.

15. See Chapter 10—Unification Unleashes the Mob.

16. The president of the employers' organisation DIHK (Deutsche Industrie- und Handelskammertage), Ludwig Georg Braun, said "Politicians and representatives of commerce must make it clear to people that xenophobia damages not only the image of the country but also its economic development." See "Ostdeutschland—Zoegerliche Investoren," *Capital*, October 14, 2004. He was commenting after a survey showed that German companies, especially larger companies, because of worries about their image internationally, resisted setting up in regions with high levels of xenophobia. The survey, by Kai Bussmann and Markus Werle for Halle University, was reported in the same issue of *Capital*.

PART ONE
THE PROMISED LAND

A FUNERAL IN BERLIN

IN HER HEYDAY, SHE CAME CLOSE enough to Josef Stalin to kiss him. In her dotage, she was a crumpled piece of cloth peering from a pile of blankets in a wheelchair.

One March day in 2002, she struggled out of her wheelchair and shuffled to a ladder propped against a bookcase in the Berlin house where she lived alone. Taking an infinity for each step, she climbed to look for a book on an upper shelf, and crashed to the floor.

When she died that night, an encyclopaedic collection of memories died with her.

Not only had she known Stalin, but she had met Lenin and drunk tea with Krushchev. She had hob-nobbed with dictators of the communist East Bloc states and even married one—Walter Ulbricht, the son of a Leipzig tailor, who rose to become the most powerful person in East Germany.

Lotte Ulbricht, the nearest the German communist movement had to a grande dame, was buried with the party's equivalent of the twenty-one gun salute on a cloudy spring Thursday, April 18, the day before her ninety-ninth birthday.

She had lived behind lace curtains in the gray, three-storied cement house she once shared with Walter at Majakowskiring 12 in Eastern Berlin. If anyone had suggested that the white porcelain polar bear and seal on her front window sill were examples of middle-class kitsch popular in the capitalist West, she would have been indignant.

This stubborn old lady refused to see visitors, apart from former party hacks, and was defiant enough to have the name "Ulbricht" displayed on the front-gate letterbox. This attracted unwanted mail. One anonymous letter read, "You shriveled bigwig pig, why don't you drop dead, you ancient lump of shit, you old East German sow. We'll fix you!"[1]

If you waited outside the house for long enough, you might see an inner set of curtains move slightly...Lotte was at home, watching.

Her East Germany no longer exists, but reminders of it are everywhere: in the abandoned brick Wilhelminian buildings, in the absence of neatness and order, in the drabness. Away from Main Street, it has a threadbare gloom, an emptiness, and a sullen resistance to the tinctured tidiness of the West. In spite of the modern Western-built cars and the neon lighting, the East remains another country. It is sometimes like looking down a street of ruins, a street where nobody comes any more, a ghost strasse. In Lotte Ulbricht's own street, Majakowskiring, a once-elegant oval boulevard, the pavements are uneven, the roadway is pitted, and the lawns overgrown. And when Lotte chose to be buried at the Weissensee cemetery, she knew she would feel at home lying in an anonymous grave hemmed in on both sides by high, crumbling brick walls. In her East Germany, the workers' and peasants' state, dilapidation was part of life.

She was present at both the birth and the death of the German party. She was manning the barricades as a fifteen year old when the party was founded in Berlin on New Year's Day, 1919, as Germany staggered from World War One defeat into anarchy. She was in Moscow when Hitler came to power in 1933 and, at the age of forty-two, she returned to the ruins of Hitler's Germany. She witnessed the division of the country into a Soviet-backed communist East Germany and the Western-oriented West Germany.

When Walter was toppled as party boss by Erich Honecker in a Moscow-backed palace coup and became a nonperson, his name was removed from public sight, and two years later he died. Lotte Ulbricht became an embittered recluse. She was eighty-six when the communist dream ended in 1989 and East Germany collapsed. She blamed Honecker.

But Lotte Ulbricht did not publicly reminisce. She wrote no memoirs and she refused to talk to either the communist or the capitalist press.[2]

Her funeral itself was hard-core party. The last boss to hold real power, Egon Krenz, came wearing a wily grin, a smart dark-blue coat and tie. Former defense minister Heinz Kessler was no longer the strutting general but just another little, cigarette-puffing pensioner dressed in his Sunday best. Burly veteran West German communist leader Herbert Mies, who once divided his party by his refusal to abandon his political 1950s time warp, came in a dark suit and trendy beige coat. He might have been some prosperous building contractor who had parked his Mercedes on the street outside.[3]

But it was the rank and file that set the tone. They were mostly tieless, wearing cheap leather jackets, windbreakers, berets, jeans, jogging shoes. These were ex provincial party bosses, secretaries, petty officials, wives of apparatchiks, and other servants of the system.

One man arrived direct from the supermarket, his battered bicycle sagging under the weight of bulging plastic shopping bags. The lack of pomp in these chipped surroundings was almost touching. This was the attraction behind the Cause—but then you remembered the price many people had to pay for an ideology that espoused egalitarianism but practised privilege.

Some of the two hundred mourners crowded into the little brick chapel while the rest remained on the steps outside or on the cobbled yard and listened to the eulogy over a loudspeaker. The speaker, Ursula Benjamin, was the daughter-in-law of the late Hilda Benjamin, the judge they called the "Red Guillotine" because of her ferocity.

Some newspapers referred to Lotte Ulbricht as the "Queen Mum" of East Germany, in reference to the late British Queen Mother. The term implies popular affection, something which neither Walter nor Lotte Ulbricht attracted. Both were almost universally disliked. Contemporaries described Walter as underhanded, overbearing and obstinate, stiff and unbending, a man who relaxed only when playing with the young Ukrainian girl the couple adopted in the 1950s, Beate. Propaganda photographs show a smiling, bright-eyed girl doing her homework at a garden table as her fawning adoptive parents look on. But there was pressure on the girl. Eyewitnesses say the Ulbrichts insisted Beate must always be top of the class. When she reached her mid teens, she was not allowed to wear stockings or other fashion clothing, unlike daughters of other party officials. She was "permanently under pressure."[4]

Former sports teacher Hans Kretzschmar recalled Beate as "a very nice, disciplined pupil who never gave me any problems...(but) her parents scared the hell outta me."[5]

She fell out with Lotte while still in her teens, and, at the age of fifteen, was sent to boarding school in Leningrad. Beate then dropped out of sight.

The disintegration of East Germany was like a fat lady removing her corsets to reveal the ugly reality. The strait-jacketed East German media had portrayed a fairy-tale world of happiness where human frailty was virtually eliminated. Job dissatisfaction, marital strife, child abuse, alcoholism, unhappiness were capitalist maladies. Under socialism, nobody was maladjusted, with the exception of "troublemakers." Corruption was a capitalist weakness. So were the concepts of "privilege" and "elitism."

The country was constantly awash with stories about excesses in high places, but no scandal ever made the press. After 1989 that changed. The first major expose was Wandlitz, the walled-off settlement outside Berlin locally referred to as "The Kremlin" where party leaders lived luxurious existences insulated from the chronic shortages endured by most of the population. After the fall of the Berlin Wall, camera teams and newspaper reporters revealed details of life in Wandlitz to a public desperate to hear about it. The ruling clique was shown to be as self-serving and corrupt as politicians anywhere. It had access to pornographic videos from the West, cars from the West, whisky from the West, fruit from the West. Here was greed, corruption, the entire gamut of human failings. The revelations helped demystify the ruling class. One of those revelations was about Beate Ulbricht and her step parents.

A tabloid newspaper revealed in 1991 that an unkempt woman regularly seen ferreting in trash cans behind a shopping complex in Eastern Berlin's Lichtenberg district was Beate, daughter of the former party boss Walter Ulbricht. The paper published a series of interviews. One photograph showed Beate Ulbricht as a pretty, raven-haired teenager, as fresh as winter dew. A second photograph, taken thirty one years later, showed a woman with a lined, puffy face and taut eyes that had seen too many empty bottles, too many midnight quarrels. Beate was on a bottle of vermouth and sixty cigarettes a day. In the series, headlined, "Nice Papa, Nasty Lotte," she placed the blame for her fate squarely on Lotte Ulbricht, whom she called "the hag."[6]

After leaving the Leningrad boarding school, she met and married Ivano Matteoli, the son of a high-ranking member of the Italian communist party, against the wishes of both Walter and Lotte. Beate and Ivano settled in East Germany, but their relationship with Walter and Lotte deteriorated so much they decided to return to the Soviet Union with their daughter, Patricia. Ivano went ahead to look for an apartment in Leningrad.

Beate Ulbricht recalled: "The blow came when Ivano had barely left Berlin. The hag arranged for my passport to be withdrawn." As a result she was unable to travel to the Soviet Union and join her husband. She suspects Walter did not relent and return her passport to her because "I might have hurt him deeply when once in jest, because of the Berlin Wall, I called him 'my dear king of the fence'."

> For two years I heard nothing from my man, and he heard nothing
> from me. Then the hag achieved what she was after: I gave in to her
> demand for a separation...the next day I got my passport back.[7]

She went to Leningrad but Ivano had vanished.

> He had moved out of his old apartment to an unknown address.
> Normally this just does (sic) not happen in the Soviet Union; the au-
> thorities always know where everyone lives—but [in this case] they
> had their instructions to keep quiet.[8]

In her despair, Beate married a former Leningrad schoolfriend, but he was a
secret drinker and violent. But, by this time, Beate was also drinking heavily,
and this marriage broke up as well. She returned to Berlin with Patricia and a
child from the second marriage, but lost custody of both. She blamed Lotte.

Referring to the many public-relations photographs of Lotte from her
Wandlitz childhood, Beate said, "If a camera were there, she played the exem-
plary, loving, mother. In reality, she was cold-hearted and egotistic."[9] In
Wandlitz, she was known simply as "the sergeant."[10]

> The hag dented my self confidence at an early age when she stuck
> me in goody-goody clothes. School was a torture. All the kids
> laughed at me for the way I dressed.[11]

In contrast, her memories of Walter Ulbricht were warm. He treated her well,
and often read stories to her in bed. She maintained that Walter only married
the infertile Lotte because Stalin told him to.

Beate spent vacations on Black Sea resorts with her parents as guests of
Soviet leader Nikita Krushchev, and, although she did not like Krushchev
himself, she remembered his wife as being "motherly, warm and heartfelt...
just the opposite of the hag."[12]

Police were called to a dilapidated apartment in Eastern Berlin late on
the night of December 3, 1991, where residents had been complaining about
loud arguments, barking dogs and a trail of men. The door had been kicked in.
Inside, they found the body of an alcoholic woman with facial injuries. The
woman, who had died from a fall or had been murdered, was identified as a
local wino. Further investigation revealed her to be the adopted daughter of
Walter and Lotte Ulbricht. The mystery of Beate's death at the age of forty-
seven, whether it was an accident, common crime or if sinister political motives were behind it, has never been solved. Possibly the killing was an act of
revenge for her vitriolic newspaper interviews a few months before. When a

Berlin tabloid reporter rang Lotte Ulbricht to tell her of Beate's death, she replied, "Fancy that."[13]

The mystery surrounding the death deepened two years later when another alcoholic, Peter Polzcyk, 49, was found dead in a room not far from Beate's former apartment. Polzcyk had been knifed and his apartment set on fire. Police said that he once been Beate's Ulbricht's lover. It is not known if the two deaths were linked.[14]

Other members of the Ulbricht family did not share Walter's politics. A brother, Erich, went in 1928 to live in New York and settled in Flushing. His sister, Hildegard, lived in a small town in the West German state of Schleswig-Holstein under an assumed name. Even in middle age, she was so terrified of being identified as the sister that, before a childhood photograph of her with Walter was published, she insisted on her face being blacked out. In 1947 Walter's daughter from his first marriage, Dora, went to the West. She often returned to visit her mother, but in 1961 her father built the Berlin Wall and stopped that.

There are about 75,000 old guard, hard-line communists in Eastern Germany, but no more than this 200 bothered to attend Lotte Ulbricht's funeral. Among the mourners were two young relatives from Texas, sons of a niece of Lotte who had gone to live in the United States.

At the grave side, a lone trumpeter played the "Internationale," the cobalt-blue urn was lowered into the ground, the faithful placed the traditional red carnations and sprinkled handfuls of sand. Lotte was gone, and in a way, so was German communism.

But Krenz did not see it that way. With his gray hair immaculately blow dried, he stepped in with his message of hope. He praised the "resolute" qualities of the deceased, then raised his voice and proclaimed, "The end of East Germany was not the death of the socialist idea." Everybody who had devoted their lives to East Germany "has no need to be ashamed."

This baring of the fangs was intended as much for himself as for his audience. Krenz had a need to indulge in self-justification. He was present only because he was on parole from prison, where he was "serving time" on four counts of killings relating to deaths at the Berlin Wall.

When the case went to the European Court of Human Rights in Strasbourg in 2001, the court not only rejected the appeal, but also said that Krenz, far from being a victim of Western "victor's justice," had himself helped create the regime of death at the Wall.

So Krenz returned to jail. But not to the dank dungeons of his East Germany, with their rubber-lined torture cells, with their nighttime interrogations where prisoners were beaten into signing "confessions," with their slop pails and with tiny, walled-off outside exercise yards where guards patrolling on catwalks could and did urinate on prisoners. There was no chance of an interrogator bashing out Krenz's teeth and forcing him to sign a declaration saying he had fallen down steps.[15] There was no chance of his being denied medical treatment for illness. There was no chance of his "disappearing" in jail because no one on the outside was told of his whereabouts.

Instead, Krenz went back to his hotel prison, where he was required only to stay overnight, protesting loudly about the injustice of it all.

His prison routine allowed him to have a daytime job in which he used his contacts in Eastern Europe for a firm of exporters. Little wonder that, even if being a convict was a blow to his ego, he had difficulty suppressing that toothy grin. (He was released just before Christmas in 2003 after serving nearly four years of a six-and-a-half-year sentence.)

The Stalinist idea still exists in dreamy time warps. The *Rote Fahne* newspaper is published in Berlin by the Communist Party of Germany/Marxist Leninist (KPD/ML), a hard-line Stalinist splinter movement. A portrait of Stalin looks down from the editorial office wall. The KPD/ML believes that East Germany was a bastion of human freedom, unlike the united Germany that, it says, persecutes people with dissenting views. *Rote Fahne* editor in chief Hans Wauer believes the 21st century will be the century of communism, and the revolutionary vanguard will lead the working class to final victory.[16]

NOTES

1. "You shriveled...," *"Lotte Ulbricht—Mein Leben—Selbstzeugnisse, Briefe und Dokumente,* (Berlin: Das Neue Berlin Verlagsgesellschaft, 2003), 251.

2. *Lotte Ulbricht—Mein Leben* was published after her death. In spite of its name, it is not an autobiography but a collection of memorabilia assembled from photographs, letters, notes by Lotte herself, and diverse contributions by other people. It was edited by Frank Schumann, a long-time journalist on state-controlled East German publications.

3. Mies was chairman of the German Communist Party (DKP) in West Germany from 1973 until 1990. It followed the orthodox Moscow line, if somewhat pragmatically, and strongly rejected the broader appeals of eurocommunism. The DKP was heavily financed by the SED. In the 1980s, Mies resisted attempts at liberalization and members deserted in droves. Membership fell from over 40,000 in the mid 1980s to 6,000 by 1990. One commentator, Rainer Poeschl, said in *ZEITmagazin*, February 24, 1989, "Mies exudes...jovial-

ity...but he is no winner. He is a 1950s-style communist, and his life has been full of missed chances...His last chance is called perestroika. He is about to miss that as well."

4. Beate was "permanently under pressure...," *Lotte Ulbricht*, 63. (The comment is presumably made by the editor, Schumann, but this is not clear). Eyewitness reports on the pressures placed on Beate were presented in a television documentary "Lotte Ulbricht privat" on *Mitteldeutscher Rundfunk*, shown on April 15, 2003, excerpts of which were published online. People interviewed included Ursula Seidler, Lotte's former householder, who said, "She [Lotte Ulbricht] never spoke about Beate, apart from saying that the biggest mistake of her life was adopting a child." And: "I know from them [contemporaries of Beate] that Lotte wanted above all for Beate to be the best."

5. "A very nice, disciplined...," Kretzschmar quoted in "Lotte Ulbricht privat" on *Mitteldeutscher Rundfunk*, shown on April 15, 2003.

6. The *Super* series ran in eleven episodes from August 27-September 7, 1991.

7. "For two years...," Beate Ulbricht quoted by Anna Meissner in "Liebe Papa, Boese Lotte," *Super*, September 2, 1991.

8. "He had moved...," *Super*, September 2 1991.

9. "If a camera...," *Super*, August 28, 1991.

10. "The sergeant...," *Super*, August 27, 1991.

11. "The hag dented...," *Super*, August 29, 1991.

12. "Motherly, warm...," *Super*, August 30, 1991.

13. "Fancy that...," Lotte Ulbricht quoted in "Sie hatte mit Fidel Castro den heissesten Flirt ihres Lebens, badete mit Chruschtschow im Meer," *BZ*, December 4, 1991.

14. After Polzcyk's body was found, Ilona Scholz, of the Eighth Murder Commission in Berlin, said it was still unclear if Beate had fallen or been a murder victim. Possibly a killer had tried to disguise her death as an accident. Presumably there was no link between the two deaths, she said, in "Erneute Morde in Berlin—Ex-Liebhaber von Ulbricht-Stieftochter tot," *dpa*, February 16, 1994.

15. Brutality in East German jails is widely documented. The author has personally talked to many former prisoners who have either been the victims or who knew first-hand of cases of such brutality. A major Knaebke, of the Stasi's Department VII/8, is quoted as saying in 1988, "The Stasi was beyond any controls. The things you hear [about it] are beyond description. For example, people's teeth are bashed out, and then they are forced to sign a declaration saying they fell down the stairs." Knaebke spoke to Christoph Hering, whose interview was made available to Roland Brauckmann and included in *Amnesty International als Feindobjekt der DDR* (Berlin: Berliner Landesbeauftragten fuer die Unterlagen des Staatssicherheitsdienstes der Ehemaligen DDR, 1996), 87. For a more comprehensive account of East German prisons, see Anja Mihir in *Amnesty International in der DDR—Der Einsatz fuer Menschenrechte im Visier der Stasi*, (Berlin: Christoph Links Verlag, 2002); and *Deutsche Demokratische Republik—Rechtsprechung Hinter Verschlossenen Tueren*, (Bonn: amnesty international, 1992). See also Chapter 13—Victims Fight to Avoid Oblivion, Chapter 14—Echoes from the Dungeon, and Chapter 22—Cold War Camera.

16. *Rote Fahne* episode related by Josefine Janert, in "Aging Revolutionaries Await Communism's Return to Glory—In Berlin Attic, Former East Germans Draw Up Blueprint for Overthrow of Capitalism," *FAZ Weekly*, March 7, 2002.

2

AN ECONOMIC FLOP

AT THE FIRST SIGNS IN 1990 THAT Germany might become united, many Europeans began quaking in their boots at the thought of a new superstate astride the center of the continent. They imagined the capitalist economic giant of West Germany integrated with the most successful East Bloc economic power, East Germany. They thought nervously of the supposed qualities of Teutonic thoroughness and industriousness, plus the German tendency toward political extremism, and, in their mind's eye, they pictured a snarling, fire-breathing monster, ready to turn on its neighbors. Memories of two world wars in the twentieth century are never far from European thinking.

The fears were at least partly based on one myth. East Germany was reputed to be one of the world's top ten economies. Western observers often overrated its economic performance. One wrote in 1985 that "this state (East Germany) is now richer than Britain, Italy, or the big power Soviet Union if Gross Domestic Product, output per head, is used as the yardstick."[1]

Far from being in the top anything, East Germany was a junkyard that had for long been teetering on the edge of ruin. Its factories were dilapidated, smoke-belching nineteenth century industrial slums.

When, in March 1990, Lothar de Maizière waved to acknowledge the applause after winning the general election as head of a conservative-oriented coalition to become East Germany's first noncommunist head of government, he kept one piece of crucial information to himself. The country was bankrupt. The State Bank had just welcomed the new leader with the news that his country owed more than 500 billion East marks, and the cash available was not enough to cover the 160 billion East marks in personal savings accounts. If de Maizière had admitted this, people would have rushed to the banks to withdraw their money, but there would not have been enough to pay them. He was afraid the streets would have run with blood.[2]

De Maizière later wrote, "One of the strangest delusions in the history of German unification was the widespread idea of an economically strong DDR which supposedly was 'the 10th industrialised state in the world.'"[3]

But senior officials working in the economic sector knew better. Guenter Mittag, head of East Berlin's economic planning, admitted in 1992 that the country had been on the rocks and said that, without unification, "an economic catastrophe with unimaginable social consequences" would have taken place. "The situation at the beginning of the 1980s was on a razor's edge. Resources were ever thinner, more had to be paid for the same amount—but the growth of private consumption had to be maintained in the interests of political stability."[4]

At the time of monetary union and political unification in 1990, West Germany was governed by a coalition of Helmut Kohl's right-of-center Christian Democrats and the smaller aggressively pro-free-market Free Democrats (FDP). This combination introduced both monetary union and political unification so rapidly that the Eastern economy was hit by the cyclone of free trade with no time to adjust. Factories could not compete. Thousands of workers were thrown on to the streets as works doors closed permanently one after the other. The shakeout was brutal. In late 1989, East Germany had a workforce of ten million. A little over a year later that was down to 5.3 million. The rest were either working reduced hours, had gone to the West, had left the workforce permanently, were unemployed or on work-creation schemes.[5]

At the time, suggestions that a slower timetable was needed were scoffed at. Not now. As the economy went into a nosedive, it was left to West Germany pick up the pieces, and so began a huge eastward-bound traffic in money. More than a decade and a half later, that traffic was continuing with no end in sight. The hope had been that a sort of "market economy Big Bang"[6] would blast the East into orbit, and that growth would foot the unification bill. Not a chance. Cash transfers to the East amount to four percent of Germany's gross domestic product (GDP) a year,[7] much more than national growth figure.[8]

True, infrastructure has been renewed; broad new roads appeared in place of the pitted, undulating alleyways; and shiny new telephone systems have taken the struggle out of communications. But huge amounts of cash have been wasted on superfluous projects—water purification plants no one needs, new streets where no traffic comes, and bicycle tracks where no cyclists ride.

It seemed nothing remained untouched by the Western money bags. A few yards down a ragged alleyway near Quedlinburg's marketplace, a cottage gleams pearly white in the mid-morning sun. Timber uprights, warped with age, strain to hold up the walls. The house, its windows just tiny black holes, evokes the crudeness of a medieval rural nailsmith rather than the finesse of an urban master builder.

Yet, when it was built in the early fourteenth century, this must have been an architectural masterpiece. It is reputed to be the oldest house in Germany, and was in domestic use until as recently as 1965, when it became a museum. It has survived because Quedlinburg remained for centuries in a time-warp off main transport routes and of little interest to real-estate developers. When I first saw the house in the early 1990s, it was being renovated. Heinz Mueller, the town's retired museum director, said the project was going ahead because Western Germans wanted it to, and, because they were the bankers, that's the way it had to be. "It doesn't need renovating," Mueller told me. "It was already a museum, but it did not meet Westerners' ideas of what a museum should be. The money could have been better spent elsewhere."[9]

An example of wasting money, gaining nothing, and causing resentment.

Crucially, far too much money is being spent on social welfare and not enough on investment.

While the economy did grow and begin to catch up with the West, the catch-up basically ended in 1995. But, because unification was required to be a success for political and patriotic reasons, it became almost apostasy to suggest it was not working. The corner was always about to be reached, but that corner still hasn't come.

Two comments within weeks of each other in 1993 demonstrate this crass contradiction. The federal economics minister at the time, Guenter Rexrodt, of the Free Democrats, said in July, "We have passed the low point in the former East Germany." From 1995, the recovery in the East would carry itself, he said. It had a real GDP growth rate of five percent and was therefore a leading "European growth region."[10]

A month later, the *Financial Times*, London, said in an editorial, "The economy of Eastern Germany is in ruins...Eastern Germany needs a growth miracle. With hourly wages in 1992 [at] sixty five percent of the west German level, but output per worker at only forty percent, it is unlikely to enjoy one."[11]

Rexrodt can hardly be blamed. He probably would have lost his job if he had been as pessimistic at the *Financial Times* editorial writer. But the signs showed that corrective action was needed.

Warnings were also coming from other sources. The HWWA economic research institute referred to the economy's lack of competitiveness.[12] Michael Burda, of Humboldt University, lamented the migration of the most productive members of the Eastern workforce, the young and the well trained, to the West.[13]

Banks were coming under fire for failing to lend to the *Mittelstand*, the medium-sized companies that, with their innovation, flexibility, and sharp-footedness, have the drive to inspire an economy. This prompted one Western politician, Guido Westerwelle, of the Free Democrats, to say, "If the banks had in the 1950s acted in West Germany as they are now behaving in Eastern Germany, the legendary Economic Miracle would not have taken place."[14]

As the economic pressures of unification mounted, a government-appointed commission proposed in 2004 turning the East into a deregulated special economic zone.

But it was left to the federal president, Horst Koehler, finally to drag the issue out of the closet when he said in 2004,

> There are large differences in living standards throughout the republic. That applies to North and South as well as to West and East. Whoever wants to level out these [differences] is consolidating the state [culture of] subsidizing and piling up an intolerable debt burden for the next generation. We must get away from the [idea of] a state that hands out subsidies. The goal [should be] to give people room to create their own ideas and initiatives.[15]

The president has no direct political power, but his comments are highly influential. His implication was that money could not be shoveled to the East for ever and a day.

When unification took place, the intention was to bring Eastern living standards up to Western levels. Koehler seriously challenged the sense of continuing this policy.

More challenges lie ahead. With the westward extension of the European Union, the East is becoming trapped between low-cost labor countries on one side and a high-tech giant on the other. The outlook for recovery within the next decade is not good.[16]

Klaus von Dohnanyi, a close observer of the Eastern economic scene, said in 2004, "Today, after fifteen years of reconstruction in the East, we have to recognize that we haven't yet reached half way and the next half will be even stonier and steeper."[17]

The status quo suits some. Too many Western commercial interests would rather see the East attached to the drip of cash transfers rather than becoming competitive. Most Eastern companies are owned in the West. Their assembly lines are in the East, but their management, research, and marketing elements are in the West. Western companies prefer the transferred cash to come back to them via consumption rather than go toward developing a healthy, and thus competitive, commercial region. They do not care about the larger picture. This also has the effect of narrowing employment opportunities and driving the most able and ambitious young people to the West. Western cities like Hamburg and Munich, bustling, innovative, and attractive, are the beneficiaries. The result is a vicious circle. The more better-qualified people go West, the less attractive Eastern towns become for investment. As a result, the East doesn't even have big-spending executives and their wives who would at least pump cash into local stores.

The problem go wider. Trade unions wanted new members in the East, and pushing for higher wages would attract them. But they had another, more compelling reason. If the East remained a low-wage area, it would attract Western industry and eliminate Western jobs. That was already beginning to happen and the unions did not like it. Some Western employers agreed with the unions and did not oppose Eastern wage claims because that helped eliminate potential competition. By 2001, Easterners were still not earning as much as Westerners, but Eastern Germany was no longer a low-wage area. Eastern Europe was much cheaper.

The situation is not simply the results of political or economic measures. Mental attitude is a major contributor. People who for forty years were expected to show no enterprise or initiative cannot suddenly be expected to change. The mood of resignation caused by unemployment and rising costs tends to erode initiative and stifle incentive to self-help or to come up with ideas, especially among older people.

For those who have jobs, production is often low because many managements are not good at motivating their workers. The concept of staff motivation in Germany, in any case, often seems to be little more than abstract.

Anecdotal evidence suggests that, while the situation is improving, insufficient thought is given to what causes people to perform better.

Monetary union and political unification, which followed each other in 1990, were steps into the unknown. They were like going to war. Everything can be planned on the blackboard, but once the guns start firing, plans tend to fall apart. Recovery has been dogged by many factors.

In the run-up to monetary union, a row over the proposed West mark/ East mark rate of exchange caused a public slugging match between Chancellor Helmut Kohl and Bundesbank president Karl-Otto Poehl. Kohl wanted monetary union quickly. Poehl said it was too soon. Kohl had initially favored a less hasty form of association between the two states, but with the exodus of people heading West hitting record proportions, and demonstrators demanding monetary union with savings and wages to be converted at 1:1, he was coming under increasing pressure to act. Poehl said 1:1 would keep wages too high and kill off Eastern industry by making it uncompetitive. It would lead to high debt and high interest rates. Yet, if wages had been exchanged at 1:2, the average Eastern pay of about 1,100 marks would have been cut to a miserable 500-600 marks a months—a recipe for potential social disaster that would have turned the exodus westward into an uncontrollable migration that only rebuilding the Berlin Wall could stop. No solution was ideal. Kohl disregarded Poehl and decided on the politically expedient solution—and the one likely to store up problems. Wages, rents and pensions were converted at 1:1, commercial debt was to be halved by converting it at 1:2, and savings were to be corsetted in a set of conditions that meant everyone getting some changed at 1:1 with the rest at 1:2. Officially, the effective overall rate for savings was 1-1.8.[18] Easterners were getting their West marks, but the foundations for the future were now shaky.

Poehl remained in office until 1991 before quitting in disgust.[19]

Yet it was not as if no thought had ever been given to the practical difficulties of merging the two states at some, unknown, time in the future. During the 1950s, various notional plans were drawn up. Among the authors were Ludwig Erhard, a former Christian Democrat finance minister who was credited with getting West Germany's postwar economic recovery off the ground in 1948; and Helmut Schmidt, a Social Democrat with a reputation as a problem cruncher. Both subsequently became chancellor.

According to Harry Nick, their schemes both "envisaged conceding Eastern Germany real competitive advantages...Schmidt maintained that West Germany would need immediately to open its markets for Eastern products, while East Germany would have to be allowed to protect its industry for a temporary time through trade restrictions.

"But, in the 1990s, exactly the opposite happened. At a stroke, the West German economy took over the East German markets."[20]

Schmidt proposed in 1959 a three-stage, five-year timetable under which public investment in infrastructure would be made to absorb some of the unemployment which he saw as inevitable. He did not believe that the entire process should be left to market forces, adding that an interim period of "considerable state activity and financial/economic aid" was unavoidable.[21]

After unification, Schmidt was scathing about the fact that these reports were ignored, and he had no hesitation about allocating blame: "Clearly, the puristic market-economy ideological mania of a Free Democrat economics minister prevented the conclusions of such studies coming to the attention of the chancellor."[22]

Trouble was not long in coming. With unemployment rising, wages much lower than in the West, and prices for many food items higher, dissatisfaction simmered. Prime minister de Maizière took the unusual step of warning against profiteering. About 120,000 workers in the metal-bashing and electrical industries went on strike.[23]

Between 1933 and 1989 hundreds of thousands of people fled Hitler's Germany, Soviet-occupied Germany, and the communist state of East Germany. Many abandoned property, willingly accepting the loss in exchange for freedom. None can have had realistic hopes of ever reclaiming, or receiving compensation for the house or factory or mansion they had left behind. Their properties were quickly reoccupied and the status quo enforced by political realities became accepted on both sides of the West-East border.

When East Germany disintegrated, the question of property ownership was thrown wide open. Former refugees or their descendants living in the West suddenly faced the dazzling prospect of reclaiming a house some of them had never even seen. But what would this mean for East Germans? The issue, which arose in the run-up to unification, was emotion-laden and delicate. Changing the status quo, if not handled carefully, was certain to cause social disruption and resentment.

Three schools of thought contested this issue. One was to do nothing. Another was for property to be handed back to the original owners, with financial compensation to be made only in cases where restitution was impossible. This was the course favored by the coalition of Christian Democrats and Free Democrats. The latter seem to be obsessed with property ownership. The third school wanted financial compensation to take priority over restitution. This was favored by East Germany's first, and only, non-communist prime minister, Lothar de Maizière, himself a Christian Democrat, who warned before legislation was drawn up: "It was clear to me then that the result (of restitution) would be unbelievable social and psychological discord. I was opposed to it because after the completion of privatisation, the owners would be in the West and this would only exacerbate the traditional poverty of the East."[24]

The dispute was between dogma and realism. De Maizière tried to push through "compensation before restitution," but admitted it was politically impossible. The dogmatists of the Bonn coalition won.[25]

It was a victory for stubbornness, myopia, and a lack of imagination. De Maizière observed caustically that proponents of restitution "were just unable to imagine that anything else would be as reasonable as the resurrection of the old ownership situation."[26]

The result was disastrous. At street level, the situation became a nightmare. Easterners watched big, shiny cars with West German license plates cruising the streets of towns and villages as drivers looked for houses that had once been owned by them or their families. The claimants wanted them back, and they wanted vacant possession. During the 1990s, some claimants pursued aggressive, personal confrontation aimed at forcing tenants out. Telephone terror, direct physical threats, stones thrown at windows in the middle of the night. Properties changed hands, and rents often increased sharply without justification. Easterners were seeing the dark side of capitalist "freedoms." Tenancy laws prevented widespread evictions, but the upshot was mistrust and hatred towards Westerners.[27]

I experienced this mood of distrust personally. For a time in the early 1990s, there was no mistaking the hostile looks people gave when they saw cars with Western licence plates. Several times as I was driving with Westerners and we needed to ask directions, I was deputed to do the questioning. When Easterners heard my accent, they simply took me for a foreign tourist and their hostility vanished.

One Eastern pastor, Friedrich Schorlemmer, gave his opinion of property claimants:

> That is their right. Yes, that is law. It is like in the best of families when it comes to inheritance…sisters and brothers become vultures. Because it is all about right, not about need—in our special case it is not about who held out and stood by one's post, but about who is able to register a claim.[28]

Claims came in at such a rate that they choked the system's capacity to deal with them. Soon more than two million packed the shelves. Some claims, especially competing ones, were mind-numbingly complex. Many involved different members of the same family whose forbears had fled Nazi Germany and gone to the United States, where they had died. Brothers and sisters fought each with competitive claims. In one famous case, descendants of one family which fled the Nazis in the 1930 claimed back an estate which over the years had been broken down into more than 900 parcels of land with hundreds of owners.

More then ten years after the fall of the Wall, 150,000 claims had still not been resolved. If the effects at a personal level were unpleasant, the economic results were disastrous. Uncertainty over ownership of commercial real estate delayed investment, and many properties remained disused and unimproved because potential investors held back or went elsewhere. In 1992, the law was amended to give priority to cases involving commercial investment.

Yet there shouldn't have been a problem at all. Schmidt was clear about that when he wrote in 1991: "…there is no pressing economic or social reason to rush headlong into (a system of) restitution or compensation."[29]

The new Germany missed the chance to create in the East a new administrative order without the throttling bureaucracy of the old West Germany. East Germany itself was one huge, cumbersome bureaucracy, where sallow-faced clerks dispensed favors from drab offices regaled with the obligatory wall photos of party boss Erich Honecker. Ironically, the efficiency of this bureaucracy lay in its clumsiness. Its goal was to control, to stifle initiative, and to keep people servile. The more hidebound and meaningless the pencil pushing, the more it did exactly that. But, as long as people showed no initiative, they barely noticed the bureaucracy.

Now, living in a state that expects them to do the opposite, to be innovative and to demonstrate initiative, Easterners find themselves ensnared in a nerve-sapping battle of red tape. Whether they want to alter their employment status or set up a roadside sausage stall, deal with doctors and medical insurance schemes, negotiate with a retirement fund, the paperwork is endless. A more imaginative approach by the Bonn government after 1989 could have made life easier. The chance was lost. By some estimates, there are twenty percent more civil servants per head of population in the East than in the West.

Disaster hit many new enterprises before they got off the ground. In the chaos, it was often hard to tell whether the cause was incompetence, inexperience, bad luck, red tape, or a combination of all four.

One Western firm bought a defunct plant from the Treuhand, the agency set up to privatise the economy. The firm invested 3.5 million marks ($2.4 million) to modernize the works and received a state subsidy of 900,000 marks ($600,000). The staff of twenty-four was soon working twelve hours a day, six days a week. Six months later came the shock. The local authority said the works were unauthorized and ordered them closed. The managers protested that the authority had issued a permit to reopen the works in the first place. The bureaucrat in charge was unimpressed. The modernization did not interest her. Neither did the fact that people would lose their jobs. The firm at first geared itself for a legal battle but then decided to cut its losses, lay the workers off, and close the plant. A local official told the firm, "You had bad luck with this woman. That department is full of red socks and meddlers."[30]

Former Chancellor Schmidt described some regulations as relics from the Middle Ages and added that Eastern states should be allowed to suspend or simplify federal laws and regulations which inhibit development. He was also pessimistic about the prospects for change: "There is little to suggest that there will any fundamental changes to the German mania for regulation."[31]

An industrial leader, Lothar Spaeth, complained that "it is not the revolutionaries who want change who sit at the bureaucratic tables but, increasingly, the foot draggers intent on self preservation."[32]

The alarm bells rang in Dresden when, on September 19, 2004, the neo-Nazi NPD party won 9.2 percent of the vote in Saxony state elections. Party leaders came together in a television studio for the post-polling interviews. As the interviewer turned to NPD top candidate Holger Apfel, the leaders of the other parties demonstratively turned on their heels and stalked out. At a television studio in Potsdam, where another neo-Nazi party, the German People's Union (DVU) the same night also polled well in the state of Brandenburg, a similar walkout took place.

The other parties wanted to demonstrate their revulsion at the neo-Nazis themselves and their anti-foreigner policies, but the calculated rejection was more than that. The neo-Nazi success was a setback to efforts to efforts to build the state economy. The last thing any region battling for growth needs is neo-Nazis in any form. They have nothing sensible to offer. Most of their deputies are unable to contribute to effective legislation. The mischievously simple solutions they offer to solve complex problems are not "solutions" at all but part of the problem itself. Outsiders do not want to live in a place where they might be attacked. Firms do not want to set up in places where their international reputation might suffer by association.[33]

The echoes of the election went far beyond the state's borders. A month later Saxony received some unwanted international advertising. As the state assembly reconvened on a tension-filled day when many people feared something would explode, media people arrived from Britain, France, Denmark, Japan and Italy, and watched the twelve NPD members enter the building past thickets of microphones, a broadside of camera flashes, and about 250 anti-neo-Nazi demonstrators calling "Nazis Out!". The footage went round the world, taking the message to potential investors that this was a place to be avoided.

It was small comfort that all parties were on their best behavior, and that the session ended without incident. Saxony is economically the most successful Eastern state but, as one commentator expressed it, "urgently needs jobs, more training, and to be able to offer perspective for young people. The state coffers are empty and the mood is bad—and that is what washed the right-wing extremists into parliament."[34]

NOTES

1. "This state…," Martin Jaenicke in "Der Primus seiner Klasse—Die Wirtschaft der DDR hat laengst Weltniveau," *Geo Special* (Hamburg: Gruner + Jahr, February 13, 1985).

2. De Maizière, described the scene in *Anwalt der Einheit, Ein Gespräch mit Christine de Mazières* (Berlin: Argon Verlag, 1996) 94. Indications of East Germany's economic plight had emerged earlier, but apparently not the full extent.

3. "One of the strangest…," Lothar de Maizière in *Anwalt der Einheit*, 94.

4. "An economic catastrophe…," Guenter Mittag in *Um Jeden Preis* (Berlin: Aufbau Verlag, 1991) 356.

5. Bundesbank statistics. The ten million figure includes the armed forces.

6. "Market economy Big Bang...," is a term used by Jan Priewe, professor of economics at the Berlin University of Technology and Economy. He said, "Whatever drove the political protagonists of unification in the Chancellor's Office, they did not have an economic conception of even the most rudimentary sort. Their actions were exclusively directed by [considerations of] power politics and election tactics...precisely because economic unity had to lead to such great problems, flanking economic, financial and social policies with long-term effects were necessary." In a contribution to *Ostdeutschland—Eine Abgehaengte Region?* (Dresden: Junius Verlag, 2001), 19.

7. Former German Chancellor Helmut Schmidt points out that this figure of four percent is roughly equal to the percentage of the United States GDP taken up by the U.S. defense budget. In "Ich habe noch nie was von Visionen gehalten..." *Wirtschaft & Markt*, July, 2004.

8. Germany's GDP grew 1.6 percent in 2004 and by 0.9 percent in 2005, according to the Federal Statistics Office. GDP declined 0.1 percent in 2003, according to a joint report by the six leading German economic institutes, Ifo in Munich, HWWA in Hamburg, RWI in Essen, IfW in Kiel, IWH in Halle, and DIW in Berlin.

9. "It doesn't need...," Heinz Mueller in a talk with the author in March, 1992. The house needed further renovation after being damaged by fire in 1997.

10. "We have passed...," Guenter Rexrodt in "Der Aufschwung Ost 'greift'," *Hamburger Abendblatt*, July 13, 1993.

11. "The economy of...," in "Germany's Challenge," the *Financial Times*, August 20, 1993.

12. HWWA Institute for Economic Research in Hamburg, in "Forscher: Ostdeutschland faellt wirtschaftlich weiter zurueck," *dpa*, May 23, 1996.

13. Michael Burda, Humboldt University, Berlin, in statement by the Center for Economic Studies and the Ifo Institute (CESifo), November 30, 2001.

14. "If the banks...," Guido Westerwelle quoted by Klaus George and Steffen Uhlmann in *Zur Sache Ost* (Berlin: Edition Klageo, 2000), 28.

15. "There are large...," Koehler quoted in "Einmischen statt abwenden," *Focus*, September 13, 2004.

16. According to Rudolph Hickel, professor of Financial Sciences at Bremen University, it was unlikely that, as had been hoped, Eastern Germany would be able to stand on its own feet from 2020. "That is why it is important for economic development...to be strengthened. That includes rethinking the present subsidy philosophy and developing new priorities." In a contribution to *Ostdeutschland—Eine Abgehaengte Region*, 61. Edgar Most, an Eastern banker who is a member of a government-sponsored body, Discussion Circle East, warns that the East "is aging, becoming dumber, and impoverished. . . Either we succeed in ending the decline or we prepare ourselves...to be in the long-term propped up by the West as we simply drift aimlessly along." He says in the latter case, the population of the East might drop to, say, twelve million [from the present fifteen million]. See "Komma fuer Komma abgestimmt," *Wirtschaft & Markt*, August 2004.

17. "Today, after fifteen...," Klaus von Dohnanyi in "Wende im Kopf noetig," *Wirtschaft und Markt*, October, 2004.

18. Average rate taken from David Marsh, in *Germany and Europe—The Crisis of Unity*, (London: Mandarin Paperbacks, 1995) 75.

19. For an analysis of Poehl's dispute with Kohl over monetary union, see Marsh, Chapter Five, "A Difficult Transplant."

20. "Envisaged conceding…," Harry Nick in "Treuhand im Spiegel," *Wirtschaft & Markt*, December, 2005.

21. "Considerable state…, " Helmut Schmidt in *Auf dem Weg zur deutschen Einheit*, (Reinbek bei Hamburg: Rowohlt Verlag, 2005), 118.

22. "Clearly, the puristic…," Schmidt, 118. The Free Democrat economics minister at the time, Helmut Haussmann, came under fire from other directions as well. "Instead of plunging into crisis management, he blustered on about a second Wirtschaftswunder. In February 1990, a senior civil servant in the Bonn Finance Ministry complained, 'The government has nothing in the drawer to pave the way economically for reunification.'" See Peter Christ and Ralf Neubauer in *Kolonie im eigenen Land*, (Reinbek bei Hamburg: Rowohlt Taschenbuch Verlag, 1993), 103.

23. See "In der DDR waechst die Unzufriedenheit—De Maizière warnt Handel—120 000 Metaller streikten," *Koelner Stadt-Anzeiger*, July 7, 1990.

24. "It was clear…," de Maizière in *Anwalt der Einheit*, 103.

25. The arrangement excluded property expropriated between 1945 and 1949, during the Soviet administration. The reasons for this exclusion have become the subject of an acrimonious dispute.

26. "Were just unable to imagine…," de Maizière in *Anwalt der Einheit*, 103.

27. According to Daniela Dahn, an Eastern journalist, many Easterners had occupied disputed properties two or three times as long as the claimants once had. She quotes one survey as finding that only three percent of claimants were former owners, and ninety seven percent were inheritors, often of the second generation. See *Wir bleiben hier oder Wem gehoert der Osten—Vom Kampf um Haeuser und Wohnungen in den neuen Bundeslaendern* (Reinbek bei Hamburg: Rowohlt Taschenbuch Verlag, 1994), 11. She also points out that most absentee claimants did not even bother to try and lay claim to ownership when East Germany existed, even though it was possible for them to pay ground rent. Payment was expected not in West marks but in East marks, which meant the amounts involved were small. Making payments would have been signal that a claimant felt his or herself still to be the owner, Dahn says. "However, many Western owners were not prepared to meet the demands of East German local authorities…East Germans assumed that those who had left had taken a life [changing] decision that included giving up property." (Dahn, 12). She adds, "Some individual claims for restitution involved entire streets, localities, and even [entire] villages…One Freiherr laid claim to no more and no less than an entire city: Putbus." (Dahn, 13).

28. "That is their right…," Friedrich Schorlemmer, in *Deutschland ungleich Vaterland*, (Hamburg: Sternbuch im Verlag Gruner + Jahr AG & Co, 1991) 34.

29. "…there is no pressing…," Schmidt, 70.

30. Clash with bureaucracy related by Klaus Iwan in *Nach der Wende, Chaos ohne Ende* (Leichlingen: Verlag C. Loeer, 1995) 94.

31. "There is little…," Schmidt quoted in "Ich habe noch nie was von Visionen gehalten…," *Wirtschaft & Markt*, July 2004.

32. "It is not the…," in *Was jetzt getan werden muss getan—Seitenblicke auf Deutschland*, by Lothar Spaeth (Stuttgart/Leipzig: Hohenheim Verlag, 2002) 179. Success stories are so rare they stand out like a spill of diamonds on black cloth. Spaeth is associated with one of them. The East German Carl Zeiss Jena once supplied the East Bloc armed forces and the Soviet space program with precision-optics equipment. At unification, a new firm, Jenoptik AG, was formed, which was headed by Spaeth. The new firm split off from this former state combine, slashed the Stalinist-era workforce from 28,000 to 8,000, and turned its attention to computer chips, communications, and laser technologies. In 1991 it recorded a loss of one billion marks ($588 million). But when it made a common stock offering in June 1998, the offer was oversubscribed thirty times. On the first day of trading, its shares rose from 34 marks to 45.30 marks. By June 2003 Jenoptik had orders worth a company record of $2.8 billion.

33. For a list of the major employers in Eastern Germany, see "Die Top 100 im Osten," a list compiled by the *Die Welt* newspaper and reproduced in *Wirtschaft & Markt*, December 2005.

34. "Urgently needs jobs…," Olaf Kittel, in "Landtag—Erste Pruefung bestanden," *Saechsische Zeitung*, October 20, 2004. See Chapter 11—A Swing to Extremist Parties.

3

LIFE BECOMES COMPLICATED

AFTER THE FALL OF THE BERLIN WALL, everyone stumbled on surprises. When a singer from a Dresden operetta company visited West Germany for the first time, he noticed that "everything in the West is so tidy. Even the piles of dung are tidier…"[1] An East Berlin couple went shopping in West Berlin and did what they had always done: they left their baby in its buggy outside the supermarket. When they came out, it was no longer there.

Westerners quickly began making unsound assumptions about the East. A Hamburg acquaintance of mine who shall be identified only as Dieter, visited the East for the first time early in 1990. He went alone in the belief that the communist order was no longer a threat, and he found a bar where the atmosphere was congenial, the beer cold, and the customers apparently friendly. The longer the night grew, the more Dieter loudly denounced the party and Stasi "red socks." But Dieter had misread the signs. When he finally emerged into the night, it was late, he was drunk, and they were waiting for him. Dieter got in at least one blow in before the attackers overwhelmed him and beat him unconscious. He came to and staggered to a hospital, where a sympathetic night nurse washed the blood from his beard and patched him up.

The woman was drunk, garrulous from the red wine. Her lipstick was smeared, and her black hair was in disarray. Here, at a trestle table in an open-air restaurant in the town of Wittenberg, 100 yards from the church where Martin Luther had nailed up his ninety-five theses nearly 500 years before, she held court. Her message came clearly through the melancholia: unemployment, rising costs, debt, and the threat of eviction were sending Easterners into a spiral of decline, hopelessness, and inertia. The easy option was to sit at home and do nothing.

The evidence backs her: increases in domestic rents have led to increases in eviction. Apartments that once cost 120 marks a month were soon costing 900 marks a month. The spending boom on consumer goods eroded savings and people borrowed from banks that enthusiastically shoveled out cash to fuel the spending frenzy. Unemployment and debt followed. Housing companies report millions of marks in unpaid rents. Not enough cash was coming in to pay for repairs. Under the communists, rent defaulters were not evicted. Nonpayment was merely a misdemeanor. No longer.

Werner Bley, deacon at St Servatius church in Quedlinburg, told me, "This rush for consumer items took place when people had no idea they would soon be out of work. I tell people not to renovate their homes, to wait until things improve. It doesn't matter if old houses stay old a little longer. They won't fall down overnight. Why should they be made beautiful just because Westerners like it that way?"

Into the twenty-first century, the economic outlook remains bleak. Job opportunities are still few, wages for industrial workers are much lower than in the West. A disturbing trend has emerged: the exodus from East to West of the 1990s, which had slowed to a trickle, has accelerated again to nearly 40,000 a year. The migrants, predominantly the young and the talented, see no future in the East, where more than a million apartments are empty.[2] A total of 2.5 million people have left since 1990, said the Berlin-based *Sozialreport 2002.*[3] Two thirds of 2,000 people questioned neither felt at home in the united Germany nor wanted East Germany back, the report said. In Leipzig, a city of under 500,000, a total of 60,000 apartments are empty and almost 900,000 square meters of office space is on the market.[4] For those who remain, things that had once been simple are now more complicated. Like shopping. Big Western retail chains moved in and bought up corner stores, pulled them down, and built bigger and ritzier stores a long way from main shopping centers.[5] The profits go back to the West. In village after village, little shops have been boarded up or bricked in. In the cities, big out-of-town shopping malls on low-rent sites have been putting city-center shops out of business. About 300,000 people now have no local shops at all.[6] Many without cars are forced to travel by bus to shopping centers or buy at inflated prices from grocery vans which tour outlying regions.

Business is not always better in the capitalist world. Richard Peck, a cheerful, wiry little ex-gymnast, runs a down-market clothing shop in Eastern Berlin's Tucholsky Strasse. The street's Wilhelminian apartment blocks were home for generations of gunnery officers from the kaiser's army to the Third Reich, but the area plunged into decay during the communist era. The view from Peck's shop in those days was of the soupy-brown tones of urban decay, of chipped concrete, exposed brickwork, and decades of accumulated filth. Freedom came, and squatters moved in, bringing with them a quality of psychedelic anarchy.

Peck was better off financially when the view was soupy.

He told me he worked for the state-owned HO retail organization for a six percent commission on sales that made him a profit of between 48,000 and 60,000 East marks a year. His rent was 208 marks a month. By the mid-90s, the rent had risen to 1,400 marks a month, and the turnover was not enough to make up the deficit. He was worried that the rent would rise even more.[7]

The old East German mark was worth little more than monopoly money. Monetary union in 1990 came like the crack of a starter's pistol, signaling the arrival of the West German currency, the deutsche mark. Bounty hunters from the West picked up the scent. Men dressed in sharp suits lent money hand-over-fist to people who would have trouble paying it back. Money grubbers and cowboys from the capitalist fringes sold bogus investments, cars, encyclopedias, and insurance policies that were neither wanted nor needed. Easterners had been warned about the sharp practices of capitalism, but they had not confronted them directly and they were suckers for every scam in the book. Another shock: the realization that deceit was not limited to professional shysters but that cheating your neighbor was a mass sport. Giant used-car markets sprang up to meet the sudden demand by cash-flushed customers for Western cars.

BERLIN—Eastern Germans seeking credit are being looted by firms acting like bandits, the Berlin working group, *Neue Armut* (New Poor), said yesterday. The firms...systematically exploit the economic difficulties and lack of experience of Easterners, *Neue Armut* said. It named ten of the firms and said they were merely the tip of the iceberg. Prosecutors are investigating.

— *ddp/ADN*, December 20, 1993

Easterners abandoned their plastic two-stroke Trabants and drove away in shiny BMWs. These "new" cars broke down about the time the buyer became unemployed.

Easterners and Westerners have different mentalities. Cox (Cornelia) Habbema, a Dutch actress who spent many years in East Berlin in the seventies and eighties, recalls meeting some of her old crowd a decade after East

Germany collapsed. Many had settled in the West, and Cox found they had become like Westerners. They all talked "about money. The food is plentiful and
good. I listen, just like I used to. But in those days we talked about entirely different things. What made life worthwhile, for example. What was no longer
tolerable. About rights and wrongs. If someone needed help. Those were our
themes then. I understood what they were talking about. But now they are
Westerners but don't seem to know it. After the topic of money is exhausted,
the old wounds break open. The aggression between East and West comes
bouncing back."[8]

Yet, at the same time, Easterners are in some ways becoming like the very
Westerners they criticise. One who came West thirty years ago says he doesn't
like going back so often now. "All they think about is money," he told me. "And
they moan all the time. I tell them, 'You wanted unification.' I say, 'Of course
there's unemployment.' I tell them they've forgotten what it used to be like."

East-West divisions emerged well before unification in 1990. In December
1989 East Germany's new communist prime minister, Hans Modrow, met
Chancellor Kohl in Dresden. It was a good-neighborly affair. They reached
agreement on several fronts and issued declarations of cooperation. In February 1990 Modrow went to Bonn to meet Kohl again. But, by now, three
months after the Wall had come down, the mood had begun to change. Westerners were looking at Easterners as a nuisance. Curiosity had turned to im-
patience. Unofficial rule bending to allow the chugging Trabant cars to break
parking rules and pollution laws in the West was ending.

Modrow sought financial assurances. But Kohl sensed the mood change.
The history-making atmosphere of Dresden had vanished. Kohl was distant
and patronizing. All Modrow got was an agreement on the shape of economic
union. He was publicly insulted. One of Kohl's cabinet ministers said he was
surprised Modrow did not get up and storm out.[9] Modrow later said that
Kohl's only interest was winning elections. This act of disdain probably did as
much to forge a separate Eastern identity as any other single event. Modrow
was not one of the Berlin-based clique that ran East Germany but had been
brought in from Dresden, where he had been party boss. British Labour Party
politician Denis Healey told me that Modrow was the only senior East German official he had met who appeared to have any human qualities at all: "I
saw Hans Modrow at his house above the river (the Elbe) in Dresden and
found him both impressive and human."[10] Modrow might have had blots on

his record, but he was an Easterner and many Easterners held him in high esteem. They resented Kohl's high-handedness. It was a taste of things to come. Western arrogance was becoming a major irritant.

HAMBURG: "The worst mistake was that the government gave the impression that German unity could be...more-or-less financed out of petty cash."
—Former Chancellor Helmut Schmidt, in "uns Deutsche kann der Teufel holen," *Die Zeit*, May 17, 1991.

HAMBURG—Chancellor Kohl made a "serious error" when he failed to appeal to the German people to tighten their belts to cope with the burden of unification, President Richard von Weizsaecker said. —*Stern magazin*, quoted by *dpa*, May 11, 1994

NOTES

1. "Everything in the West...," Steffen Friedrich quoted in "Es ist wie auf einem anderen Stern," *Hamburger Abendblatt*, November 27, 1989.
2. Statistics from *Sueddeutsche Zeitung*, April 19, 2002.
3. According to the Federal Office of Statistics, two million people went from Eastern Germany to Western Germany between 1991 and 2003. But just over a million have returned, leaving a total decline of 848,000, the Office said. According to a report by the *Hamburger Abendblatt* on June 30, 2005, the Office said 91,000 people left Eastern Germany in 2004, reducing the population to 13.4 million. Other sources say the population of the region has declined from 16.7 million in 1989 to 15.3 million in 2004. An estimated half a million Easterners live in the East but work in the West.
4. Statistics from Nicola Dickmann, in "Housing Surplus in Leipzig has Landlords Pulling all Stops to Attract Tenants," *Frankfurter Allgemeine Zeitung*, English-language edition, March 20, 2002.
5. The Western German Spar supermarket chain reported that, of 1,600 small stores in Eastern Germany it had taken over, it had either closed or otherwise disposed of 1,500. Their floor area of as small as 300 square feet was "not suitable" for the grocery trade, board chairman Bernhard A. Schmidt said in "Spar startet im Osten durch," *Hamburger Abendblatt*, February 23, 1992.
6. See "Ostdeutsche Doerfer verlieren ihre Geschaefte," *Hamburger Abendblatt*, May 29, 1993.
7. The author spoke several times with Pech between 1990 and 1993.
8. "About money...," Cox Habbema, in *Mein Koffer in Berlin—Oder das Maerchen von der Wende* (Leipzig: Militzka Verlag, 2004), 59.
9. Education minister Juergen Moellemann quoted in "Das war wie eine Ohrfeige," *Der Spiegel*, February 19, 1990.
10. "I saw Hans..." Letter to the author, May 15, 1996.

4

RETREAT INTO NOSTALGIA

A WAVE OF NOSTALGIA IS WASHING across the East. It is a matter of reaching for a bottle, taking a laudanum fix, and entering a make-believe time warp of warmth and benevolence cloaked in a romantic pink haze. The trimmings are all there—F-6 cigarettes, communist-style cola, the smoke-belching Trabant joke car, a supposed look alike of former party boss Erich Honecker stepping out at East German-style dances.

A television show takes a walk down memory lane, and stores sell items of East German miscellany. People who lived for forty years under a regime they loathed have invented a new past. They forget the oppression and the tedium, and yearn for the days they used to hate. For some, especially the young, this nostalgia is more of a gag relating to a world they were too young to know. They take part rather like people in Western countries once bought Mao's *Little Red Book*. But for others the nostalgia drips heavily with *Wehmut*.

Erika Riemann is not nostalgic. When she was fourteen years old, she used lipstick to paint a red bow on Stalin's mustache. The artwork was performed in 1945 on a photograph in a school building in the town of Muehlhausen, part of the Soviet zone of occupation. She was too young to know that the Soviet sense of humor did not run to enjoying a teenage jest. Soldiers arrested her, and she vanished into the Gulag, where she remained for eight years. When she fell ill, doctors removed her appendix without anaesthetic. She was released in 1954.

Riemann wrote a book about her imprisonment.[1] She was interviewed on television in 2003, a year when the nostalgia reached a crescendo in a series of television shows portraying the former dictatorship as a vaguely cartoon-like place with quaint customs where funny little cars bounced along bumpy streets. Millions of Easterners tuned in. The promoters were accused of prettifying an unjust society. One critic said East Germany was being presented "as a soap opera in a way that could not be more incompetent, more dumb, or more twisted and that plumbs the depths of the media's handling of recent German history."[2]

It was a gray country, with an occasional strange purple or pink stripe some-where, because someone had gotten a plastic truck from a West German grand-mother. (Artist Norbert Bisky commenting on his childhood in East Germany, in "German painter draws on images of youth.")
— *Wall Street Journal,* December 16, 2005.

The Riemann interview was beamed during one show in which ice-skating champion Katarina Witt and boxer Henry Maske, both of whom led privileged East German childhoods, took viewers down memory lane. Viewers in the packed studio revelled in Witt's enthusiasm as she relived her youth, accompa-nying a camera team to her old school, and visiting old friends. The producers did not spoil the party by inviting Riemann to the studio. Instead, they filmed the interview in advance and cut it into the telecast, which made it impossible to gauge audience reaction.

This nostalgia feeds on itself and rationalizes all it touches. This conver-sation was overheard in a Berlin train.

Woman A: I don't know any more how I can afford these things with my tiny pension. When I think of how cheap a bread roll was in the old days. Only five pfennigs...And medicines, I didn't have to pay anything extra, and I didn't have to think about where the ten-euro surcharge [to visit a doctor] was coming from.

Woman B: And when I think about how long my daughter has been out of work. East Germany was not so bad. We all lived well. Okay, there were limits to travel, but with present-day prices few can af-ford that anyway.[3]

A popular form of *Ostalgie* (a composite of *Ost*, meaning "East," and *Nostalgie*, meaning "nostalgia") is owning a Trabant car. No single product underlined East Germany's industrial arthritis as obviously as the Trabant. Based on a pre-war design, it had a top speed of about sixty-five mph. Its motor, which burned a mixture of gasoline and oil, discharged clouds of blue exhaust fumes.

When, in November 1989, lines of Trabis chugged through the holes in the Wall sounding like motor mowers needing a tune-up, almost every traffic regulation in the West was broken. The little chuggers had inadequate lights for the fast-moving autobahn traffic, and they were structurally unsafe. After a simulated crash using dummies in which a stationary Trabi was hit from be-hind, an assessor declared with a shrug of the shoulders that no one inside it would have had the ghost of a chance.[4]

East Germans had to wait on average more than ten years for a new Trabant. The wait could be longer. One youth put in his order at the age of eighteen, but by the time unification came in 1990 he was at thirty-five—and still waiting.[5] Easterners swarmed to buy BMWs, Mercedes and Volkswagens, with their power, comfort, and for a time, prestige. But the Trabant survived to become a cult car and about sixty fan clubs have sprung up. One Berlin garage fits battery engines to them while other works have found niche businesses turning them into convertibles, stretching them, or changing them into small treble-axled trucks.

The Trabi as a prism through which to view the past.

Eva-Maria Storbeck finds the nostalgia just as revolting as Erika Riemann. I had Storbeck's name from the official report of a government investigation into abuses by the East German dictatorship, and knew she had a harrowing story to tell.[6]

I met Eva-Maria at her home in the village of Vieritz, west of Berlin. She is a trimly built woman in her fifties, friendly but reserved. Her demeanor and appearance combine vivacity with grittiness. Her first son, Bernd Schewe, died on October 22, 1971, at the age of thirteen. His eight-year-old sister, Birgit, discovered the body sagging from a silk scarf tied round the neck and fixed to a door handle. Bernd was too tall to have hanged himself. The marks on his neck showed he had been strangled.

No one knows if the police in the Brandenburg town of Premnitz even bothered investigating. If they did, there were no results. She smelled a cover up, especially when two investigators from Berlin implied the crime must have been committed by a West German visitor. But Eva-Maria had a shrewd idea of who had killed her son.

Her first contact with the Stasi had been in 1963 in Leipzig, where she was studying to become a librarian. Two men took her to Halle, where she was questioned in the glare of two spotlights. What was her opinion of the Soviet Union? What were her political views? Why had she played the West German national anthem on the piano? (The anthem is sung to music composed by Haydn). She was shown a piece of blank paper in which holes had been cut. Eva-Maria recognized the cutouts as the tracing lines of a dress pattern from a magazine. What information was encoded in the holes? To whom was she sending the information? She was four months pregnant, but the questioning continued day and night, day after day. She was released after four months. She was arrested again and held for fourteen days. Later that year, her daughter, Birgit, was born. But the arrests continued. She lost count of how often she had been pulled in.

When a second son, Heiko, was born in 1977, Storbeck ran into a sustained program of harassment from teachers and doctors. After unification, her Stasi file revealed that the Stasi had several times lured her away from her home with bogus reasons and, during her absence, had searched it. The method was common. They entered the house, photographed the contents, examined them, and then used the photographs to replace them exactly as they were.

Eva-Maria thought back to her dead son. The day he died she had been working at a local school on holiday duty. Birgit was with her. The Stasi would have known her whereabouts if they wanted to search the house. They might have mistakenly thought Bernd was with her at the school. She asked herself: if the Stasi had entered the house and if they had been disturbed by a thirteen-year-old boy, what would they have done? The probable answer is: killed him. There was otherwise no motive for the death. No other crime had been committed.

Vieritz is a sleepy little rural community. Like people all over East Germany, the villagers made their pact with the dictators in East Berlin, which meant accepting the restrictions of a dictatorship in exchange for a peaceful, if frustrating, existence. These days, the villagers are unwilling to admit their tacit pact. The past was not that bad, they believe. Unsurprisingly, this comfortable little world does not sit comfortably with Eva-Maria Storbeck's story.

She knows the villagers ridicule her.[7]

NOTES

1. *Die Schleife an Stalins Bart*, by Erika Riemann (Hamburg: Hoffmann und Campe Verlag, 2003).
2. "As a soap…," by Peter Kruse in "Die DDR als Seifenoper—Wie das deutsche Fernsehen Millionen von Menschen verhoent," *Hamburger Abendblatt*, date unknown.
3. "I don't know…," Ekkehard Schultz, in "Gar nicht so schlimm, gar nicht so schlecht—Zu Ursachen und Wachstumbedingungen von DDR-Nostalgie," *Stacheldraht*, January 31, 2005.
4. Simulated crash results reported in *Auto Motor Sport Magazin* 19 (1990): 190.
5. Long wait on buying list related by Rosemarie Gramsch in a letter to the author, August 1, 1997.
6. For Storbeck's statement on September 27, 1993, to the government-sponsored panel investing injustices in East Germany, see *Enquete-Kommission, Aufarbeitung von Geschichte und Folgen der SED-Diktatur in Deutschland—Staatssicherheit Seilschaften, VIII* (Frankfurt: Suhrkamp Taschenbuch Nomos, 1995) 745.
7. Report largely based on talks with Storbeck and her sister, Rosemarie Gramsch, as well as on papers from Storbeck's Stasi files.

5

THE BOXER

FEW PEOPLE BELIEVED AXEL SCHULZ could win the world heavyweight boxing title. But this 220-pound Nordic warrior from Valhalla, a product of the communist amateur boxing machine, was getting his chance against George Foreman. He was not supposed to be in Foreman's class, but his two handlers, trainer Manfred Wolke and manager Wilfried Sauerland, thought otherwise.

But even if Schulz did avoid getting knocked out by the big-punching Foreman, would he be allowed to win on points? What happens inside the ring, with the butting, eye-gouging and kidney punching, is almost puritanical compared with much that happens outside it. Whatever the result, I hoped it would be sufficiently clear-cut to prevent arguments. There would be hell to pay in Eastern Germany if there were any hints of professional boxing's notorious corruption.

East Germans knew the writings of Dashiell Hammett, who was one of the few American authors they were allowed to read. Hammett, a Marxist, wrote about the seedy side of American life in the 1920s.[1]

In this excerpt, Hammett writes about fight night in a town known, because of its lawlessness, as "Poisonville." Ike Bush, a capable battler, is supposed to take a dive in the sixth against a bum called Kid Cooper. Bush has other ideas. He "threw his right hand…Everyone in the house felt the punch. Cooper hit the floor, bounced, and settled there. It took the referee half a minute to count ten seconds…A high twinkle of light caught my eye. A short, silvery streak slanted down from one of the small balconies. A woman screamed. The silvery streak ended its flashing slant in the ring with a sound that was partly a thud, partly a snap. Ike Bush…pitched down on top of Kid Cooper. A black knife handle stuck out of the nape of Bush's neck."[2]

Few of the thousands of Easterners turning on their television sets in the early hours of April 23, 1995, as Schulz and Foreman prepared to enter the ring in Las Vegas, were thinking about Dashiell Hammett. Fewer still had ever heard of a former cop named Robert W. Lee. In 1956, Lee, whose heavily hooded eyelids half hidden behind dark glasses give him a deceptively benign appearance, had become the first black patrolman in the history of the New Jersey town of Scotch Plains. Lee must have stood out from the crowd because, in 1965, he was singled out to become a detective with the county prosecutor's office.

Manfred Wolke won the welterweight boxing gold for East Germany at the 1968 Mexico City Olympic Games. After the medal ceremony, he went back to the changing rooms, showered, dressed, and returned to ringside to watch the later fights. He was surprised to find himself seated beside the hulking form of George Foreman, clad in a dressing gown, and waiting for his heavyweight final. Wolke believed that Foreman's Russian opponent, Ionis Chapulis, would be too good, and he thought Foreman should have been warming up in the dressing room instead of sitting still. He said as much, but Foreman ignored the advice, and remained seated until his trainer came. Then he rose to his feet, yawned twice, stepped into the ring, and knocked out Chapulis in the second round.[3]

Afterwards Wolke and Foreman went their different ways. Foreman turned professional. Wolke returned to a communist country that allowed no professional boxing. At the 1972 Olympic Games in Munich, he had his moment of transient glory when he carried the East German flag at the opening ceremony. But inside the ring, he was eliminated with a cut eye against the eventual gold medal winner, Cuba's Emilio Correa. Wolke retired with a brilliant career record of 236 wins in 258 bouts, was promoted to lieutenant-colonel in the *Volksarmee*, and turned to training young boxers in the *Armeesportklub Vorwaerts* gymnasium in Frankfurt an der Oder.

Frankfurt was a transit point on the caviar run from East Berlin to Moscow via Warsaw. It was a forlorn Eastern outpost, scarred from wartime bombing, with remnants of north German brick Gothic architecture, but without a trace of the allure, energy, or money of its illustrious namesake of Frankfurt am Main. Yet in the world of East German boxing, all roads led to the cluster of low, gray buildings of the *Armeesportklub* complex up on a hill at the edge of town.

As Wolke faded into obscurity in this grim city, things were happening elsewhere. This was the era of Muhammad Ali and Joe Frazier. They were suddenly joined by another stellar figure. In January 1973 George Foreman, full of bruising menace, knocked Frazier out in Kingston, Jamaica, to win the heavyweight title. In 1975 Ali knocked out Foreman in Kinshasa, Zaire, to regain the title. Closer to Wolke's own weight class, Roberto Duran and Jose Napoles blazed trails through the world's best lightweights and welterweights.

Wolke's own success had helped fire a boxing boom throughout East Germany, but he was an ambitious man and wondered what might have happened if he had been living in the West.

A turning point came in 1977, when a lanky thirteen-year-old boxer was sent from the East German provincial club of BSG Motor Ludwigsfelde to Frankfurt an der Oder to be given the best tutelage the state could provide. From the windows of the state sports school, Henry Maske could look down on to the squat buildings of the Armeesportklub Vorwaerts complex where the pick of East German athletes were trained with an iron discipline to take on the world. Four years later, Maske himself would be sent over the road to join Wolke's senior boxing team.

About the time Maske arrived in Frankfurt an der Oder, Foreman retired, and Detective Robert W. Lee was appointed to the New Jersey Athletic Commission, which is supposed to monitor professional boxing.

In 1982, in the New Jersey town of East Orange, a preliminary boxer named Anthony Adams was knocked out in the first round of a bout against Tony Coster. Adams had lost all his five previous bouts while Coster had won all three of his. Adams weighed 176 pounds while Coster weighed 217.5 pounds, a huge difference of 41.5 pounds. Clearly this was a mismatch that never should have taken place.

The bout would normally have attracted no attention, except Adams was called as a witness at an commission of inquiry hearing into boxing malpractice. Adams testified that Deputy State Athletic Commissioner Robert W. Lee had not only raised no objection to the contest taking place but had adjusted the published weights to 190 pounds and 210.5 pounds to minimize the impression that a grotesque mis-match was being arranged.[4]

Because nothing ever happens in professional boxing without money changing hands, alarm bells were now ringing about Lee. In 1981, the FBI uncovered evidence that Lee and his boss at the commission, former heavyweight champion Jersey Joe Walcott, were extracting bribes in return for issuing promoters with licences.[5]

If reports such as these had reached the Armeesportklub officers' mess, there would have been some heavy tut-tutting.

After the commission of inquiry findings, Walcott was shunted off into retirement. Lee was reprimanded, but, instead of being sacked, was promoted to take Walcott's place. It was only when the commission of inquiry dug out more evidence against Lee that Lee's appointment was suspended.

But Lee had new fields to spread with muck.

A young heavyweight, Axel Schulz, who had been outpunching rivals around East Germany was in 1987 sent to join Wolke's boxing team. The same year, the veteran Foreman came out of retirement, and went on to win the International Boxing Federation (IBF) version of the title at the grandfatherly age of age of forty-five.

If both Maske and Schulz seemed destined for big things, Wolke's life was not all glory. At international tournaments behind the iron curtain, it was customary for national team trainers to sit together, bring out their bottles of vodka, slivovitz, and other national firewaters, and drink. It was not mere indulgence, but a duty.

Wolke explained, "I hadn't touched a drop until my thirtieth year…[but] when I began in 1973, it was like everything else I did: without ifs and buts. When I drank it was for keeps."[6]

He became an alcoholic. The Volksarmee turned a blind eye, but late one night he was picked up intoxicated, wandering in an industrial area where he should not have been, and was sent to a health farm to dry out. He was demoted to major and taken off the main boxing team.

He was reinstated only after giving up drinking.

As army officers, Wolke and Maske worked full time at boxing. This was both the communist way of ensuring success and a reward for bringing the country the prestige it desperately sought. As members of a privileged elite, they should have had no further aspirations, especially not for the professional version of the sport, which was officially detested. The idea of the pot-bellied, cigar-chewing manager lugging bulging money bags to the bank while the broken-nosed boxer counts his coppers to pay to heat his hovel was the sort of exploitation scenario that won support for communism in the first place. There were also other objections. An East Berlin sportswriter said: "…it is the moral aspect that distinguishes the professionals from the amateurs. The sensationalism, the inhumanity, the smaller...gloves, the absence of headgear, the lax medical care."[7] In the paper's view, professional boxing neglected the health of the competitors, a charge that could not be leveled at the professional versions of other sports.

East German amateurs watched big-time professional fights on television, especially when they traveled to foreign countries for tournaments, and they dreamed of the fortunes they could earn if they had the chance. But, in the insular communist world, it was a taboo theme. They talked about it, but not openly.

Any doubts Wolke, Maske, and Schulz had about their future were dispelled in December 1989 when the East German boxing team competed in Manila. After the tournament, the East German embassy rang, warning them to remain in their hotel rooms. A coup was taking place. Military police lined the streets and gunfire rumbled in the distance. The hotel staff had disappeared, so the boxers watched television. The networks were running hours of professional boxing, perhaps to deflect the attention of sports-mad Filipinos from politics. The boxers remained glued to the screens for two days and saw a world they wanted to be part of. One, Andreas Otto, recalled: "For the first time, we discussed openly what it would be like to be professionals."[8]

The team returned home to a country where everything was changing. The back of the ruling party had been broken, and the Stasi secret police was on the run. New, democratic political forces had been unleashed and the country was engulfed in a *rausch* of renewal. Color came to the gray streets as traders from the capitalist West drove across the border and set up roadside kiosks selling exotic merchandise people had never before been able to buy.

It was like one long birthday party with balloons and crackers.

The best of the country's cyclists, its top soccer, ice hockey, and handball players, signed lucrative professional contracts. It seemed that its boxers, top performers on the amateur world stage, merely needed to apply for professional licenses, choose any of the hungry managers waiting in the wings, provide bank account details, step into a ring, become famous, and make lots of money.

But boxing was not other sports.

That team in Manila had been trained by Guenter Debert, himself a professional in the days of post-war deprivation in the late 1940s. But now he toed the Stalinist hardline. Upon his return, he told an East Berlin newspaper he would do all he could to prevent professional boxing from gaining a foothold. He told about the televised bouts in Manila.

> It was not the sport that was predominant but the business side …brutal scenes showing battered boxers being allowed to continue purely with the aim of being destroyed physically…[it] appealed to the basest instincts of humans, and our athletes looked on astounded as their eyes were opened to this reality.[9]

The rumor mills churned. The mass-circulation West German *Bild Zeitung* said Maske had decided to turn professional. The state-run East German *Neues Deutschland* said Maske had decided no such thing. Maske himself equivocated, saying on East German television he did not have an aversion to becoming a professional.

Maske and Wolke did turn. The news shocked the Stalinist establishment. The officers' corps branded the pair as turncoats. Major Wolke and Lieutenant Maske were drummed out of the Volksarmee, and the amateur boxing association expelled them.

The two continued to use Armeesportklub training facilities, although they now had to pay. Then Schulz turned professional as well. That was too much. The establishment reacted with knee-jerk anger and banned all three. Wolke searched for a place to train and ran into a wall of resentment. The Volksarmee's influence extended to the sullen, gray Stalinist bureaucracy, and no one would make property available. Wolke saw the three of them as victims of a "conspirative smear campaign" and he suspected former team trainer Debert was behind it. "He's an old Stalinist," Wolke added.[10]

His luck changed. The East German rail company, the Reichsbahn, made available an old engine shed smelling of diesel oil. The shed, wedged in a tight triangle of land between a shunting siding, a disused brick signal box with broken windows and the main track to Berlin, was 650 square feet, barely big enough for a ring and punching bags. Wolke had to buy rope and make the ring himself. The three new professionals bought paint and renovated the shed themselves. When the heating did not work, which was often, they had to train in temperatures close to zero. But this shack was a home. The three musketeers were on the way.

Wolke met a West German manager and promoter, Wilfried Sauerland, who gingerly brought the team into the jungle of boxing capitalist style with its ballyhoo and venality.

The combination worked. Maske began his professional career in London by knocking out a flabby Mexican, Teo Arvizi, in 54 seconds. He won fight after fight.

Not only did he pick up a huge following, but he gave boxing in Germany a certain acceptibility. As well as film-star good looks, Maske had gravitas and depth. He could think and he could articulate. When he boxed he looked not like a gladiator taking part in a bloody and meaningless battle but a philosophy student who believed he was locked in a contest to solve humanity's problems. People who would normally not dream of watching a boxing bout switched on when Maske entered the ring.

On March 20, 1993, he beat "Prince" Charles Williams in Duesseldorf to win the IBF version of the world light-heavyweight title.

At last, Wolke was having his overdue success on the world stage.

Money was coming in, and the team was able to move out of the tiny training shack and into a larger room just a few yards away. It was still in the railway sidings, but the three had become used to the metallic screech of shunting carriages. Wolke himself was happy not to be in an opulent setting. He just wanted a place to train. "The railroad yards are dismal, but this doesn't bother me," he said.[11]

Schulz also kept winning. The extent of his improvement had not been noticed in certain places, notably in the backrooms of the IBF, where the deals were worked out under the scrutiny of a certain Robert W. Lee. Lee himself had set up the IBF, ostensibly to clean up boxing.

Frankfurt an der Oder's main shopping avenue, Karl Marx Strasse, puts on a brave face. The stores these days are neat and painted, but the street itself has a strange desolate feeling, as if most people have gone home. The commercial focus is on two capitalist-era shopping complexes facing each other that attract almost enough shoppers to stave off a mood of emptiness.

One complex, known as the Oderturm, consists of a tower block rising above an airy shopping atrium. It was here, late on the night of Saturday, April 22, 1995, that 2,500 people paying $3.60 each crowded beneath a big projection screen for an all-night session to watch the ice blonde Schulz, his eyebrows like medieval battlements, challenge Foreman, black, paunchy, and menacing, for the IBF championship.

Thousands of miles away in the tinsel of Las Vegas, 12,000 people paying up to $700 a head took their seats in the MGM Grand Garden Arena to watch the action at close quarters. Among the spectators were Hollywood stars Bruce Willis, Burt Reynolds, and Jack Nicholson.

It was in this extravagant setting that, twenty-seven years after their paths first crossed, Wolke—working Schulz's corner—and Foreman once more came face to face.

As events were to show, Las Vegas was an appropriate venue. This former desert stopover was given its name of "the Meadows" by nineteenth century Spanish traders. When a railroad linking the East Coast to California was built early in the twentieth century, Las Vegas was just a sleepy town along the route. But in 1931, new laws allowed quickie divorces and casino gambling. The East Coast mobs moved in. Bugsy Siegel built a luxurious gambling hotel known as the Flamingo. Territorial disputes happened, and Siegel was gunned down in 1947. Between 1948 and 1958, eleven of fourteen casino resorts that opened in Las Vegas were run by the mob. These were the years when professional boxing in America was firmly in the hands of luminaries such as Frankie Carbo, who determined who fought whom and who won. Big-time boxing arrived in Las Vegas in the early 1960s. The scowling Charles Sonny Liston, who was controlled by a mob run by Carbo and Blinky Palermo, defended his title there against Floyd Patterson in 1963. Liston settled in the town. In January 1971 his wife returned from a trip and discovered his bloated body. He had been dead for about six days. Whether he died from a heroin overdose or was rubbed out by the mob is unknown.[12]

All this was far from the minds of the jostling, beer-swilling crowd inside the Oderturm atrium. They knew Schulz was the underdog—the bookies were offering 8-1 against him—but they were optimistic. A good performance would lift their spirits in much the same way that East German swimmers and athletes once had and enable them for a few hours to forget the spiral of industrial collapse, joblessness, rising personal debt, and the spy-society accusations.

Schulz, twenty years the younger, began nervously, but his confidence grew and he used his quicker reflexes to slip and counter. He won the twelve rounder by a street, and Foreman knew it. The veteran's head sank to his chest as he walked back to his corner at the final bell, and it remained bowed until the decision was announced.

But this was not the way the men holding the purse strings had planned it. The judges followed the plot. One called the bout even, but the other two awarded it to Foreman. In the Oderturm atrium, shouts of disbelief rang out, and half-empty beer cans tossed in disgust thudded against the big screen.

The anger was more than just disappointment at a loss in a sporting arena. People saw it as another blow by the market-dominated economy—the same system that had given them unemployment, high prices, crime, and a host of other real or imagined injustices. The fight was a metaphor for the fortunes of the East after the fall of the Wall: high hopes followed by disappointment and resentment. People felt cheated.

Anyone imagining the leering ghost of Frankie Carbo drifting across the night sky after the fight would have been right. Two years after the bout, in May 1997, an FBI agent stopped IBF official Douglas Beavers in the garden of his Virginia home.

"Agent (Theresa) Reilly told Beavers that she had a tape that implicated him in bribe-taking. Beavers simply asked, 'What took you so long?'"[13] But it wasn't Beavers the FBI was hunting. It was Lee and some of his other cronies. Beavers agreed to turn informer in return for immunity from prosecution. His part of the bargain was to meet Lee and make secret audio and video tapes of the meetings.

Jack Newfield, a long-time observer of the boxing scene and a reporter for the *Village Voice* and the *New York Daily News*, watched fifteen hours of secretly filmed video footage. He recalled, "In the most graphic of the undercover videos, recorded on December 18, 1998, in a Portsmouth, Virginia, hotel room, Beavers arrived with the payoff money taped to his leg in a plastic bag." The sum of $5,000 changed hands. "On the tape you can see Lee sliding the money into the pocket of his suit," wrote Newfield.[14]

The amount in this case was small, but that was hardly important. Evidence assembled from witnesses as well as subpoenaed IBF records on rankings, fight contracts, checks, invoices, expense forms, and telephone records, revealed an organisation soaked in graft where little happened without undercover payments.

In 1999, Beavers appeared as a witness in a New Jersey court. In the dock was Lee who, together with other IBF officials, faced more than thirty corruption charges. Beavers told the court that that the Foreman-Schulz bout had been "fixed."

Jim Brady is a boxing writer who specializes in exposing corruption in the sport. In his account of the hearing, he wrote, "Beavers...testified that in 1995, George Foreman won a terrible split decision over Germany's Axel Schulz in Las Vegas. Nobody but the two judges thought Foreman had won, but with George bringing all the fans and TV money, there was almost no way the rugged German could get the decision."[15]

Part of the testimony was from a Las Vegas-based boxing promoter, Bob Arum, who promoted Foreman's fights. He said he had paid the IBF $100,000 in 1995 so Foreman could fight Schulz. Lee had demanded $500,000, Arum said. He refused.

The picture that came out of the probe was that Foreman needed to defend the title to retain IBF recognition as champion, but he needed an opponent he could beat—and not any stumblebum, because he would have to generate big television revenues. Arum thought Schulz would be ideal. He would put up a bit of a fight, but would be a pushover, and German television had the cash to pay lucrative sums for live coverage. There was one problem. Schulz was not rated in the top ten and thus not eligible for a title fight. So Arum paid the $100,000, Schulz was included in the ratings, declared a valid challenger, and given the bout.[16]

So Eastern Germans were vindicated. Schulz had been robbed of the heavyweight title.[17] Gamekeeper-turned-poacher Robert W. Lee, was banned from boxing for life and sent to jail.[18] The IBF was placed in the hands of a court-appointed monitor. But the damage had been done. The result stood. It was no consolation that the term "world title" is, in any case, a nonsense because of the number of organisations, one as rapacious as the next, siphoning off money by running their own championships. Neither was the fact that fighters have been victims of shady dealing throughout professional boxing's seamy history. The warnings of party functionaries had been justified. Professional boxing was a dirty business.

NOTES

1. According to one biographer of Hammett, some critics had described Hammett's novel, *Red Harvest*, as "a Marxist assault on capitalism, and certainly Hammett forcefully dramatized the evils of a system driven by greed." See William F. Nolan, in *Hammett—A Life at the Edge* (New York: Congdon & Weed, 1983), 77.

2. "Threw his right hand...," Dashiell Hammett in *Red Harvest* (London: Pan Books, 1975), 71.

3. Foreman episode at ringside from Torsten Schulz, in *Der Boxermacher—Manfred Wolke & Seine Champions* (Leipzig: Gustav Kiepenheuer Verlag, 2002), 51.

4. Adams received $250 dollars for the fight but was suspended for not putting up a good fight, according to Jeffrey T. Sammons in *Beyond the Ring—The Role of Boxing in American Society* (Urbana: University of Illinois Press, Illini Books edition, 1990) 255.

5. The FBI mounted in 1981 a sting operation known as "Crown Royal," in which an undercover agent posed as a man wanting a promoter's licence, taped a conversation with Lee at a meeting where he handed Lee cash. See Jim Brady, in *Boxing Confidential—Power, Corruption, and the Richest Prize in Sport* (Lytham, Lancs, U.K.: Milo Books, 2002) 271.

6. "I hadn't touched...," Schulz, 66.

7. "It is the moral aspect...," Klaus Schielke in "Steht das Profi-Boxen schon vor unserer Tuer?," *Berliner Zeitung*, December 22, 1989.

8. "For the first time...," Andreas Otto, quoted by Klaus Weise, in *Henry Maske—Auf Eigene Faust* (Berlin: Verlag Sport und Gesundheit, 1995) 55.

9. "It was not the sport...," Guenter Debert quoted by Klaus Schielke in "Steht das Profi-Boxen schon vor unserer Tuer?," in *Berliner Zeitung*, December 22, 1989.

10. "Conspirative smear...," Manfred Wolke quoted by Mary Thuermer and Markus Goetting, in *Henry Maske—der Gentlemanboxer* (Munich: Wilhelm Heyne Verlag, 1995), 57.

11. "The railroad yards are...," Wolke quoted in Weise, 68.

12. For detailed assessments of the Carbo-Palermo era and corruption in boxing in general, see, for example, Sammons and Brady.

13. "Agent [Theresa] Reilly...," Brady, 307.

14. "In the most...," Jack Newfield in "The Shame of Boxing: Favors for Sale—On Tape," in *The Nation*, on-line edition, November 12, 2001. http://www.thenation.com/doc/ 2011112 /newfield/6

15. "Beavers...testified...," Brady, 311.

16. Hearings against Lee and the IBF gained widespread press coverage. For a detailed account of both Beavers's role and of Lee's career with the IBF, see Brady, 268; for other accounts of Beavers's role, see "How a Portsmouth Man Put the International Boxing Federation on the ropes," in Associated Press Sports Editors, the *Dallas Morning News*, online edition, by Ed Miller, March 23, 2004; "Boxing Body Faces Corruption and Bribe Slur," the *Examiner*, San Francisco, January 31, 2000; and "'Magic' may have run out for IBF," in the Associated Press's online service, February 5, 2000.

17. The Foreman fight proved the high point of Schulz's career. He was never able to repeat his form of that night and retired in 1999. Maske defended his title eleven times before retiring in 1996 with just one loss in thirty-one fights. Wolke still trains boxers from his Frankfurt an der Oder gymnasium.

18. Lee was convicted on six criminal charges money involving laundering and tax fraud. Another twenty-seven charges, including bribery charges, were dismissed. He was sentenced to jail for 22 months, fined $25,000, and agreed to a lifetime ban from involvement in boxing. He was due to go to jail after exhausting his appeals procedures. See Case No. 03-1691: Robert W. Lee, Sr. v. United States. Other IBF officials to face charges include Lee's son, Robert Lee Jr., Donald Brennan, and Francisco Fernandez. Fernandez made no court appearance and a warrant had been issued for his arrest.

6

THE MAN WHO GAVE
HISTORY A NUDGE

A FEMALE VOICE, SHRILL AND spitting outrage from the back of the hall, ripped through the atmosphere like a trumpet blast.

Cut off in mid sentence, the speaker at the rostrum fell silent. Guenter Schabowsi, ex member of the East German ruling SED, ex member of the Politburo, the highest decision-making body of the old Stalinist state of East Germany, paused and listened.

The interjector, a gray-haired woman in baggy jungle green trousers, shawl thrown across one shoulder, complained that she had lost her house and land, and none of the political parties cared. None except the reformed communists of the PDS, she said.

As she warmed to her task, it became clear that her real agenda was not just a personal dispute about property. It was political. The PDS, she continued, was the only party that opposed military participation in Afghanistan and Kosovo.

This was too much for Schabowski. Raising his voice, he said the PDS was simply the SED, and the SED had been a friend of former Serb president Slobodan Milosevic [who, until his death, faced war crimes charges in The Hague]. The sharp retort drew sustained applause.

The interjector slowly walked toward the rostrum, talking and ignoring Schabowski's calls to order. Schabowski said, "Under the SED, you would not be allowed to come here and speak like you are doing."

She slowly left the hall, still complaining about injustices.

Her departure from the meeting in Hamburg on April 30, 2002, left Schabowski and a second panelist, Guenter Nooke, to continue on the evening's theme: political extremism and the PDS.[1]

Nooke, broad shouldered, combative, black bearded, is a former East German civil rights activist. In the days when Schabowski was a member of the Politburo, Nooke worked in church peace and environmental groups—and walked a tightrope between state harassment and arrest. Schabowski once edited the official party newspaper, *Neues Deutschland*. Nooke helped found an illegal church information paper called *Aufbruch* (Awakening).

In the united Germany, Nooke became a Christian Democrat deputy in the *Bundestag* (parliament), while Schabowski withdrew from active party politics after undergoing a sort of road-to-Damascus conversion and rejecting his communist past. Now, more than a dozen years later, both men broadly agreed on their contempt for the PDS.

But the audience this spring evening in 2002 took as much interest in the controversial figure of Schabowski as in the discussion itself. After taking a question from the floor, he explained his position by saying, "I am a sinner." He added, "When you are given a kick by people you are purporting to represent, you have to ask why."

When another questioner asked which political party he now supported, he simply replied, "It would border on tastelessness if I were now to ingratiate myself with a political party."

Nooke's thoughts might well have gone back to a turbulent day on November 4, 1989, when more than half a million East Germans, caught up in the rushing tide of revolution, pushed into Berlin's Alexanderplatz. One after the other, the regime's apparatchiks took the microphone, and, one after the other, were jeered and catcalled and whistled down. One of the speakers was Schabowski. Down in the huge crowd was Nooke, who later recalled the moment. "What could be worse for a dictatorship than to be ridiculed? As I stood, eyes damp, in the midst of this mass of humanity…I knew that what was happening was irreversible."[2]

Five days later, the Berlin Wall fell.

When Guenter Schabowski rose on the morning of November 9, 1989, he knew he had a busy day ahead. But, as he said good-bye to his Russian wife before being driven from the stockade at Wandlitz, outside East Berlin, to a meeting of the party's Central Committee, he had not the slightest inkling that he was stepping into the center of a political storm that was to change the world.

The previous day, Schabowski, the jowly Berlin party boss, had survived a purge of the Politburo, the party's policy-making committee. The purge was a desperate attempt to control the frenetic pace of events as people fled in their thousands to the West through Hungary and Czechoslovakia and others went on to the streets in protest marches. Now, as information secretary of the Central Committee, Schabowski faced a big test: telling an international televised meeting what the party proposed doing to stop the disintegration. One crucial procedural change took this meeting into uncharted waters: for the first time, questions party hacks had not vetted were to be allowed. Schabowski would need all his skills to deal with spontaneous questions put from the floor by an aggressive and nimble foreign press corps. It was an innovation that was to stretch the party's competence to beyond breaking point.

The Central Committee meeting began in the morning with a proposal to ease travel regulations. The new Politburo had already approved the proposal, but the Central Committee debated the wording and agreed on some changes.

But none of the leadership, now headed by Egon Krenz, had ever needed to react quickly to rapidly changing events. Neither had it ever had to account to a critical public. Schabowski was not present when the proposal was discussed. As one of the few senior apparatchiks who acted like a person rather than a soulless political hack, he had become the publicity man entrusted with the hopeless task of improving the party's image. And now he was at another press meeting. When he returned to the Central Committee meeting, Krenz handed him the paper containing the new travel rules. The harassed-looking Schabowski barely had time to glance through the paper before the televised conference began at 6:00 p.m. in the charmless artificial-wood and crystal-lighting ambience of the press center, a hall in a grimy building less than 200 yards from the Wall itself.

He began as if he were trying to bore everyone. He spoke about new plans to hold elections and other business the "renewed" party was dealing with now that Honecker and the others had been kicked out. He read the paper quickly, obviously unfamiliar with its contents. It was two minutes to seven when, in reply to a question, he said that people would be able to travel to the West at short notice and without restriction. A questioner asked when the change would apply. Schabowski, the light glinting from his metal spectacle frames, looked uncertain. He picked up the papers again as if searching for something he had missed. After hesitating, he replied, "As far as I am aware, it takes effect immediately, without delay."

There have been plenty of famous quotes in history, but few to equal this for impact. What precisely had happened is still unclear. One version is that his reply was based on information contained in a separate piece of paper carrying the wording of the decision to relax travel restrictions. Point Two of this paper said, "The following regulations apply immediately...." What, according to this version, he had not seen was a crucial piece of information buried at the bottom of the page like an afterthought that said, "The attached press statement dealing with the regulations is to be published on November 10, 1989." That is, the next day. This note is said to have been found after the meeting, screwed up on the floor.[3] Another, less credible, version is that Schabowski was part of a KGB plot to force the slow-moving East Germans to enter the world of perestroika and glasnost. A third theory is that he decided on the spur of the moment to act alone for his own reasons.

Then the questions came in a rush. What was "short notice"? An hour? A week? A month? What would the reasons for refusal be? He had said exit to West Germany. Did he also mean West Berlin? What did this mean for the Wall?

The Western agencies all sent out slightly different messages. Reuters had its initial report on the line at 7:00 p.m., the West German *dpa* agency a minute later, and *AP* a minute after that. The official East German agency, *ADN*, whose director general was a member of the Central Committee, was aware that an embargo on the story until 4:00 a.m. the following day, but shortly after seven, someone saw the lack of sense in that and sent the news out anyway. *ADN* did not correct Schabowski's version. If it had, events might have taken a different turn. The delay would have given the army, police, border guards, and Stasi time to deploy their forces and to interpret the new regulations as they wanted.

But it was too late. The sheer speed and force of the reaction was like a dam bursting. The purpose of the Berlin Wall had been to keep people from leaving. Within hours it had become little more than a curiosity.

After his speech, confusion reigned. It was not immediately apparent what his announcement meant in concrete terms. Most of the media were unsure what to make of it. But any doubts among East Germans themselves were removed by the official East German *Aktuelle Kamera* news program at 7:30 p.m. that said, "Private trips abroad can be applied for immediately without special reasons." The rush to the checkpoints began. Just after 8:30 p.m., about sixty people were allowed through at Chaussee Strasse.

What happened that night revealed the increasing confidence of a people who were seeing signs of collapse on all sides and the decreasing confidence of border troops who were equally aware of the disintegration around them. After its first announcement, *ADN* said no more at all until 10:25 p.m., when it dutifully added that travel visas would be issued by "the relevant departments of passport departments of *Volkspolizei* local bureaus." But by then it was far too late.

In the Hamburg headquarters of the English-language service of *dpa*, Ernest Gill came on for the night shift at 11:30 p.m. and was told that travel restrictions had been eased. But no details were available. Western television channels were no help. Gill cheerfully went away and made a cup of coffee, not knowing that, before his shift finished, the world would be a different place.

Thousands of people demanding information telephoned police stations. The pressure built up at checkpoints closest to heavily settled residential areas of East Berlin. Lines lengthened. People were told to go away and come back in the morning. But a Politburo member had said that exit was "immediately," they protested. The lines grew until they became crowds, and the mood became more and more insistent. Guards counted their bullets. They saw that if crowd turned to mob, their Kalashnikovs would be useless.

Telephones rang hot as border posts sought instructions. But on this night communications between Stasi, the *Volksarmee* and border guards broke down. Individual attempts to find out what was happening and bring events under control came to nothing. For forty years, the party's great fear was being overwhelmed by street power. It had nearly happened in the workers' revolt of 1953. East Germany's security forces were trained to smash troubles before they began, yet the entire system failed on the night it was needed.

At the Bornholmer Strasse checkpoint a tailback of cars had grown three miles long. By about 11:00 p.m. about 20,000 people were lined up at the checkpoint. One guard was heard to say, "We'd better let them through or they'll lynch us." Two Stasi officers on duty, fearing that the situation would explode, gave the order to lift the barrier. At 11:20 p.m. the crowd charged through. The dam was broken. In the pandemonium, identity cards and exit visas were irrelevant. The crowd was uncheckable.

The Central Committee meeting continued to 8:45 p.m., when members adjourned to a nearby restaurant. Word of Schabowski's press conference was getting around. Committee members were shocked. Events were running out of control.

Between 11:30 p.m. and midnight, the barriers went up at other Berlin checkpoints, Heinrich-Heine Strasse, Oberbaumbruecke and Chaussee Strasse—where the first group had been tentatively allowed out. By 10:00 p.m. thousands of Easterners had reached the center of West Berlin. By now, American and other foreign networks were beaming live reports from Berlin.

About midnight, an urgent report arrived on Gill's computer in Hamburg. It said Easterners were being allowed out to the West. He switched from one television channel to the other in the hope of seeing an on-the-spot report but found nothing. One channel was showing a program about Oriental culture. In the early hours, they went off the air. As Gill was sitting slumped in front of his computer screen in the early hours, the Wall was no longer an effective barrier to the free movement of people. People in the West had climbed on top of it at the Brandenburg Gate, where it was twelve feet wide, made that way to stop any Soviet tank driver from bulldozing through it to the West.

Shortly after midnight, a lavatory attendant at an East Berlin bar went across to the West for the first time in her life. When she got there, she telephoned her husband, rousing him out of his sleep: "Willi, guess where I am." "Rubbish!" he snorted. It was that sort of night.

—episode related by *dpa* staffer Steve Chadwick

During the night, Gill sent out several small news items that had arrived on his screen from correspondents in Berlin about Easterners coming West, but none captured the drama or the importance of what was happening. By the following day, Friday, at least half a million Easterners were out in the West.[4]

In the chaos, East Germany's generals had been given no direct information. They placed motorized army units on full alert, but, with the streets jammed with Trabants and Wartburgs chugging bumper-to-bumper for the exit points, the military vehicles could not have gone anywhere. An estimated two million people poured into West Berlin over the next three days, while another three million crossed into West Germany at points along the inter-German border. The genie was out of the bottle. East Germany had stripped itself of its self-imposed isolation.[5]

Twelve years later, Schabowski gave me his account of the fall of the Wall. On November 6, three days before the fateful press conference, Krenz had telephoned him. That morning, the East German newspapers had published the draft of new travel regulations. But the proposals were vaguely formulated, and the public, becoming increasingly self confident, had immediately seen their limitations. At this time, mass demonstrations on the streets were dictating the pace of events, and the regime was becoming nervous. Krenz sounded worried. He and Schabowski agreed that something needed to be done quickly. So, another set of travel rules was drawn up. They were ready by November 9 and were submitted to members of the Central Committee, who, numb from the rising unrest on the streets and the sacking of Honecker on October 18, signaled their acceptance.

It was agreed, in Schabowski's absence, to impose a blackout on the new rules until 4:00 the following morning. Then the changes were to be announced over the radio. It was calculated that the news would seep out slowly, because few people listened to the radio at that time of the morning. More important, the information would, in the meantime, be passed to the border checkpoints, which would be prepared when the first people started arriving to head for the West.

During the day, Schabowski had spent several hours at a press conference. He arrived back at the Central Committee meeting just before 5:00 p.m. Krenz handed him a copy of the new travel proposals. Schabowski looked over it quickly. He and Krenz agreed the changes should be announced at the international press conference scheduled to begin in less than an hour.

Krenz said to Schabowski, "This will be a sensation." But Krenz had not mentioned any news embargo—perhaps because he had not known about it, Schabowski said.

He maintains that if he had been told of an embargo, he would have pointed out the futility of announcing world-shaking news and then requesting that no one breathe a word of it for nine hours.

> If Krenz had come to me with such a crackpot idea, I would have talked him out of it. Not even the East German press—which was used to taking orders—would have (by then) accepted that, let alone the assembled press of the world. But I had no need to make any such protest—Krenz mentioned nothing about it.

Schabowski insists that the paper he was given contained no indication of a with-effect date.

After the press conference, Schabowski returned to his home at the walled-off Wandlitz settlement outside Berlin, thinking that by its actions, the East Berlin leadership would be praised as reformers. He came back to earth when the telephone rang. A party official on the other end said something strange was happening at the border at Bornholmer Strasse. A crowd had assembled but were not being allowed through.

> Schabowski: I said, 'that cannot be true'...I was certain that the government apparatus would have taken all the necessary measures before my announcement.

He drove back to Berlin and stopped at a tailback of Trabis and Wartburgs all trying to drive to the border. When he got out, an official in civilian dress approached him and said in the tone of a public announcement, "Comrade Schabowski, the guards began a short while ago letting people through. Nothing unusual to report."

> Schabowski: The civilian was probably one of Mielke's men posted near the border. It was a joke. It had taken twenty-eight years for the Wall to be removed and now a Stasi man can see 'nothing unusual.' I wanted to go and pat him on the shoulder.

He continued,

> I was extremely relieved. The danger of events running out of control appeared to have been averted. I walked up to the crowd slowly heading to West Berlin. The mood was happy and full of expectation and, despite the crush, it did not seem agitated. The people were carrying their blue identification papers...East Germany did not appear to have been lost.
>
> I returned to Wandlitz and rang Krenz. 'It's okay now,' I told him. 'There must have been a damn hitch in informing the checkpoints. But now it seems to be going smoothly. An unbelievable crowd, but the mood is good.' When I said, 'This is a plus for us. The people will return,' he agreed. Not a word about any embargo not being observed.

Krenz himself gave the order to raise the barriers after a telephone discussion with Mielke, Schabowski said. He added, "We had just managed to scrape past a catastrophe. It remains a miracle that no shot was fired and no blood was shed."

Under different circumstances, the urbane Schabowski might have been a hero—the man who smashed the last frontier of a totalitarian system. He was instrumental in toppling party boss Honecker in September, 1989, and, as the state of East Germany tottered, he was sufficiently composed to go out on to the streets and talk with people. None of other Old Guard dared risk that. But that is all forgotten. Schabowski lost out in all directions. He was a member of the Politburo and thus part of the old hated establishment, so for most people he was beyond rehabilitation. But he was also vilified by members of that same old establishment as the villain who pulled the plug on the East German state. He has never been forgiven. The party brass and the generals blamed Schabowski then and they blame him now. But, like the Council of Ministers and the Politburo, the party hacks were not used to working quickly. Their work under pressure had been slapdash. It was obvious no one had briefed him properly.

Fourteen years after the event, the bickering was continuing. Krenz says he informed Schabowski of the situation when he handed over the papers. Schabowski denies it.

Schabowski went on trial together with other Politburo members on charges related to murders at the Berlin Wall and, in August 1997, was jailed for three years.

NOTES

1. The author was present at the meeting.
2. "What could be worse...," Guenter Nooke in *Eine Revolution und ihre Folgen—14 Buergerrechtler ziehen Bilanz,* edited by Eckhard Jesse. (Berlin: Ch.Links Verlag, 2001), 97.
3. What really happened at the press conference is simply not known. If there had been an embargo on the paper Schabowski read, then Krenz's recollection is astoundingly vague. In his book *Wenn Mauern Fallen* (Vienna: Paul Neff Verlag, 1990) he notes on pages 180/181 that, at the Central Committee meeting, a final amendment was made to a document which contained the embargoed date, but does not even mention handing any paper to Schabowski, let alone what it might have contained. He merely refers to a "small error" by Schabowski and that "the world noted what really it should have found out the following day." Nine years later, Krenz says in another book, *Herbst '89,* (Berlin: Verlag Neues Leben, 1999, page 245) that he gave Schabowski his (Krenz's) own copy of the document, but, apart from adding elaborate footnotes explaining that Schabowski had announced the wrong date, he is still short on detail. Why was the mistake made? Where was the embargo date in the paper? Did anyone tell Schabowski, who had spent much of the day carrying out press work and commuting between the Central Committee and elsewhere? Several versions of the press conference exist. None are entirely convincing. A photograph purporting to show the Schabowski note has also been published, but its origins are not clear.
4. This account of the events of November 9, 1989, has been drawn from sources too numerous to name, including eye witness accounts and the author's own observations.
5. There is no better blow-by-blow report of the turbulent events of 1989/90 at street level than Ken Smith's *Berlin: Coming in From the Cold* (London: Penguin Books, 1991).

7

THE MIDNIGHT GUERILLAS

URSULA POPIOLEK WOKE WITH A sore throat at 4 o'clock on the morning of Sunday, February 17, 1995, at her Eastern Berlin home. As she went to fetch a glass of water, she noticed a light flickering outside. She went to the window and what she saw made her forget her throat. A car in her driveway was ablaze. The police and fire brigade arrived and discovered that the fire had been caused by a bomb.

Popiolek knew that the attack was connected with her reference center and meeting place in downtown Berlin, the *Gedenkbibliothek zu Ehren der Opfer des Stalinismus* (Memorial Library in Honor of the Victims of Stalinism).

A few weeks earlier a pile of car tires had been set alight in the stairwell of the home of a Popiolek ally, Siegmar Faust, but the suspicion arose that the real target this Sunday morning was not the Popiolek house but the library itself and that the bombers had misunderstood their instructions.

More trouble was on the way. When I arrived at the library in Berlin's Hausvogteiplatz one October evening in 1996, it was clear something was wrong. Popiolek, uncharacteristically somber, showed me a letter from the Berlin city council ending the modest state subsidy with immediate effect. The letter, which had arrived a few hours previously, was terse and gave no reason. It was signed by Martin Gutzeit, a former dissident who is also a Protestant minister of religion. Gutzeit is himself a member of the Gedenkbibliothek. I wrote to Gutzeit asking for clarification but received no reply. Perhaps the letter did not get through.

Popiolek took legal action.

The midnight guerilla campaign continued. The library moved to new ground-floor rooms at Rosenthaler Strasse 36. Slogans were smeared on the outside wall. One said: "Raus!" ("Out!"). On the evening of Friday, January 22, 1999, the premises were closed for the day and locked. Sometime that night, intruders entered the building and forced their way into unoccupied rooms directly above the library, a hole was cut into the floor, a hose pushed through, and the tap turned on. Water flooded the library. By the time passersby had noticed something was wrong and notified the fire brigade, the damage amounted to about 50,000 marks ($30,000). The Gedenkbibliothek moved yet again, this time into a state-owned building in the patrician Nikolaikirchplatz, away from the constant noise of rattling trams in the Rosenthaler Strasse that had provided cover for troublemakers in the night-time emptiness.

On December 17, 1999, a court ruled that the subsidy cut was not lawful.[1]

Mysterious cases of intrigue and violence have been common over the years, and former Stasi secret-police mischief makers are usually blamed.

I assure you that the idea of your institution and the small library that emerged from it have my unconditional support. For the future I wish you a more secure place where you and your project are no less visible but where you can work safely...I continue to remain available for library events.

—letter from former dissident Uwe Kolbe to Ursula Popiolek on March 1, 1999 after the January attack

---

But not in this case. Instead, political rivals are suspected. East Germany's opposition forces were once united by their common enemy, the communist state. But political freedom shattered this unity. It was not long before Easterners were arguing with each other across the political spectrum. Personal rivalries developed. The disputes were for funds, for influence, for publicity. Newspapers often published unchecked reports and so fueled disputes.

As East Germany collapsed, dozens of organizations were set up to help victims of Stalinism and to keep alive memories of the state's villainy. Museums, libraries, research centers, societies, places where people could meet, were set up one after the other. They were funded by state subsidies, donations, and membership fees. The Gedenkbibliothek was founded jointly in 1990 by Popiolek, a Slavic studies specialist; Faust himself, an author; and other former civil rights activists.

In the 1970s the Stasi arrested Faust on political grounds, and he spent 401 days in solitary confinement in a damp, airless cell, during which time he saw no natural light and his health deteriorated because of bad diet and lack of medical care. He was allowed no lawyer and no visitors. At the time, East Germany was itself protesting the incarceration of people on political grounds in Chile and Spain. Faust managed to smuggle a letter to his wife. An international uproar followed after the details his case were released. Singer Wolf Biermann composed a song about Faust and his cell ("With Running Water [down the wall]"). Faust was released in 1976.[2]

The library was plagued by internal differences of opinion and became the target of harsh words in some sections of the press. Critics have accused the Gedenkbibliothek of having neo-Nazi sympathies but there is no sustainable evidence of that. Author and film director Dirk Jungnickel believes the neo-Nazi issue was used as a pretext in an effort to destroy the organization. "I only hope that the Gedenkbibliothek can now get down to performing its real, important tasks with sufficient public money and without the quarrelling."[3]

It certainly has a list of high-quality speakers of various political persuasions, including left-wing American Jewish writer and political commentator Melvin Lasky; former dissident clergyman Rainer Eppelmann; a former high-ranking communist who fled East Germany in 1948, Wolfgang Leonhard; and an author once kidnapped by the Stasi, Karl Wilhelm Fricke. Popiolek herself blames the difficulties on forces from left wing sources of the ex-civil-rights camp.[4]

The dispute is a Machiavellian tale of intrigue in which many things remain unclear. One Easterner who escaped to the West in the 1950s and emigrated to the United States told me he was concerned about the unknown forces at work in the case.[5] The campaign against the Bibliothek seems to have run its course. There have been no more attacks. And the subsidy has been restored.

NOTES

1. Ruling by the Twentieth Chamber of the Administrative Court in Berlin in VG 20 A 421.96 of December 17, 1999.
2. Faust's story as a dissident is related, for example, by Juergen Aretz and Wolfgang Stock in *Die vergessenen Opfer der DDR*, (Bergisch-Gladbach: Bastei-Luebbe, 1997) 84. A detailed account of his dealings with the East German government is contained in Faust's book, *Ich Will Hier Raus* (Berlin: Verlag Klaus Guhl, 1983). Faust did not endear himself to dissident groups in East Germany and sections of the political left in West Germany by respectively allowing himself to be expelled to the West instead of remaining behind and trying to change the system from within; and for talking to the right-wing Springer press.
3. "I only hope...," Dirk Jungnickel, in "Viele brechen ihr Schweigen—Der Regisseur Dirk Jungnickel ueber seine Filme und die Opfer der SED-Herrschaft," *Junge Freiheit*, August 2, 1996. Jungnickel himself fled East Germany in 1985 and has since been making documentary films.
4. See "Sehnsucht nach dem Totalitaeren," *Der Spiegel*, March 15, 1999.
5. The author based this chapter on many conversations with both Ursula Popiolek and with a number of other people both with and without connections to the Gedenkbibliothek; and on diverse press reports, including "Erst Opfer des Stalinismus, dann Opfer der Demokratie?—Wer will die 'Gedenkbibliothek zu Ehren der Opfer des Stalinismus' e.V. vernichten?" in *Deutschland magazin*, March 1999; and "Wasser floss auf die Buecher—'Gedenkbibliothek' fuer Stalinismus-Opfer durch Anschlag geschaendet," *Welt am Sonntag*, January 31, 1999.

PART TWO
THE POST-COMMUNISTS

8

THE CONJUROR

AVALANCHES OF SOLID WATER pummeled the mountains of Bavaria, upper Austria, and Bohemia. The torrents hit the forests like sheets of rippling steel and smashed into the sleepy hollows below. In three days some regions were deluged with eighty inches, four times the monthly average. The water surged into Eastern Germany, turning its gentle river valleys into threshing rapids. It tore away thousands of homes. Helicopters flew round-the-clock to rescue people from the rooftops of buildings caught in the rapids. Forty-five thousand people were evacuated. At least twenty people were killed. In Dresden, where the River Elbe rose from 2 meters (6 feet 7 inches) to a record 9.4 meters (30 feet 9 inches), priceless works of art were winched to safety from the city's baroque palaces.

This was August 2002. The twenty-first century had only just begun, and the deluge was already being called the Flood of the Century.

The flood hit during a general election campaign. The left-of-center Social Democrat chancellor, Gerhard Schroeder, raced to the devastated region and promised immediate cash assistance. The disaster produced one unexpected result: heavy political damage to the "reformed communists" of the Party of Democratic Socialism (PDS), the party that had emerged from the ruins of the East German Socialist Unity Party (SED).

The PDS's pacifist platform had already been undermined when Schroeder vowed in election speeches not to back the United States' war in Iraq. Now, as vast reaches of Eastern Germany were submerged, local resentments the PDS liked to play on suddenly seemed unimportant.

On election day, 630,000 voters walked away from the PDS. Its vote dropped to under two million and its deputies in parliament declined from thirty-six to just two. At last, it seemed that the party's decade-long spoiling game in German politics was at an end.

The PDS had never been able to win support in the West, where it was broadly regarded as a club for former communist officials and Stalinist apologists, and now its power base in the East appeared to be declining as well.

Three years later, in 2005, it defied the predictions and bounced back. Now calling itself The Left Party, it won nearly nine percent of the vote across the nation and was returned to the Bundestag with 54 deputies.

This revival emerged from a strange turn of events. At a time of economic decline, Schroeder's government introduced reforms that divided not only the nation as a whole but also the chancellor's own Social Democrats. Some rebel Social Democrats in the West broke away and formed a group known as WASG (Voter Initiative for Work and Social Justice). In the election, the breakaway group, headed by Oskar Lafontaine, once Schroeder's finance minister, ran candidates on The Left Party's list. The alliance, billed in the election as "The Left.PDS," won over voters in the West who would otherwise never have dreamed of voting for the old PDS and its tainted political background. But Lafontaine had in effect issued the PDS with a decontamination certificate and the PDS had its coveted foothold in the West.

How long this alliance would last was in the lap of the gods. The two groups were planning to merge but, behind the election euphoria, resistance on both sides was evident. Some Western WASG members feared they were merely providing the former communists with a passport to the West, while the PDS feared that loose cannon among WASG deputies with their own quirky political agendas would buck party discipline and torpedo the combination.

East Germany came crashing down in 1989, bringing the ruling SED with it. The party panicked in a reflex of self-preservation, sacked senior apparatchiks, changed its name by tacking on a label, "Party of Democratic Socialism," aimed at demonstrating that here was a new political force with a hip approach. As the mood of public revulsion gathered pace, and the sleaze and corruption of the ruling class and the excesses of the Stasi were exposed, people mocked the SED-PDS as the "Party of Democratic Stalinism."

It had just two assets. The first was Gregor Gysi, an East German lawyer, who had built a reputation by taking the cases of high-profile dissidents. He was born in 1948 into a nonworking-class family. His father, Klaus, was a diplomat who became East Berlin's culture minister. Curiously, the son had been trained as a cattle breeder. This happened at a time when eucation minister Margot Honecker, wife of party boss Erich Honecker, decided that children from families of intellectuals ought to develop an closer understanding of the working class. When the time came to discuss careers, the school director asked Gysi, then aged 15, if he was interested in animals. The unsuspecting boy blithely answered "yes," saying the family had once had a pet dog. The school director said "excellent," a training place for a cattle breeder was available, and that place was Gysi's. "In this way, Gregor Gysi learned better to understand farmers, just as Margot Honecker intended."[1]

On November 4, 1989, a massive crowd gathered in East Berlin's Alexanderplatz to call for free elections and other freedoms. Half a million people waving banners stretched as far as the eye could see, as the SED party faithful watched their world fall apart. Speaker after speaker stepped forward on the wooded dais and held the party and its leaders to account for forty years of misrule and oppression. Then came the former cattle breeder. Wrapped in in a trenchcoat, his tie comfortably loose, Gysi hit all the right notes. From behind his metal-rimmed spectacles, he seemed to exude warmth, clarity, logic and, above everything, hope. The SED rank-and-file knew this was the paladin they were looking for.

There was no turning back. He was not just the party's vision of the future. He was the future. On December 3, under grass-roots pressure, the entire Politburo and Central Committee quit. Five days later, Gysi was elected new party chairman. He boosted party morale by declaring that socialism did have a future, but he drew a line between the East German form of socialism and the new "democratic" movement the PDS claimed to represent. He explained, "So-called Marxism-Leninism did not prove itself a success as (the) intellectual foundation of socialism. Its system of dogma allowed no variation of thought, so that left-wing theoretical thought became impoverished and degenerated into apologetic propaganda."[2]

The party dumped the SED tag in 1990 and called itself simply the PDS. When East Germany held its first and only free general election in March, it polled just 16.4 percent. It might have done better to form a new party and cut its links with the past, but it did not because of the second asset—money. The SED had had huge amounts of it and the PDS claimed, as the successor party, to be the lawful inheritors. Investigators wanted these millions too on the grounds that they had not belonged to the party but had been embezzled from the East German state and were, therefore, state property. Much of the cash was a product of wheeling and dealing in capitalist countries by the East Berlin smuggling organization, KoKo. Much of it had been placed over the years in foreign and West German bank accounts, but some of it was domestic cash that had been hurriedly smuggled out of the country—and away from nosy regulators—in late 1989 and early 1990.

A scandal broke in Oslo when a PDS official, Karl-Heinz Kaufmann, tried to withdraw seventy million marks from a branch of the Norske Creditbank.

The bank telephoned Interpol, but Kaufmann fled to Moscow. Hours later, a flying squad raided the PDS headquarters in Berlin and discovered that 107 million marks ($67 million) had been transferred from the Deutsche Handelsbank to accounts in Norway and the Netherlands. Kaufmann later left the safety of Moscow to return to Oslo and again tried to withdraw money. The security forces were ready for him. He was arrested and extradited to Germany.

The PDS could not afford to admit knowing about financial shenanigans. One official, Gerhard Lauter, claimed, "We were simply too naïve...We had no idea how deep the graft in the old SED was."[3]

Support for the PDS continued to plummet. When the first all-German election since World War Two was held in December, it polled just 11.1 percent in the East and nothing in the West. Its only success was Gysi himself. In the electoral district of Hellersdorf/Marzahn, a cement jungle of Stalinist-era high-rise tenements and home to diehard SED hangers-on and low-level ex Stasi heelers, he polled almost 36 percent of the vote, enough to win.

The party welcomed any support it could get. Some of that support came from the West, where followers of splinter left-wing and anarchist groups applied for, and were given, membership. Warnings that Western groups were intent on pursuing their own brand of politics inside the PDS were ignored. But the warnings were well founded and, within a short time, the party was rejecting Westerners.

The party's fortunes began to change. As voters became increasingly disenchanted with unification, they slowly turned to it. A grateful PDS saw its chance. It stepped in with the clucking concern of a mother tending a sick child. It gathered its skirts, went on to the streets, and dealt with the everyday problems of ordinary people, something its predecessor party had not given the slightest thought to in forty years. In the words of one contemporary, SED bosses Walter Ulbricht and Erich Honecker "knew little about what was happening to the people and cared even less."[4]

But now the PDS could not do enough. It offered a refuge from unpredictabilities and a wall to wail at. And there was Gysi, radiating charm and holding his own in televised debates with all comers, often under hostile conditions. He was the person increasing numbers of East Germans identified with. Of course, the party had its thinkers, people who performed the intellectual plumbing and carpentry, but without Gysi, it would have been merely a store without a display window. Gysi was the conjuror. Gysi was able to create a mirage just by making an appearance. He used his charisma and a few broad strokes of his brush, leaving his ever increasing audience themselves to paint the details into this shimmering image of a better, easier life somewhere on a distant horizon.

There was one drawback to these mirages. To see them, you had to want to believe in them.

Gysi quit as chairman to give more time to his job as party floor leader in the Bundestag, and was succeeded by another reformer, Lothar Bisky, a former rector of the East German cinema university.

The year 1994 marked a major change. The PDS moved towards the mainstream of politics when it agreed to back the minority Social Democrat-Green coalition government in the parliament of Saxony-Anhalt, the poorest federal state in Germany. In the general election the same year, the PDS entered the Bundestag by winning four electorates in Eastern Berlin.

Although the PDS officially broke with Stalinism in 1995, many questions about it remained unclear. It seemed to accept a free-market economy, but with many reservations. It rejected European Monetary Union, it wanted higher taxes on both the rich and on companies, and it said policies should contain a greater social element.

One researcher, Dan Hough, in 2001 expressed it this way:

> The all-encompassing Marxist-Leninist ideology of the SED has been replaced, and the PDS now attempts to portray itself as a broad socialist party to the left of the SPD, having denied the importance of the leading role of the working class and chosen, even if in a guarded way, to admit that the market may have a role to play in its future ideal world.[5]

The PDS exploited a widespread rejection of Western values represented by the world of Mercedes, Joop, Jil Sander, Cartier, Gucci, Calvin Klein, fur coats, and absentee landlords with no commitment apart from profit. It played on irritations over what was seen as Western condescension, and it offered a feeling of security by igniting a cozy campfire for people who felt they were the losers of unification to huddle round and forget the outside world.

The message was that Easterners were being discriminated against across the board.

In the 1998 general election, it won almost twenty-two percent of the Eastern vote and, under the proportional representation system, gained thirty-six seats in the Bundestag. More significant were events in the northern state of Mecklenburg-West Pomerania, where it became a partner in a coalition government with the Social Democrats.

This was astounding. Less than nine years after the fall of the Berlin Wall, the "post-communists," the pinch-hitters of the SED, had come to power in a democratic election.

But not all members were happy. They didn't approve of rubbing shoulders with the mainstream parties. The PDS consists of many factions, most pulling in different directions. They include the Communist Platform, the Marxist Forum, the Alliance of West German Communists, Trotskyites, ecologists, and a group of Hamburg-based anarchists. The common ground is non-parliamentary opposition—anything except taking part in government.

The unspoken corollary to this is that power has been tried once—by the SED for forty years—and found to be too mercurial to handle on its own, without the backup of terror.

Much as some extremists rage about how communism's day is still to come, this is simply a case of a little dog barking from behind the safety of a fence. The extremists are happier on the streets. This reached ludicrous proportions in 2003 when the PDS organized demonstrations against reforms in unemployment regulations at the same time as it was, as part of a state coalition in Mecklenburg-West Pomerania, enforcing those very changes.

The hard-line Communist Platform is personified by a young (born in 1969), unsmiling brunette, Sahra Wagenknecht, whose pompadour hairdo strikingly resembles that of Rosa Luxemburg, a pioneer of German communism who was murdered in 1919. Wagenknecht believes the revolution of 1989 was the work of dark counterrevolutionary forces and that everything will run smoothly next time round. She was only nineteen when East Germany collapsed. To her mind, any suggestion that the party make concessions to the united Germany's constitution, to the market economy, or to a democratic parliamentary system is treachery. She says the party is "anticapitalist." Her attitude warms the hearts of the unreformed old guard, the aging members of the rank and file who hanker for the rosy days when Stalin was in charge of the Soviet Union.

The factionalism did not matter when the party was gripped by a siege mentality, when attacks from outside caused it to close ranks around the campfire. But, although the political resurgence encouraged the demoralized rank and file, it also exposed these strong internal differences.

Many members have no ideology at all for the new age. They live in the past, dreaming of the old East Germany and refusing to admit that their lives were committed to a flawed ideal. They are a sort of legion of the lost that has damned itself to roam a path going nowhere.

One former member of the West German communist party (DKP), Christian von Ditfurth, said, "For many comrades, if not the most, it [the PDS] is more of a therapeutic self-help group in which the losers of 1989 encourage each other [to believe that] they always wanted only the best."[6]

The lost legions were assured of a political home in the party on the condition that they kept their mouths shut. They were allowed to hand out pamphlets and run errands, but that was all. Gysi never had a high opinion of the sentimentalists who rue the end of East Germany, or former SED functionaries. He never misses an opportunity to emphasize the democratic intentions of the PDS, but the reality was that he, Bisky, party theorist André Brie, and the other reformers were in a minority. The show of unity worked as long as the siege lasted. Success changed all that.

The reformers knew that the PDS would only flourish long-term if it won significant support in the West. The difficulty of the task was demonstrated one drizzly Friday night in 2001, when Gysi spoke at an open-air meeting in Hamburg. Most of the crowd were casual passers-by who wanted to see and hear Gysi in person. He was in his usual sparkling form, yet in the twenty minutes I was there, he was unable to draw either great enthusiasm or hostility. There was no heckling. Not a sign of Gysi's mirage.

Hamburg is neither introspective Eastern Berlin nor some inward-looking provincial Eastern town. It is an affluent, cosmopolitan, outward-looking city with a history of foreign trade. It was here that hundreds of thousands of emigrants once boarded their ships to travel to the New World. Gysi's appearance here was of little more than curiosity value.

A shoot-out between the party's reformers and the conservatives had to happen. The reformers decided to test the mood of the party, which claims to be pacifist, by drawing up a discussion paper that proposed approving "in exceptional circumstances" peacekeeping military operations by NATO if backed by a United Nations mandate. It was a mild motion, merely suggesting that military operations should not automatically be vetoed but, instead, looked at on a case-by-case basis. The Communist Platform reacted predictably. One member, Michael Benjamin, accused Gysi of seeking confrontation, while another, Wagenknecht, warned him not to take risks with the party's "anticapitalist character."

The dueling ground was the party conference in 2000 in the western city of Muenster. When the NATO motion came up for debate, the turning point was an emotional appeal by Sylvia-Yvonne Kaufmann, who urged the 500 delegates to oppose it. As she stepped down from the rostrum, she broke into tears. Her message hit the hearts of the lost legions. The motion was defeated, and so was the master plan of the reformers. It seemed ten years of work by the Gysi-Bisky forces was down the drain.

Bisky, tired of the role of peacemaker, quit as party chairman. Gysi, the flag bearer, blasted the conference's NATO decision and said he was resigning as party floor leader in the Bundestag. He angrily attacked delegates who looked back with nostalgia, and said they were simply closing their minds to the truth. When one anarchist from Hamburg demanded the right of reply, Gysi angrily told her to "shut up."

What is the PDS doing for the victims of the SED regime? The answer: nothing. The PDS still lives in the world of the evildoer. It still knows only the perspective of the oppressor. —Christian von Ditfurth, in *Ostalgie oder Linke Alternative —Meine Reise Durch die PDS* (Cologne: Kiepenheuer & Witsch, 1998) 127.

He said minorities were "terrorizing"[7] the party and suggested that the anarchist clique should be smashed. In the chaos, the lachrymose Kaufmann disingenuously said she had not intended to cause any controversy.[8]

The Gysi-Bisky defeat at Muenster ended any immediate chance the party had of developing beyond an Eastern party of protest. That suited many members. But two years later, when disaster struck in the 2002 general election, the reformers would rue their failure to use Muenster as a chance of clearing out the stables.

Gysi continued to appear on talk shows and give interviews. His chance to break back into political significance came in 2001, when he ran for mayor of Berlin. He didn't win, but nobody expected him to. However, the PDS polled heavily in the elections, and entered coalition talks with the governing SPD.

As part of the negotiations, the Social Democrats insisted the PDS clarify its position on the past, notably its stance on the Berlin Wall. Once again, the PDS ambivalence towards both the past and the present was exposed.

The pragmatic Helmut Holter, a key member of the PDS in the Mecklenburg-West Pomerania governing coalition, demanded "no dithering" and a public apology for the victims of the Wall. He saw the issue as deciding "in which direction the PDS will march."[9] Wagenknecht said an apology would be "totally absurd" because the PDS had not decided to build the Wall.

She presumed the order had been taken in the Soviet Union and that "[former U.S. President John F.] Kennedy gave the green light for it."[10]

The national executive negotiated a gritty session and agreed on a formula, with only one dissenting vote—Wagenknecht's. She left the meeting without saying a word.

The *Berliner Zeitung* reported under the headlines, "PDS regrets building of Wall but rejects apology," and "An apology without an apology."[11]

Although the party did issue a statement regretting the "injustice," it was mainly an explanation for the creation of the Wall. The statement declared that "the PDS has irrevocably liberated itself from Stalinism."[12]

Few outside the PDS bought that. Guenter Schabowski, once a member of the East German Politburo but who now uncompromisingly rejects the East German past, said the statement had "nothing to do with morality . . . [The declaration] is so hesitant, so full of qualifications. . . They [party members] still haven't understood that socialism is in the final analysis is a system which cannot exist without a wall of concrete and ideology."[13]

But the PDS did join the Berlin city coalition, and Gysi became economics minister, a position that carries responsibility for encouraging investment in the heavily indebted city. One conservative politician compared this to making a fireman out of an arsonist. Yet, soon, Gysi, the man who has never been able entirely to clear himself of suspicions that he once worked for the Stasi, was being praised by commercial organizations as a man they could do business with. "He sees the big picture," said one commentator.[14]

Gysi's aim in joining the Berlin government was to try and undo the Muenster disaster by dragging the party toward the mainstream. Governing gave it a voice in the *Bundesrat*, the upper house of parliament, thus forcing other parties to listen to it. Gysi intended maintaining the momentum, but he failed.

As events were to show, the Muenster conference was a bigger disaster for the reformers than anyone had imagined. It staggered the PDS and set it up for its knockout in the general election of 2002.

The first setback came well before the election when, out of the blue, Gysi quit all public offices, including the ministerial post. This was ostensibly over a minor scandal about the private use of airline bonus miles acquired from flights used on state business. But the offence was somewhat technical. Members of other parties were also caught up in it, and not even Gysi's political opponents demanded his resignation. Without its ringmaster, the party suddenly looked vulnerable. His decision angered the grass roots. They could not see why he had quit. Neither could most other people. Gysi explained that if he had remained, the party would have been hounded throughout the election campaign: "I was convinced that, of all people, those who had elected me would not understand."[15]

A more cynical view is that he decided there was no political advantage for to be wrung out of occupying a crucial job in a highly indebted city. Better let someone else run the risks.

By now the Gysi stardust seemed to be losing some of its twinkle. Sections of the party were more closely examining the substance behind the magic. He was said to be a good tactician but accused of being short on strategy.

One biographer, Jens Koenig, wrote that Gysi didn't want jobs where he needed to attend meetings lasting eight hours, and added, "He doesn't strive for power. He wants to talk. He seeks a political platform from where he can barge into the fray."[16]

Koenig took the example of a play, "The Demagogue," written by Florian Havemann, in which the main character runs for mayor of a city. The candidate doesn't just inspire people, he bewitches them. He switches on his big Illusion Machine, and explains in detail how everything could be better. This character, Koenig said, "is no firebrand. He is a modern demagogue."[17]

The demagogue, he added, is Gregor Gysi himself.

The example is interesting, because in the 2002 general election, Havemann ran for parliament on the PDS ticket.[18] Both men have known each other since they were teenagers in East Berlin. Although Gysi didn't achieve what he set out to do when he ran for the Berlin mayoralty, he did have his Great Illusion Machine switched on, said Koenig. He talked about sanitizing the city's finances but without cutbacks here, without staff sackings there, and with increased spending here, he wrote. "He played on the great Capital City Stage, where it was all about vision and nothing to do with numbers,"[19] Koenig said. He quoted Havemann as saying,

> The modern demagogue is well-meant. He doesn't know he is a demagogue. He cannot know this, otherwise he would lose his credibility. A politician today in only credible if he himself believes what he says. The pure cynic, who thinks differently from what he openly professes, no longer makes the grade.[20]

In Gysi's absence, the general election-campaign television appearances were dominated not by Gysi but by Bisky's successor as party chairman, Gabi

Zimmer. Gysi was an impossible act to follow. Zimmer was unable to radiate that sense of warmth and cleverness with which Gysi made Easterners feel better about themselves.

The party might just have weathered the Gysi storm but for the floods, which acted as a spectacular catalyst for other electoral forces. For the first time, many Easterners looked beyond their own backyard. Some thought the PDS was not adjusting quickly enough to meet national needs, that its policies were inadequate to help a country overcome its problems of unemployment, sluggish growth, and structural rigidity.

The closer polling day came, the worse the party's predicament seemed to be. One PDS candidate told me that in the final week of the campaign, he sensed the election drifting away from the party.[21] Political commentator Oliver Michalsky wrote, "If the party is not reelected to parliament, it will have become what it deserves. A regional Eastern party without federal political claims; with communal roots; and, because of its old links, a discussion partner for the little difficulties of everyday life. Nothing more. But you don't need a political party for that."[22]

The election was the predicted disaster. Before sunset on election day, the knives came out as the factions turned on each other. The conservatives accused the reformers of taking the party away from the people it claimed to represent by going into government in Berlin and Mecklenburg. The party was becoming like other parties, the conservatives said. It lacked a battle strategy. For their part, the reformers blamed blinkered conservative attitudes.

The dispute set the scene for a titanic battle at the party conference. But the battle was not even a skirmish. The reformers were given a bloody nose when the grass roots opted for a return to the reassurance of the campfire. Party chairwoman Zimmer spoke of "constructive opposition" instead of involvement in government. No one explained how this was meant to equate with the PDS's role in state coalitions in Berlin and Mecklenburg.

Another commentator, Martin Lutz, wrote, "For the first time, [Zimmer] spelled out clearly what she wanted: a return to socialism, but this time with feeling. [She] hit the mood of the delegates. The [delegates]...celebrated Zimmer for telling them, 'Backward, and Don't Forget.' In doing so, they gave a thumbs down to those who wanted to keep heading westwards."[23]

The conference divided the party into the pragmatic north and the campfire south. Delegates elected a new national executive without a single reformer. The reform-minded Berlin party, the biggest branch in the country, was not even represented. By June 2003, less than a year later, the party's poll standings had not improved and the internecine battle was continuing. As the criticism mounted, Zimmer stepped down. The grass roots elected a new executive, and brought back Bisky as chairman, simply because there was no one else. It was a desperate move designed to unite the ununitable and to win credibility. Yet, when one new executive member demanded a twenty-hour working week and free metropolitan transport—and this at a time of economic crisis—Bisky seemed to face defeat before he had even started his salvage work.

However his hand was much better than it appeared. The figure of Gysi loomed large, despite his absence, and the post-election infighting was, for many voters, irrelevant. They could interpret the party as they wanted, and they did just that. In the 2004 European Parliament elections, the party improved its all-German share of the poll to six per cent in a result that suggested it had now found its real, if limited, role as a toreador with a red rag, tormenting Westerners as a reminder that not everyone is happy with the united Germany.

The perceived refusal of Western politicians to accord the PDS its proper dues and the continued disdain by Westerners (one observer ironically referred to a Western view of Eastern Germany as "a region somewhere near Poland, with strange people")[24] is part of the reason for a more sinister development—a drift toward political extremism. In one 1998 state election, the PDS and a neo-Nazi party won a combined third of the vote.[25] The electors were saying, in part, that if the West does not take us seriously when we vote PDS, we will show them that we mean business by voting neo-Nazi.

One Western Christian Democrat, Otto Hauser, was so enraged after that state poll he hinted that the supply of federal funds for the East might dry up. "Western Germans continue to support the East, even if some do it with clenched teeth. The people in the East should realise that the readiness to help should not be over-extended by votes for extremists," he said.[26]

The extremists Hauser was concerned about were not the neo-Nazis. He was aiming for the PDS. "We are building up the East, and they go and vote left," he said. Hauser's outburst was another case of the Western arrogance that Easterners resent. And it was not as if Hauser was a low-level politician in some provincial backroom. He was spokesman for Chancellor Kohl. In making the threat, he was saying what many Westerners thought, but even his political allies knew he had gone too far. One, Joachim Herrmann, said he did not think much of the idea of "connecting in any way at all voting habits with transfer payments."[27]

By September 2004, Bisky felt cocky enough to admit, shoulder-shrugging, the divisions within his party. He said some members were urging him to leave the Berlin government, end the alliance with the Social Democrats, and to turn the party into one purely of protest. "But as party chairman, I stand for another course. I continue to favor taking part responsibly in decision making—inside parliament."[28]

A few days later, the PDS justified his hubris with a dynamic performance in two state elections, in Brandenburg and Saxony, partly helped by resistance to welfare and labor law reforms. The Saxony result was grotesque. The PDS polled twenty-two percent, behind only the Christian Democrats. The Social Democrats—the party of August Bebel and Willy Brandt that was formed from the German workers' movement in the 19th century—picked up under ten percent, less than one percentage point ahead of the neo-Nazi NPD, a party of the rabble that draws its inspiration from the cesspit politics of Hitler.

Another layer of muck splashed across Eastern Germany's already grubby image. Tourist officials reported a rash of hotel and tour cancellations, and authorities announced a concentrated tourism marketing campaign to counter "the (region's) threatening image as a neo-Nazi stronghold."[29]

But, in contrast to Hauser's cavalry charge six years before, another Western politician, Hans-Ulrich Klose, took a far more pertinent view of the high vote for extreme parties in this election. Klose, a former Social Democrat mayor of Hamburg, said that while the PDS performance could be explained in several ways—and he refrained from criticising people who voted for it—the vote for the NPD "cannot be explained by gullibility...but by malevolence, ignorance and stupidity."[30]

The PDS is a limited party with more potential for dividing than uniting. Its attempts to ascend some moral Mount Everest come across as hypocritical in the face of its predecessor party's behavior. The PDS's pacifist stance, when its roots are soaked in blood, is a mockery of the 1,000-plus people killed at the state's fortified border. But the PDS is likely to remain a political force, with its popularity rising and falling in time with Eastern moods.

Gysi survived a heart attack in 2004, gave up smoking, and bounced out of his self-imposed exile to run in the 2005 election, when his and Lafontaine's

GHOST STRASSE

faces beamed out from posters across the nation. The PDS was dependent on its relationship with the WASG. Together, they were in a position to dominate the far left of the political spectrum. But if the alliance did not hold, the PDS would be once more consigned to the provinces of the East—regardless of whether it continued to call itself The Left.PDS or something else.

NOTES

1. "In this way…," Jens Koenig in *Gregor Gysi—eine Biographie*, (Berlin: Rowohlt Berlin Verlag) 108.

2. "So-called Marxism-Leninism…," Gregor Gysi in *Wir Brauchen Einen Dritten Weg—Selbstverstaendnis und Programm der PDS*, (Hamburg: Konkret Literatur Verlag, 1990) 14.

3. "We were simply…," Lauter quoted in "Der dicke Filz—Einige Spitzenfunktionaere in Haft, Parteichef Gysi als verfolgte Unschuld—die PDS kaempft, vergebens, um ihre Glaubwuerdigkeit," *Der Spiegel*, November 5, 1990.

4. "Knew little about. . . ," Wolfgang Leonhard in *Das kurze Leben der DDR –Berichte und Kommentare aus vier Jahrzehnten*, (Stuttgart: Deutsche Verlags-Anstalt, 1990) 200.

5. "The all-encompassing…," Dan Hough in *The Fall and Rise of the PDS in eastern Germany*, (Birmingham: University of Birmingham Press, 2001), 10.

6. "For many comrades…," Christian v. Ditfurth in *Ostalgie oder Linke Alternative—Meine Reise Durch die PDS* (Cologne: Kiepenheuer & Witsch, 1998) 273.

7. Gysi was reported as saying, with an eye on Western German sectarians and Eastern German old communists, that it was a "misunderstanding of democracy" if a minority in the PDS could "terrorize" the entire party. Now "clear decisions" and "symbolic acts" were needed. This did not inevitably mean initiating procedures to expel representatives of the Communist or Marxist Platform, but certain dogmatic positions in the PDS had to be rejected "with all force." Report in "Appell an PDS—Gysi bangt um sein Erbe—'Eine Minderheit terrorisiert die Partei,'" *Hamburger Abendblatt*, April 12, 2000.

8. For details of the Muenster conference and its consequences, see Christoph Seils in "PDS in schwerer Fuehrungskrise—auch Gregor Gysi gibt auf," and "Personaldebatten fallen der PDS schwer," Brigitte Fehrle in "Parteitag—Die Abrechnung," and "Kampf in der 'Friedenspartei,'" *Berliner Zeitung*, April 10, 2000; "PDS gegen Aktionaers-Kapitalismus," *Frankfurter Allgemeine Zeitung*, April 10, 2000; Brigitte Fehrle and Christoph Seils in "Gegen die 'Diktatur' der Minderheiten—Erstmals denken fuehrende Politiker der PDS auch an Ausschlussverhahren," *Berliner Zeitung*, April 11, 2000; "Appell an PDS—Gysi bangt um sein Erbe," *Hamburger Abendblatt*, April 12, 2000.

9. "No dithering…, " Holter quoted by Brigitte Fehrle in "PDS streitet um Entchuldigung fuer den Mauerbau," *Berliner Zeitung*, June 30, 2001.

10. "Totally absurd." Wagenknecht quoted in *Berliner Zeitung*, June 30, 2001.

11. "PDS Regrets…," Brigitte Fehrle in "PDS bedauert den Mauerbau, lehnt aber Entschuldigung ab," and "Eine Entschuldigung ohne 'Entschuldigung,'" *Berliner Zeitung*, July 3, 2001.

12. The statement, "Die PDS hat sich vom Stalinismus der SED unwiderruflich befreit," was published on the PDS web site http://www.pds-online.de/partei/aktuell/01017/pv_13august.htm.

13. "Nothing to do with...," Schabowski quoted in "Koepfe aus den Kellerluken," *Der Spiegel*, July 9, 2001.

14. "He sees the...," Thomas Holl in "Der rote Wirtschaftsliberale—Fuer die PDS hat Gysi als Senator in Berlin einen Imagegewinn verbucht. Doch handfeste Erfolge gibt es nicht," *Frankfurter Allgemeine Sonntagszeitung*, June 2, 2002.

15. "I was convinced...," Gregor Gysi in *Was Nun? Ueber Deutschlands Zustand und Meinen Eigenen*, (Hamburg: Hoffmann und Campe, 2003) 150.

16. "He doesn't strive...," Koenig, 332.

17. "Is no firebrand...," Koenig, 319.

18. See Chapter 9—The Meticulous Maverick.

19. "He played on...," Koenig, 319.

20. "The modern...," Koenig, 319.

21. Florian Havemann, in a talk with the author in Berlin the week after the election.

22. "If the party...," Oliver Michalsky, in "Anfang vom Ende der PDS," *Berliner Morgenpost*, September 9, 2002.

23. "For the first time...," Martin Lutz in "Auf dem PDS-Parteitag ist Ratlosigkeit spuerbar," *Berliner Morgenpost*, October 13, 2002.

24. "A region somewhere...," Jochen-Martin Gutsch in "Wir Holzmichl—Es gibt viele Bilder vom Osten. Manchmal ist schwer zu erkennen, welches das richtige ist," *Berliner Zeitung*, November 8, 2004.

25. In 1998, in Saxony-Anhalt, the PDS won 19.2 percent of the votes polled and the neo-Nazi DVU (German People's Union) 12.7 percent for a total of almost thirty two percent. See Chapter 11—A Swing to Extremist Parties.

26. "Western Germans continue...," Hauser quoted in *Freie Presse*, Chemnitz. The quote was published in "Schnelle Lippe—Kohls neuer Pressemann Otto Hauser ist eine Fehlbesetzung: Fuer die Doppelrolle als Regierungssprecher und Rambo ist er nicht raffiniert genug," *Der Spiegel*, June 8, 1998.

27. "Connecting in any way...," Hermann, quoted by Andreas Thewalt in "'Der Regierungsschwaecher'—Kopfschuetteln ueber Otto Hauser: Kohl's neuer Sprecher gilt auch in der Koalition als 'glatte Fehlbesetzung,'" *Hamburger Abendblatt*, June 5, 1998.

28. "But as party...," Lothar Bisky quoted in "Oskar wuerde uns passen," *Der Spiegel*, September 6, 2004.

29. "The (region's) threatening...," in "Sachsen kaempft gegen Nazi-Image," *Hamburger Abendblatt*, September 27, 2004. See also Part Three—Hitler's Shadow.

30. "Cannot be explained...," Klose in "NPD waehlen—dafuer gibt es keine Entschuldigung," *Hamburger Abendblatt*, September 25, 2004.

9

THE METICULOUS MAVERICK

THE BEANPOLE OF A MAN CLASPED his cigar between middle and ring fingers as if he wanted to perform a party trick, tapped off the ash, and insisted he had been guilty.

"I don't see myself as a victim. On the contrary, I was an offender."

As smoke curled round his peppery two-day growth and rimless spectacles, I said, "But you were only a teenager."

"I knew what I was doing. When I made the protest, I knew the rules and broke them. I knew I would go to jail if they caught me."

Well, I said, that is a highly constructed position. "In most countries, what you did would not be a crime."

At the age of sixteen, Florian Havemann, a citizen of communist East Germany, helped write a pamphlet protesting against the Soviet invasion of Czechoslovakia in 1968. He was convicted of "inciting hatred against the state," and jailed for four months.

He came out of jail determined to flee to the West. Three years later. Florian and a girlfriend went to a secluded parking area where they climbed into the empty tar container of a tank truck and crouched in the noxious inkiness. When the pair hauled themselves out, they were surrounded by the glitz of capitalist West Berlin.

The son of Robert Havemann, East Germany's best-known dissident, had flown the coop. Within hours, the story of the escape was on the news wires.

Three decades later, and a dozen years after the collapse of East Germany, here was I perched on a chair of a spartan, uncarpeted room in the Havemann apartment in Berlin trying to find out why, in 2002, he was running for election to parliament on the ticket of the PDS.

I was not optimistic about getting answers. On the Internet I had discovered an example of Florian Havemann's writing, headlined, "Attempt to Define an Elite Temptation, or an Essay about the Essayist Elite." What followed was 7,000 words of impenetrability, apparently the work of an intellectual who reveled in explaining the inexplicable. If he insisted on circling in the clouds, I knew I would never catch him.

The Havemann home overlooks the broad Kottbusser Damm, where every second store is in Turkish hands. I walked up the steps to the graffiti-daubed entrance, pushed the intercom button, and went inside. Frau Havemann ushered me into a second-floor room, where I sat alone, waiting for the haughty academic with his firewall of lofty language.

This was not the room of a Western politician. Here were no lush leather swivel chairs or shiny steel-and-glass furnishings. Instead, a parquet floor darkened with age, a tiled oven backed against one distempered wall, and books and papers piled offhandedly on a small table all gave a mood of both space and clutter. Two works of art—both photographs of that icon of German communism, Rosa Luxemburg, and elaborated by Havemann himself in acrylic colors—looked out pensively from one wall. A promising start. This was the den of a someone unconcerned with the conventional trappings of status or affluence.

Florian Havemann was neither aloof nor self-consciously learned. When I showed him the Internet essay, he gave a boyish laugh. "Complicated," he said wryly.

He talked a lot, chain-smoked those thick cigars, and drank coffee. Occasionally he hesitated before answering. It was difficult keeping him on my track and off his (they did not always coincide) .

He believes Germany needs the PDS as a party of the left and not as a socialist party. He places the SED in a good light, saying it took much responsibility for keeping the revolution peaceful. As if this explained everything. When I pointed out it had merely tried to save its own skin, he hesitated and replied, "Whatever its motive."

Florian's decades in West Berlin have been mixed. He worked as an electrician and as a supermarket hand. He studied graphic design and stage design. At night, he wrote plays. He formed a theater group. He cleaned office buildings. In 1976 he went to Stuttgart with Achim Freyer, a stage designer who was his professor at Berlin's Arts University. Together, they set up the stage for Claus Peymann's production of Goethe's *Faust*. Florian continued to write plays. He drew up plans to stage them. He negotiated with theater companies to put them on. He cleaned more office buildings. He traveled. To London, where he helped set up an art gallery for an exhibition and where he met his French wife, Agnes. To France. To Peru. There was always something: music, poetry, plays, dance music. But nothing got off the ground.

And the cleaning. Always the cleaning. Like an act of catharsis.

In 1999 came change. He was not a PDS member, but he let the party nominate him as its political representative to the Brandenburg state constitutional court.

Just days after the end of the war, a tall, gaunt figure with thinning hair waited at a commandeered army barracks in Spandau with a ragtag band of released prisoners to hear communist leader Walter Ulbricht, who had returned from wartime exile in Moscow. Robert Havemann, thirty-five, scientist, inventor, communist, and member of the anti-Nazi resistance, had been sentenced to death by Nazi judge Roland Freisler. Havemann had survived, and he felt a huge personal debt of gratitude to Stalin.

Havemann's first direct contact with the Nazis had been in 1929, when he heard Hitler speak at the Loewenbraeu beer hall in Munich. It was a traumatic experience for the nineteen-year-old student and, he resolved that the Nazis must be stopped in their tracks. The communist dogma appealed to him, and so did the communists' determination to oppose the fascists.

He graduated in chemistry and was taken on at the Kaiser Wilhelm Institute for Chemistry in Berlin. When Hitler came to power in 1933, Havemann joined resistance movements. The Gestapo arrested him in 1943 and jailed him. Scientist friends on the outside arranged for a laboratory to be set up in his cell so he could test organic substances for chlorine. They told the Nazis the work was essential to help develop poisonous gases. Havemann said later that the work was not even marginal to the war effort, but no one really knows.

In 1945, he returned to his old job at the Kaiser Wilhelm Institute as part of Ulbricht's plan to place communists in key jobs throughout the city.

In 1952, the year Florian Havemann was born, Stalin ordered *Aktion Ungeziefer* (Action Vermin) to stop the westward exodus of people out of the Soviet zone. A 500-yard swathe was slashed into forests so guards could better aim their rifles, border areas were placed off limits to the casual visitor, and 8,000 families were resettled. The first many knew of their fate was the sound of rifle butts battering on front doors in the middle of the night.[1]

A few people bucked the westwards trend and headed East. One was a sixteen-year-old Hamburg youth, Wolf Biermann, who had dreamed of world revolution. Biermann, a communist just like his father, who had been murdered by the Nazis in Ausschwitz in 1943, arrived in East Germany in May 1953, shortly after Stalin's death.

By this time, East Germany's postwar optimism had degenerated into frustration. The economy was shattered from the twin ravages of war damage and Soviet reparations. The pace of reconstruction was slow, unlike the West, where currency reform and different economic rules were producing wealth.

A few weeks later, the unthinkable happened: workers in the workers' state went on strike. The spark that ignited the powder keg was an order to increase industrial production norms. Everyone knew that "higher norms" was a fancy term for pay cuts. The mood reached boiling point on June 16.

The lead came from construction workers at a huge building site in the center of East Berlin, the Stalin Allee, who downed tools and walked away. By the time the march reached the ministerial building, it had swelled to 10,000.

The marchers chanted, "We want Ulbricht," but he was said to be at a meeting. Instead, an industrial minister, Fritz Selbmann, appeared at a window of the building, which had once been Goering's Air Ministry, and told the crowd that the pay norms were to be withdrawn. Robert Havemann, now the head of the physiochemical faculty at East Berlin's Humboldt University, went into the yard in the drizzling rain to plead with the strikers. With him went Heinz Brandt, a Berlin party official. Brandt climbed on to a bicycle while Havemann stood on a table. Their appeal was ignored.

The strikers extended their demands—withdrawal of the norms, reduction of living costs, free and secret elections, and no punishment. The demands were broadcast by the American-controlled Radio in the American Sector (RIAS), a crucial factor in the absence of a reliable telephone system. RIAS announced the time and place of demonstrations, and reported on events.

The next day, June 17, armies of workers marched from their factories to the center of Bitterfeld in the industrial heartland south of Berlin. By 11:00 a.m., a crowd of more than 30,000 had pushed into the Platz der Jugend, where they listened to a schoolteacher, Wilhelm Fiebelkorn, speak. Fiebelkorn said Ulbricht must resign. The government must resign. Border controls with West Germany must be demolished. Food prices must be cut forty percent.[2]

Strike turned to riot. Mobs stormed a police station, smashed doors and windows, and set prisoners free.

In Berlin, the Stalin Allee workers from Block 40 marched in pouring rain, and other angry workers joined in. They smashed shops, set fire to kiosks. They set alight Columbus Haus, the Vopo headquarters, sending clouds of black smoke billowing into the sky. The building was gutted. By 9:00 a.m., Soviet tanks were on the streets, droning toward the crowds, turret motors whining, guns swiveling. Rioters threw stones, pieces of brick, and lengths of iron. Steel beams wrenched from ruins were rammed into tank tracks and running gear.[3]

Protests, strikes, and demonstrations erupted in 250 towns, big and small. In Berlin, the CIA's man, Henry Heckscher, asked for permission to arm the rioters with rifles and Sten guns, but Washington turned him down.[4] In the town of Rathenow, a mob attacked a loathed party member, Wilhelm Hagedorn, and threw him into the river. He died in hospital.[5]

The Soviet high commissioner, Vladimir Semyonov, told Ulbricht that RIAS was saying that East Germany no longer had a government. And he added, "They're not far wrong."[6]

By the time the revolt ended, 55 people had died, including a woman run down by a Soviet tank. About 20 people were shot dead, and more than 5,000 others arrested. Eighteen Soviet soldiers were themselves shot when they refused to shoot demonstrators who smashed their way into a prison.[7]

Years later, Robert Havemann wrote,

It was clear to me that the revolt…was not a derailing of the workers movement or a plot of foreign secret services, but a completely extraordinary political event.[8]

When Heinz Brandt had addressed the demonstrators outside the ministerial building with Robert Havemann, he was already becoming disillusioned. Brandt, who had spent eleven years in Nazi concentration camps, "had recognized that Ulbricht and his colleagues had betrayed everything he had fought for and suffered for twenty years"[9] In August Brandt was expelled from the party."

Krushchev became Moscow party boss in September. He delivered a blistering denunciation of Stalin at the Soviet Party congress in 1956 and set off a wave of de-Stalinization in Eastern Europe. For many party members the denunciation was traumatic. One of those people was Robert Havemann.

> At a stroke I realized that I had been a victim of hopes, illusions, and deceptions. I had believed that all reports about conditions in the Soviet Union, about the persecution, about Stalin's ruthless, inhuman concentration camps, about the Moscow [show] trials of the 1930s, to be pure lying propaganda by the Nazis and the capitalists.[10]

From 1957, his lectures defied the official line, and he came on a collision course with the party.

Florian Havemann and his brother Frank, three years older, were growing up in the spacious upper-floor family apartment at Strausberger Platz, close to the center of town. The Havemanns were among the communist aristocrats, member of a privileged class in the workers' state. They possessed two cars, owned leisure boats, and were allowed the capitalist privilege of servants. At weekends, they family left town for their a weekend house in a green oasis at Gruenheide.

Gruenheide was a retreat for the elite. At weekends, the place came alive with children and, in the evenings, visitors came and drank cognac, and the talk drifted through a haze of cigarette smoke. Frank and Florian, barely in their teens, always joined in. And they learned, but not always as their elders would have liked.

Wolf Biermann had meanwhile studied at Humboldt University and found work as a theater production assistant. But it was his singing that gained him a following as he put his own acidly worded verse to guitar music. Soon he was a leading figure among intellectual dissidents.

The little man with the sharp tongue was walking a tightrope.

He first clashed with the regime in 1962 after building a backyard theater that the Stasi closed it before the first performance. The authorities banned Biermann from performing publicly, and canceled his application for party membership. In 1965 his travel privileges were rescinded. His works could no longer be published in the East, although cassettes of his songs continued to circulate among student and intellectual groups.

Wolf Biermann and Robert Havemann first met in the late 1950s. If this combination of the balladeer and the scientist, a specialist in the esoteric world of colloidal chemistry, was an unlikely one, the binding force was their similarity. Both were fighters and both were battling the same opponent. Both believed that East Germany was the better Germany. Both wanted socialism without the Stalinist oppression.

Biermann, of the sad eyes, Zapata mustache, and Beatles hairdo, regularly visited the Havemann homes, where, in between talking politics, he played his guitar. He and Florian became close in spite of a fifteen-year age difference.

Yet the two didn't always agree. Years later, Florian recalled the frustration as he listened to endless—and what he regarded as futile—discussion about changing the system. Biermann and his prickly songs were irrelevant to the real world, he thought. The two boys were more interested in new stars from the West, the Beatles, the Rolling Stones, Bob Dylan, Jimi Hendrix.

Children from many prominent East German families preferred a mixture of "rock 'n roll, dancing, necking, and sudden bursts of political discussion," Florian Havemann recalled.[11] One of this elite was Gregor Gysi.

Meanwhile, Professor Havemann's lecture hall was always filled to capacity, and party officials looked on with gritted teeth as students lined up to get inside. Havemann, a tall man with a cupola of a forehead crowning a bony face, was just one of several academics disenchanted with the regime. There were also rumblings outside academia. In 1957 the Central Committee's farming specialist, Kurt Vieweg, advocated an end to farm collectivization. He was thrown out of the party, fled to the West, but was lured back by an "amnesty" that was ignored. He was jailed for twelve years.[12]

A year later, Heinz Brandt also fled to the West. In 1961 he was kidnapped by a Stasi gang, taken back, and jailed for thirteen years for "spying." The case generated international protest and prompted British peace movement activist Bertrand Russell to hand back to Ulbricht a peace medal he had been awarded.[13]

In 1963 the DEFA film studios shot footage of one Havemann lecture for a documentary, but the Stasi raided the hall and removed the film.[14]

Havemann's uneasy standoff with the party flared into full-scale confrontation. A student from West Germany turned up at a lecture in 1964, and put questions to the professor. Upon his return to the West, the student talked to his local newspaper, which ran an article.[15] The reaction in the East was sharp. Some things were excusable, but talking to the Western press—the enemy of the people—was not one of them. Havemann could have said he thought he was dealing with a student, but he was too stubborn. The party expelled him and dismissed him as head of the physiochemical faculty. The next year, it expelled him from the Academy of Sciences and banned him from publishing. He had been muzzled, or so the regime hoped.

He later told his third wife, Katja, "I was no longer one of them, and they just let me drop like a stone."[16]

Hopes that the communist system would become more democratic were dashed in August 1968, the year of the "Prague Spring." Alexander Dubcek, the new first secretary of the Czech communist party, tried to introduce liberal reforms. The Soviet Union assembled a force together with its Warsaw Pact allies and marched into Czechoslovakia to smash the "counterrevolution." In East Germany, workers and intellectuals openly protested. The Czech flag became the symbol of protest. Hundreds of people were arrested.

Among the protesters were four young people from prominent communist families: Frank and Florian Havemann; Thomas Brasch, son of deputy culture minister Horst Brasch; and Rosita Hunzinger, daughter of a well-known artist and SED member. They hung a Czech flag outside a window ten floors up from the Strausberger Platz apartment, from where it could be seen from the downtown Alexanderplatz. The symbolism of the act was clear, but the four could hardly be charged with displaying the flag of a friendly nation. However, they had also authored pamphlets opposing the invasion and containing a poem written by the enemy of the state, Biermann.

All four were charged with "inciting hatred against the state," and given short prison terms.[17]

After his release, Florian was sent to work as an apprentice electrician at the railways. He hated it. Any lingering hopes he had harbored about improvement in East Germany were dashed.

The brothers reacted to their jail terms in different ways. Frank Havemann joined the SED. He wanted to change the party from within, claims Florian. Florian himself decided to go to the West. Anywhere would do. Even China would be better, he thought.

Three years later his chance came. When he told his father, Robert Havemann, the idealist for whom remaining in the country and fighting the system from within was an article of faith, said, "You're mad. Get out of here. If you're still here in twenty-four hours, I'll call the police."

Florian Havemann never saw his father again.

Florian Havemann made a spectacular entry to the heady atmosphere of the West, but, even as he was being interviewed by the press and lionized by rebellious left-wing West Berlin students, trouble was brewing. Biermann, angered by his departure, wrote a poem accusing him of betraying socialism. When the poem was published, the left-wingers who had been lining up at the door to meet and talk with the son of Robert Havemann instantly dropped him.

The ban on Biermann's concerts was unexpectedly lifted in September 1976, and he marked the new freedom with a public performance. In an equally un-expected move, he was handed an exit visa and allowed to go on a concert tour in the West. He began in a blaze of publicity with a live, televised perfor-mance in Cologne on November 13.

Late on the night of November 16, the official East German *ADN* news agency announced that Biermann's right to live in the East had been with-drawn. He had been banished from the kingdom like a deviant knight.

East Germany was rid of the prickly lyricist, but the uproar on both sides of the border exceeded the regime's worst expectations. Writers, musicians, and artists in the East distributed handbills and scrawled protests on house walls. In one village, a large sign saying "Biermann hat recht" (Biermann is right) was painted on the road. Welding torches were used to burn it off. A singer, Nina Hagen, then twenty-one, daughter of Biermann's girlfriend, ac-tress Eva-Marie Hagen, protested, and she was deported as well. Eva-Marie Hagen herself signed a protest petition and was dismissed from her television job.

Robert Havemann wrote an article criticizing the expulsion that was published in the West, and he was placed under house arrest. His lawyer, Goetz Berger, was struck off the register for taking up Havemann's case. The street outside the house in Gruenheide was sealed off, and placed under round-the-clock surveillance.

Biermann's banishment was a watershed. Many who had hoped the re-gime would steer a more humane course now realized their optimism was misplaced. Arguments still take place about whether this was the point where East Germany signed its own death warrant.

Havemann's house arrest was technically lifted in 1979, but his move-ments remained under surveillance. The same year, in an attempt to criminal-ize him, he was fined 10,000 East marks for alleged violations of foreign-exchange regulations. The charges related to royalties from publications in the West. He remained defiant, saying, "It is not socialism when the vast majority of people are completely at the mercy of the decisions of a tiny group. It should be the other way round."[18]

If Florian Havemann had been dropped by the Western left intellectual scene because of Biermann's taunt, the breach became unbridgeable in 1978, when he wrote an article for *Der Spiegel* in which he harshly criticized his father. Robert Havemann was an icon of the Western left wing. He was the heroic dissident who enabled a distinction to be made between the excesses of the East German state and the idea of communism itself.

Attacking him was to trample over ideals with heavy boots. And the son trod with all his weight. He condemned his father's "communist utopia," saying it had not been developed from reality, had nothing to do with any concept of world history or with economic ideas, and was not even derived from Marxism. "I ask what is communist about it?" Florian Havemann wrote.

His father was part of an illegal and elite undemocratic political class, and a person who had never had any real contact with the workers' movement, Florian said. "I put the question: did Robert Havemann really become a communist at all?"[19]

Armchairs creaked all over the country as critics rose to their feet. Dozens of readers' letters, most critical, landed at *Der Spiegel*; and Florian stumbled into a political no-man's-land from which he has never emerged.

When he wrote the article, he was just twenty-six, an age when rage rather than caution often dictates actions. I put this point to him, but, a quarter of a century after writing the condemnation, he stands by it. He insists that he was fond of his father but wanted to point out that the Robert Havemann as portrayed publicly did not exist. That was mere legend, he said.

Robert Havemann was no average scientist. He showed an early practical bent and developed a talent for inventing apparatus for chemical analysis. His later work on photosynthesis was important for the Soviet space program. He could have spent the war years in relative comfort and with both status and money. He chose the tough option. After the war he could have had fame, status, and material wealth in either of the two German states. But he followed his ideal, and, when that did not measure up, he again took the tough option and spoke out.

His time in a Nazi prison had permanently impaired his health. In 1945 tuberculosis had laid him low and, over the years he was plagued by lung and heart problems. He was sent to hospital when in 1971 he suffered a tuberculosis relapse but he refused an operation because he did not trust the doctors. His suspicion was justified. Years later, his Stasi files showed that one of the doctors who treated him was an informer. Katja Havemann believes the doctor tried to prevent Robert recovering.[20]

By 1982 Robert knew he was dying. One visitor, pastor Rainer Eppelmann, recalled, "He lay there, very thin, the oxygen canister larger than he was. I wondered at his composure. That he could talk about his own death, which he knew was just hours away, with such calmness...and about what we all should now do...impressed me deeply."[21]

Havemann asked that Biermann be allowed to visit him. The lyric poet was granted a four-day visa, returned to East Germany for the first time since his expulsion five-and-a-half years before, and stayed with his old comrade. Katja Havemann, at Robert's request, took video footage of Biermann sitting at the deathbed.

> There were a lot of people there...and Wolf talked and played his
> tunes. I stood behind the camera for hours. Afterwards I noticed
> that in parts I had forgotten to switch on the microphone.[22]

It was the last time Biermann would see Robert alive. The rebel idealist died a few days later, on April 9, at the age of seventy-two. Florian Havemann, now able to return to the East, attended the funeral, but Biermann was turned back at the border.

Florian accuses his father of being a lazy professor. Students had complained about that. He painted a picture of a philandering bohemian who reveled in talking to an audience but who, by the mid-60s, no longer read or wrote. His inspiration came from discussion. He was a social person who, after losing his job, became increasingly isolated. When the stream of visitors stopped, he stagnated mentally. Sometimes his opinions descended to the level of tabloid newspapers, Florian remembered.

It was only some time later that Robert again received the company he enjoyed, when dissidents made their way to his door. In the words of Eppelmann, "for a certain group of people, Gruenheide was like a Mecca."[23]

The 2002 election was a disaster for the PDS. Voters deserted it, and it was sent back to the new Bundestag with just two deputies instead of thirty-six. So Florian Havemann failed in his first attempt to enter politics.

How difficult would it be going back to cleaning? "Tough," he said. He gave that wry, boyish laugh again, and said, "But I use the time to make notes for my plays."

A year later when I rang him, he sounded more cheerful. He was no longer cleaning, he said. He remained a constitutional court judge and was spending time drumming up ideas for a PDS think tank.

But he clearly keeps a distance from the party. He hasn't joined it, and, by the time of the 2005 general election, was no longer working for the think tank. After taking a stand during internal party feuding in 2002, he was not invited to run again for election.

All of which seems entirely consistent with a maverick who seems to be meticulous in his efforts to remain one.

NOTES

1. A total of 8,422 people were resettled in the 1952 action and another 3,640 in 1961, according to Klaus Kinkel, German foreign minister in the Kohl administration, in a speech at the third congress of the Alliance of Victims of Forced Resettlement in East Germany, in Magdeburg. Reported by *dpa*, date unknown. For details of both operations, see *Zwangsaussiedlungen an der innerdeutschen Grenze—Analysen und Dokumente*, by Inge Bennewitz and Rainer Potratz (Berlin: Christoph Links Verlag, 1994).

2. Fiebelkorn escaped to the West together with another strike leader, Horst Sowada, according to Thomas Flemming, in *Kein Tag der deutschen Einheit—17. Juni 1953*, (Berlin-Brandenburg: be.bra Verlag, 2003) 96. A third leader, Paul Othma was denounced, arrested and sentenced to 12 years' jail. He served 11 ½ years.

3. The accepted version for many years was that the Russian tanks put down the uprising. But evidence has emerged in recent years to suggest that, in fact, they were not decisive, and that the rebellion was losing steam of its own accord.

4. Request by CIA Berlin chief related by Thomas Powers in *The Man Who Kept the Secrets, Richard Helms and the CIA* (New York: Alfred A. Knopf, 1979), 46.

5. Details of the lynching emerged only in 2003. See "Tod in Rathenow," *Der Spiegel*, June 16, 2003.

6. "They're not far…," Semyonov quote recalled by an eye-witness, Rudolf Herrnstadt, in *Das Herrnstadt-Dokument—Das Politbuero der SED und die Geschichte des 17. Juni 1953*, (Reinbek bei Hamburg: Rowohlt Taschenbuch Verlag, 1990) 83.

7. Assessments of the death toll vary wildly. Western sources had put the death toll at over 500, while the East Germans said it was 25. A study in 2004 by the Potsdam-based *Zentrum fuer Zeithistorische Forschung* (ZZF) (in "17. Juni 1953: Zahl der Opfer korrigiert," *ap/Hamburger Abendblatt*, June 16, 2004) concluded that the toll was 55. This

included 34 demonstrators, passersby and onlookers either shot dead over the six days or who died from bullet wounds, five people sentenced and executed by Soviet occupation forces and another two sentenced to death by East German courts. The study does not mention any shooting of Soviet troops. The most reliable source for this came from a Red Army officer who deserted.

8. "It was clear to me...," Robert Havemann in *Ein deutsche Kommunist: Rueckblicke und Perspectiven aus der Isolation*, (Reinbek bei Hamburg: Rowohlt Verlag GmbH, 1978) 76.

9. "Had recognized...," Wolfgang Leonhard in *Das kurze Leben der DDR—Berichte und Kommentare aus vier Jahrzehnte* (Stuttgart: Deutsche Verlags-Anstalt, 1990), 112.

10. "At a stroke...," in Havemann, 77.

11. "Rock 'n roll, dancing...," Florian Havemann quoted by Jens Koenig in *Gregor Gysi—eine Biographie*, (Berlin: Rowohlt Berlin Verlag) 121.

12. Vieweg was released in 1964, and remained in East Germany until he died in 1976.

13. Brandt was released in 1964 was allowed to go to West Germany, where he worked a trade-union journalist until his death in 1986.

14. Havemann himself told about this episode in an article smuggled to the West and published in "Die wollen mich hier rausekeln—Robert Havemann ueber seinen Kampf mit dem DDR-Regime," *Der Spiegel*, October 9, 1978.

15. The *Hamburger Echo am Abend* newspaper ran the article, "Wir Deutschen machen alles ganz besonders gruendlich ...," as an interview with "our reporter Karl-Heinz Ness," on March 11, 1964.

16. "I was no longer...," Katja Havemann, as told to Marc Kayser in "Der Alptraum Stasi verfolgt Katja Havemann," *Sueddeutsche Zeitung*, January 30, 1992.

17. Florian Havemann told me he learned from a reliable source that Ulbricht had ordered Berlin party boss Paul Verner to "fix" the case of the four. Ulbricht, realizing that jail would only cause more bad publicity in the West, had wanted the cases dropped. But Verner had misunderstood, and the cases went ahead. The prosecution said Robert Havemann and Biermann had systematically influenced the accused to "adopt the tactics and methods of ideological diversion of the enemy." All four accused were convicted and jailed. Ulbricht is said to have ordered all to be released. Frank, Thomas Brasch, and Rosita were freed after three months. Florian, the youngest, remained incarcerated for another month after his mother, Karin—Robert's second wife—who was a party stalwart, vetoed his release by saying she had no control over him.

18. "It is not socialism...," in Havemann, 86.

19. "I put the...," Florian Havemann, in "Alle machen aus meinem Vater eine Fall", *Der Spiegel*, October 30, 1978.

20. As told by Katja Havemann to Marc Kayser in *Sueddeutsche Zeitung*, January 30, 1992.

21. "He lay there...," Rainer Eppelmann, quoted in *Robert Havemann oder Wie die DDR sich erledigte*, by Katja Havemann and Joachim Widmann, (Munich: Ullstein Heyne List, 2003) 341.

22. "There were a lot of...," Katja Havemann quoted in Havemann and Widmann, 344.

23. "For a certain...," Rainer Eppelmann quoted in Havemann and Widmann, 5.

PART THREE
HITLER'S SHADOW

10

UNIFICATION UNLEASHES THE MOB

THE RISE OF BOXERS MASKE AND SCHULZ coincided with the rise of a more sinister phenomenon. A few months before the Schulz-Foreman bout, Maske's own training received an unexpected setback. A black American brought to Germany as his sparring partner, Adolpho Washington, was running alone one morning in Frankfurt an der Oder when skinheads threw stones at him from a passing car. A short time later, another group of skinheads threatened him. So when, in a third incident, pedestrian set his dog on him, Washington just took the next train out of town.

Washington's experience is common in Eastern Germany. But, because he was not injured, the incidents might not even have been reported in the media if he had not been a public figure.

Unification raised fears of a resurgence of an aggressive form of nationalism, and that this, in turn, would cause an explosion of gratuitous violence. The fear was that once West and East German extremists joined forces, the Nazi devil would dance again. One outspoken opponent of unification was author Guenter Grass, who believes it was a united German state which enabled the Nazi racist ideology to prevail after Hitler came to power. He said in February, 1990, before unification, "Anyone thinking these days about Germany and who seeks answers to the German question needs also to consider Auschwitz. This place of horror, an example of a persisting trauma, rules out any united German state in the future."[1]

As events quickly showed, not only were there proportionally more extremists in the East, they were also more violent. They were much quicker to target foreigners, even though most of them personally did not know any. The decade of the 1990s turned into a succession of murderous excesses as waves of thugs marched from one side of Germany to the other, attacking people on the streets, setting fire to migrant hostels, and desecrating synagogues and Jewish cemeteries. Some politicians claimed that right-wing extremism was not an Eastern German problem. They protested that the statistics were not reliable. But their protests were merely part of an widespread culture of denial which sought to defend the indefensible. Counterespionage reports over the years have consistently said that half the violence-prone extreme rightists are in Eastern Germany, which has only about a fifth of the German population. And although the days of the spectacular set-piece excesses of the 1990s, when property was besieged in front of television cameras while onlookers applauded and the police stood by, appear to be over, the number of violent youths on the lookout for trouble is increasing. According to counter-intelligence reports, about 9,700 youths were in 2001 estimated to be violence-prone, more than double the figure of 4,200 in 1991. Often it is difficult to distinguish between politically motivated right-wing crime and simple crime. But police reported 531 violent crimes by right-wing extremists causing physical injury in 2005, ninety-eight more than in 2004.[2]

The Rottweiler attitude of Easterners toward outsiders stems partly from the ideology and provincialism of East Germany. The communist establishment was obsessed about traitors in its ranks and paranoid about outsiders. Strangers were suspect. Life in such a closed, insular society gave people no more than a hazy idea about people who lived in other countries. Schools demanded almost military-like obedience, which provided ideal training for neo-Nazis. And the system bred concepts of hate toward people seen as hostile. Enemies of the state lurked in every shadow.

Even though many neo-Nazis were only small children when East Germany collapsed, the mentality of suspicion thrives, especially in the provincial towns and villages. But now, the enemy they were taught to hate can be anyone: blacks, Asians, winos, the homeless, the crippled, British tourists, Western German campers. All are blamed for life's problems. All have been attacked.

East German schools taught how the communists had resisted the Nazis —as many had, of course—and how communists became martyrs. But they barely mentioned non-communist resisters or the millions of Jews who died in concentration camps. Generations of school pupils grew up with a distorted view of the Third Reich that barely dealt with the Holocaust. Schools did not get to grips with its cause and effect. Pupils understood fascism and nazism only as remote concepts. Children were forced to visit former Nazi concentration camps, but the visits were mere ritual chores.

Few children learned to discuss ideas. Opponents were simply condemned. The East German system polarized thought into "them versus us." Youths met at clubs and in homes and discussed issues such as Hitler's Third Reich and the division of Germany and came to their own conclusions. Since these issues were taboo in the media, youth organisations and schools, dissenting views were not aired. This has left minds receptive to simple solutions for complex problems.

Two observers, Peter Koedderitzsch and Leo A. Mueller, say,

In this isolation, a simple and clear image of the enemy emerged ...the Stasi, the Volkspolizei and other identification symbols of East Germany were seen as 'un-German' and 'unworthy'...threats and militant action were directed against 'lazy, stinking punks,' all foreigners living in East Germany (Africans, Poles, Vietnamese etc) ...homosexuals and Jews.[3]

Ideas became deeds. A Soviet war grave in Radeberg was smeared with the Nazi battle cry of "Sieg Heil," swastikas were painted on a power station in Cottbus, Jewish graves were desecrated in Dresden, Potsdam, and Zittau. One group that smeared swastikas and slogans on walls, was said to have worn "beat clothing and beatles hairstyles."[4] This was an attempt to imply that corrupt Western influences were the source of the problem. Racially based incidents against foreign workers were common, but much of the activity was protest against a hated state—bored youths delighted watching the frenzied police reaction to a swastika sprayed on a wall. A group of school pupils, asked in 1966 why they had smeared thirty swastikas on house walls, replied that they "wanted to give the Volkspolizei something to do."[5] The press, held in the viselike grip of the state, said nothing. West German intelligence officers in 1960 questioned 1,000 East German refugees specifically on the issue and were told of 126 cases of swastika graffiti.

Much of the mythology of Nazism was passed on by war veterans romanticizing about their days in the Third Reich when Hitler planted fruit trees on the autobahns. Such stories found receptive minds among a youthful generation longing for more out of life than anything the colorless Stalinist state could offer.

In the 1970s a hippie sub-culture emerged in East Berlin. Long hair in those days was a strong form of protest. Hippies were superseded by the more aggressive punks, with their colored, teased hairstyles, and ready fists. Punks fought a lot, mainly with each other, and robbed Western tourists. By the early 1980s, a rock music culture was beginning to take over. An important part of this culture was high alcohol consumption and rioting at soccer matches.

Skinheads emerged out of this subculture. Skinheads became adept at organizing soccer-based violence. But they were not a single entity. Two infamous early groups, the *Ostkreuzer* and the *Lichtenberger Front*, marched with *Babyskins*, *Oi-skins* (after their battle cry of "Oi"), and *Nazi-skins*. Extremist skinhead aims include recreating Germany in its 1937 borders and deporting foreigners. They deny the Holocaust happened.

By the mid-1980s, "a massive, violence-oriented subculture of hooligans, skinheads and 'faschos' emerged"[6] that targeted dark-skinned foreigners, homosexuals, punks, and the *Volkspolizei*. In 1987 a crowd of thirty skinheads attacked visitors leaving a rock concert at East Berlin's Zionkirche and screamed "Jewish pigs," "Sieg Heil," and "communist pigs."[7]

The complex nature of this rebellion against the state was illustrated in the 1980s when a following built up round the Dynamo Berlin soccer club. Dynamo was modeled on the Moscow Dynamo club. Moscow Dynamo was the KGB (Soviet secret police) team. Dynamo Berlin was the Stasi side, the plaything of Stasi minister Erich Mielke.

Former dissident Vera Lengsfeld recalls neo-Nazis occupying the "right-hand corner" at the stadium and greeting home-team goals with Hitler salutes. Erich Mielke, sitting up in the VIP box in the grandstand could hardly have failed to notice, she said.[8]

There was other evidence about a reluctance to act. A Stasi report in August 1989 about skinheads on the rampage in the Alexanderplatz, said that when someone rang the Volkspolizei, they were told: "You're trying to make fools of us—we're not your whipping boys." The report, signed by an Oberleutnant Schmidt, comments of the "huge lack of understanding" at the "apparent lack of interest" by the Volkspolizei.[9]

About 13,000 people were sentenced as Nazi war criminals in the Soviet zone and East Germany after 1945, twice as many as in the much larger West Germany (although many of those 13,000 were innocent). East Germany sacked about 500,000 Nazis from public posts, while West Germany got rid of about 220,000. The East reasoned it was clean and that any remaining Nazis were in the West. The absence of fascism in the East was, for party and regime, an article of faith. The third party conference in July 1950 declared that "the roots of fascism have been exterminated." This was baloney. Former Nazis occupied senior posts in the East, and some were members of the *Volkskammer*. In 1950 one communist party central committee in Thuringia contained more Nazis than communists. Thuringia was a notorious laggard in denazification.[10]

In West Germany, postwar right-wing violence was a fact of life. In the 1970s Karl-Heinz Hoffmann, a mustachioed Walter Mitty figure, organized his *Wehrsportgruppe* Hoffmann (Defense-Sport Group Hoffmann), a band of youths who dressed in jungle-green uniforms and played war games in forests. One former Hoffmann follower blew himself up by accident at the 1980 *Oktoberfest* in Munich. Twelve other people died with him. The group was banned.

Seventeen deaths were linked with right-wingers in 1980. A neo-Nazi killed himself after shooting dead two Swiss border guards on Christmas Day 1980. Two other neo-Nazis were killed in a shoot-out when Munich police tried in October 1981 to impound their van, which was loaded with munitions. In 1981, near Hamburg, neo-Nazis stabbed to death Johannes Buegner, a member of the extremist *Aktionsfront Nationale Sozialisten* (ANS), as part of a campaign to rid the band of "homos, perverts, and traitors." Buegner was a homosexual.[11]

The situation in the united Germany is diffuse and constantly changing. The Verfassungsschutz counter-espionage agency says that eighty-five percent of youths who commit crimes of violence with a right-extremist background are from one of the many skinhead milieus.[12] But other excesses are committed by youths with no links with any skinhead scene. Many skinheads not only are non-violent, but are not prejudiced against foreigners. And involvement in attacks does not necessarily mean participants are connected with any neo-Nazi political parties, of which there are several.

Turks are the foreigners most hated by Easterners. But there almost no Turks in Eastern Germany. The region still has few foreigners of any origin—less than two percent of the population—and those who are there pose no cultural or economic risk to Germans. One Eastern politician, Joerg Schoenbohm, said, "I have talked with youths who reject foreigners and asked them if they knew any personally. None did."[13]

Yet foreigners continue to be attacked—and about six times more often in the former East Germany than in the former West Germany.

The extreme right offers elitism for youths who feel inadequate. An educator, Heike Fuessenhaeuser, found that "even in bars and clubs and at school, they stand out. Isolation, loneliness, an inability to establish personal relationships . . ." Instead of personal contact, abstract terms such as "nation" and "people" cropped up. "Being German" was important because success elsewhere was beyond them.[14]

A Leipzig psychologist, Walter Friedrich, said "the identification with Germany as 'fatherland,' the feeling of being a German, makes many proud, but at the same time it has generated a high level of aspiration. This can be easily fulfilled in respect of foreigners." He added, significantly, that "the Ossi does not feel an equal among equals compared with Westerners, but perceives himself as inferior in several respects."[15]

To the west of the East Germans were the rich West Germans with their all-powerful deutsche mark. To the east were the Poles, even poorer than the East Germans and generally looked down upon. In Germany, the term "Polish economy" is used to describe anything that is a shambles. In the middle were the unwanted *Gastarbeiter* (guest workers) from Third World countries working in East German factories and building sites. Foreign workers originally came to East Germany under socialist treaties signed with Mozambique, Angola, Cuba, and Vietnam. They arrived as part of international socialist solidarity to fight the evils of imperialism, colonialism, neocolonialism, racism, and apartheid. They took jobs East Germans did not want, and they were paid little. Industrially, migrant workers were important but they were seen by East Germans as competitors for scarce resources. When the country collapsed, the guest workers stayed on, generally unloved and unwanted. Their numbers were added to by waves of asylum applicants lured by Germany's liberal political asylum laws. The number of asylum applicants hit a record level of 438,000 in 1992. The newcomers were accommodated in camps and hostels in towns throughout the country.

Violence put some obscure towns on the map. One was Hoyerswerda, where refugees from Ghana, Turkey, and Cameroon were quartered in hostels. In the early months of 1990, foreigners and local youths clashed there sporadically. On May Day a Mozambican was beaten up by a gang and taken to hospital. Mozambicans went out on to the streets looking for revenge and the day ended in a pitched battle.

The tension simmered in the town for more than a year. Then, on September 17, 1991, neo-Nazis attacked a Vietnamese street vendor selling contraband cigarettes. They stole his money, were driven off by police, regrouped, and went to a hostel occupied by Vietnamese and Mozambican migrant workers. The neo-Nazis, who had been drinking all day, stoned the building and smashed windows under the gaze of 150 applauding onlookers. The fighting went on for five days and nights. A second hostel housing asylum seekers came under attack. A hundred extreme left-wing anarchists, known as *autonomen*, arrived in town to show solidarity with the foreigners. Television cameras brought the daily fare of hate to the living rooms of the nation as 400 police battled with a hundred skinheads, who were, in turn, battling 100 *autonomen*. Eighty-three people were injured.

Rolf Schmidt-Holz said in the liberal-leaning magazine, *Stern*: "In the days and nights the neo-Nazi hordes hounded foreigners, our state capitulated to the mob. Romanians, Vietnamese, and Mozambicans fled for their lives before German boots, before German Hitler salutes and German xenophobia. And all that our mighty constitutional state could do was to fill the tanks of a few miserable local buses...the xenophobia of Hoyerswerda is, on terrible historical grounds, typically German. And the applauding citizens are the accomplices of the mob."[16]

The state of Saxony interior minister, Rudolf Krause, was forced to resign. Three skinheads were sentenced to eighteen months in jail for assaulting the Vietnamese street vendor and attacking the hostel. In this autumn of 1991, attacks continued night after night. The victims were not just foreigners: Two skinheads attacked a retired German merchant marine officer, Gustav Schneeclaus, near Hamburg and left him lying on the ground with head injuries after he told them that Hitler was a "lousy crook." He died three days later.

Then came another televised spectacle in the port city of Rostock when in August 1992 neo-Nazis laid siege to a hostel housing Vietnamese, Polish, and Romanian asylum seekers. A hundred policemen were injured in brawling. As at Hoyerswerda, hundreds of people stood and applauded the neo-Nazis.

Most of the hostel residents were driven away in buses but, when the rioting resumed, the police suddenly disappeared for one and a half hours. More than 150 Vietnamese, including children, took refuge in the upper floors of the building, together with a German television team. Siegfried Kortus, in charge of the operations, denied allegations that he had slept during the violence. He said he had "merely changed a shirt"[17] The people trapped on top of the blazing building survived the flames and the chaos to tell the tale by escaping across the rooftop.

Warnings of the impending violence had been published beforehand in the local press and the Interior Ministry had been told what might happen. The man at the head of the confusion was the Christian Democrat interior minister of the state of Mecklenburg-West Pomerania, Lothar Kupfer. One editorial wanted to know why "almost all deployed police were pulled out not during the quiet afternoon, but at the hottest phase, on the Monday night."[18] In January 1993 Kupfer told a commission of inquiry that the police in Rostock had "fulfilled their task in an ideal manner." He was sacked.

One commentator wrote:

> The blame for the fatal chain reaction—from abuse of asylum, to hostility toward foreigners, to a rise in right-wing extremism, to civil-war-like unrest—lies with the state [of Mecklenburg-West Pomerania]. The incompetence of this bunch of amateur thespians …allowed…the right-wing radical raiding parties to run out of control.[19]

Prosecutions in the case, characterized by paper shuffling and inactivity, took ten years.

From Rostock, the fascist mob swept on to link up with local skinheads in other parts of the East. With them moved the international press. Some youths gave Hitler salutes as soon as they saw a media camera. Others demanded, and were often given, money. Interviews were charged for. The going rate for American journalists was said to be up to 600 marks ($367) for an interview, while the British, regarded as either poorer or tight fisted, paid a mere 400 marks ($244).

Riots erupted somewhere every day. In early September, a Quedlinburg hostel was cleared and forty-one skinheads were arrested. The deacon of the St. Servatius church, Werner Bley, told me he saw the ringleaders whipping up feelings as they drove round town in Mercedes cars with Western license plates.

Ignatz Bubis, the chairman of the Council of German Jews, and a local Christian Democrat deputy on the Rostock City Council, Karlheinz Schmidt, both attended a press conference in Rostock, scene of the televised riots. Schmidt spoke of "Israeli terror against the Arabs" and then said to Bubis, who was born in Germany, "You are a German citizen of the Jewish faith, and your homeland is Israel. Is that correct?" Schmidt was echoing the line laid down in the twenty-five-point program issued by the Nazis in 1920: Jews could not be German, because they were not of German blood. The comment drew this attack: "There are people who use their backsides to demolish within seconds everything that others have carefully built up...The sheer lack of instinct in his question to Bubis has demolished everything. Dumbness? I am afraid the man knew exactly, in this context, that a question which implies a similarity with the violence between Israelis and Palestinians belongs in the most pulpy propaganda of right-wing radicals."[20]

Within hours, Schmidt had been forced to resign.

Moelln, a hilltop town of 16,000 between Hamburg and Luebeck, is a popular destination for day-trippers attracted by its historic old-town center tucked beneath the medieval Nikolaikirche and lined by picturesque half-timbered buildings. It was in this unlikely setting that, shortly before one o'clock on the morning of November 23, 1992, the police received a telephone call. "A house is burning in the Ratzeburger Strasse! Heil Hitler!" A short time later, a second call was received. "It's burning in the Muehlen Strasse! Heil Hitler!"

Two houses, both occupied by members of the same Turkish family, were in flames. All occupants were rescued from the Ratzeburger Strasse house, but three people died in the Muehlen Strasse blaze. Germany's Turkish population is about 1.7 million. Turks began arriving in Germany at the end of the 1960s to work during *Wirtsschaftswunder*, the economic miracle.

Photographs of the burned-out Muehlen Strasse house flashed round the world. German president Richard von Weizsaecker was visiting Mexico, and the topic dominated his only international press conference.

Foreign tourism in Eastern Germany declined sharply. A French group canceled a planned stay in Quedlinburg. An American furniture manufacturer dropped plans to reopen a disused factory in Rathenow. A Chinese businessman arrived to spend thirty million marks ($20 million) buying German machinery. He was beaten up by skinheads, and he gave the contract to an American firm instead. Japanese living in Germany were advised to wear business clothing to avoid being mistaken for Vietnamese.

Senior officials seemed unable to say the right thing. Attacking foreigners did not seemed wrong for its own sake. In 1994, a mob of 150 skinheads went on the rampage in Magdeburg, chasing five Africans through the streets. Police questioned and released forty-eight of the thugs, but only one person was arrested—the Greek owner of a restaurant who had given the Africans refuge. It took a public uproar before nine prosecutions were brought.[21] Government spokesman Dieter Vogel said, "This is precisely what harms our reputation. For this reason we just cannot put up with it."[22] When Roman Herzog, a senior judge and candidate to succeed Weizsaecker as federal president, said after the Magdeburg clash that "such atrocities have a terrible effect abroad," one leader writer chided him gently, saying, "Although true enough, this is not the main reason for Bonn [then still the capital of Germany] to deal with the hate issue forthrightly."[23]

Up until the Moelln attacks, regional police dealt with the excesses. But now, with the situation reeling out of control and local law-enforcement officials hopelessly unable, or unwilling, to act, the federal prosecutor stepped in, and, a little more than twenty-four hours later, the first suspect in the Moelln case, Michael Peters, was in custody.

Peters, twenty-four, product of a special school for slow learners, the physically abused son of a local drunk in Gudow, near Moelln, was a member of the neo-Nazi National Democratic Party (NPD). His bookcase was full of magazines about weapons. On the wall of his room was a Third Reich battle ensign and a sign saying,

Im Himmel gibt's kein Bier, Drum trinken wir es hier.

(In heaven there is no beer, That is why we drink it here).[24]

Five days later, nineteen-year-old Lars Christiansen was also in custody.

In court, a lawyer representing the Turkish family, Christian Stroebele, asked Peters if he had ever been disadvantaged by a foreigner. "Not that I know of," the accused replied. Had a foreigner ever taken a job at his expense? asked Stroebele. "No. Actually, no."[25] Peters was convicted on three murder charges and jailed for life. Christiansen, because of his age, received ten years.

It had taken 2,000 fire-bomb attacks and seventeen deaths in 1992 alone to get this far. The federal interior minister Rudolf Seiters stepped in immediately after the Moelln attack and used his constitutional powers to ban two neo-Nazi organizations, the German Alternative (DA) and the National Front (NF).

Wolfgang Thierse, an Eastern politician who closely observes the extreme-right scene, summed up the situation by saying,

The police come, often very, very late, to the scene, witnesses' statements are often insufficiently recorded, cases against offenders only open months afterwards, and the punishments for causing physical injury are appallingly light. But the worst is that many attacks are not even reported to the police because of fear or apathy.[26]

Courtrooms can be intimidating for victims. "The public gallery is often packed with neo-Nazis, who look just like the defendants," said Thomas Hannich, who works for a victims' support group, Opferperspective Saxon, (Victims' Perspective Saxony).[27] Opferperspective co-founder Ingo Stange accuses local official of eagerness to ignore the problem and of funding youth clubs in which the only users are right-wing radicals. "Many victims refuse to press charges because the fear revenge attacks," Stange says.[28]

Thierse knows of cases where, during court adjournments, witnesses are intimidated by being forced to wait in the same room as the accused.[29]

Charges against extremists—insofar as charges were brought at all—generally stopped short of murder. Courts gave the appearance of leaning over backwards to rule that the accused had not set out to kill but only wanted to frighten people. One judge talked about "youthful lapses" when he handed down sentences of between two years suspended and four years jail for the 1990 killing of an Angolan. Another judge ruled, in jailing a nineteen-year-old skinhead to five years for stabbing to death another Angolan, "We must assume that the color of the skin of the victim contributed significantly to the offence." As if the victim were to blame.

Just as things seemed to be getting better, they got worse again. The city of Guben is just a few miles down the track from Frankfurt an der Oder. One cold winter's evening in February 1999, a rumor swept town shortly before midnight that a crazed black man had disemboweled a German girl with a machete.

Circumstances had brought together Farid Guendoul, twenty-eight, an Algerian, and Isaka Kaba, a seventeen-year-old illiterate from Sierra Leone. They lived at a hostel for political asylum seekers not far from Guben. Earlier that evening, as snow lay on the ground, the two had left for a nightclub on the Guben outskirts. An illuminated sign promising "Entertainment" penetrated the gloom. Admission was ten marks ($6), expensive for asylum seekers, but worth it to break the tedium of hostel life. Inside, where men and women, many from Eastern Europe, danced to throbbing music, Farid and Isaka met another Algerian from the hostel, Khaled Bensaha.

By the time the three left the club after midnight to return to the hostel, gangs of German youths were roaming Guben in cars, coordinating their moves by mobile phone as they looked for the mad machete man.

One gang of youths saw the three foreigners 200 yards from the club, and gave chase. Khaled was knocked to the ground. Farid and Isaka reached the concrete dormitories in Hugo Jentsch Strasse opposite the dance club but found their escape route cut off by two cars. They panicked. Farid pushed intercom buttons at the entrance to number 14. When no one answered, he crashed through the glass door. Isaka followed. Farid began bleeding badly. He told Isaka to take a taxi and fetch help. Isaka saw the pursuers were still outside. Terrified, he returned to the street and hailed a taxi. He could not make himself understood to the driver. With the German youths following close behind in their cars, the taxi took him to a takeaway restaurant on the edge of town. Isaka entered the takeout, and the youths stormed it. The woman on duty locked the doors and rang the police. The police saw Isaka's bloodied hands and handcuffed him. At last, they had the crazed black machete man, or so they thought. Isaka was taken to the police station, and he tried to tell his story—but no one understood him. He was thrown into the cells, where he remained for eight hours.[30]

Back in the building at Hugo Jentsch Strasse number 14, residents refused to open their doors. Someone called the police, but when the patrol car arrived, skinheads assured an officer that the situation was under control. In a way, that was true. Farid was dead. He had crawled up the stairs as far as he could and then lay, exhausted, bleeding to death. A simple tourniquet would have saved him. One resident did go to see what had happened—he said he gave the Algerian heart massage and bandaged the leg. But by then it was too late.[31]

Eleven youths were arrested and tried after Farid Guendoul's death. Three were jailed for between two and three years, six others received suspended sentences, and two were given warnings. The case dragged on for seventeen months with defense counsel delaying at every opportunity, on the principle that the more prolonged it became, the better for the accused. The tactics were so crude that Thierse said the case had been prolonged by "lawyers sympathizing with the violence-prone right-wing scene."[32] Five lawyers said they would sue him. They later withdrew their threat.

While few people openly encourage attacks on foreigners, the inherent blinkered attitude of small Eastern German societies, and their willingness to condone attacks, amount to a tacit acceptance of them. One statement after the Guben killing by the mayor of Spremberg, a town in the region, gives some insight into the mentality of some Easterners. Egon Wochatz said, "What was he [the victim] doing on the street at night?"[33]

Guben itself is a grim rump of a town of 35,000 on the banks of the River Neisse. Like other German towns along the river, it lost its Eastern part to Poland after the war when Europe was politically reshaped. The town square church and the town hall are on the Polish side. Guben is typical of Eastern towns. Its industry has collapsed, official unemployment is over twenty percent and the unofficial figure double that. People have drifted away, leaving houses empty, the night streets deserted, and an air of deprivation. Unification has brought a sharp rise in robberies, white-collar crime, and drug trafficking.

The death of Farid Guendoul remains an uncomfortable memory for the residents of the city's Hugo Jentsch Strasse number 14, a doleful prefabricated building on an edge-of-town site. Some two years later I talked to one resident, but she refused to comment. When I asked why, she said, "That was all so long ago." Across the road, the nightclub is revealed by daylight to be nothing more than a scruffy little wooden building with a tin roof.

People in Guben sought to portray Guendoul's death as an aberration, as an isolated event rather than a reflection of the community's values. One social worker, Ingo Ley, said only two of the leaders were influenced by extreme right-wing ideas. Instead, all the youths had "minor criminal tendencies."[34] But asylum hostel manager David Nicette disagreed. He believed "it [an attack similar to that on Guendoul] will happen again. If not in a week, then in a year. The political climate is contaminated."[35]

As if there weren't enough problems, Kohl worsened the situation by in 1993 naming an Eastern German, Steffen Heitmann as his candidate for the presidency.

Heitmann, a lawyer and theologian, symbolized the ranks of applauding bystanders. Kohl, worried that the Eastern electorate would turn to the parties of the far right in the next general election, wanted to siphon off votes from the extremist camp. Heitmann was seen as the key. His nomination was also intended as compensation for Easterners, who had seen little sign of Kohl's "blooming landscape."

The nomination angered many Christian Democrats, who had not been consulted. Every utterance Heitmann made came under scrutiny. He said that the "organized death of millions of Jews" could not be allowed to signify "the special role of Germany until the end of history."[36] He made no secret of his reservations about foreigners. When during a walk through Stuttgart, he came across people of various nationalities, he asked rhetorically, "I wonder which country I am living in."[37] His attitudes were winning him doubtful allies. One man almost embraced him and said, "You're a real German, not like that lefty Kanaka" (meaning incumbent president von Weizsaecker).[38]

Heitmann was, in effect, giving the green light to the hordes of neo-Nazis ready to go out and beat up foreigners.

Heitmann led a blameless, conforming life in East Germany. His inability to say the right thing was not from nastiness but naiveté. He turned down the nomination before it came to a vote.

Germany has become a country of immigration without many people realizing it. Kohl said, "Germany is not an immigration country." He was wrong. It is. The temporary *Gastarbeiter* of thirty years ago are still in Germany, and so are their children. And they are not going to disappear. The movement of people out of Eastern Europe, Asia, and Africa is increasing. Germany needs some immigration for demographic reasons. It also needs skilled workers, particularly in the information technology sector. Some people intentionally fudge the issues of political asylum and immigration, but the need for clarity was finally recognized when the political parties agreed to draw up an immigration law for the first time. The law was finally approved in parliament in 2004.

NOTES

1. "Anyone thinking...," Guenter Grass in a speech to the Evangelical Academy in Tutzing, Bavaria, on February 2, 1990.

2. See report by the Verfassungsschutz counter-espionage agency issued in Cologne on December 7, 2001, and published on-line by *Der Tagesspiegel* on December 8, 2001. See also Verfassungsschutz report http://www.bmi.bund.de/cln_028/nn_122688/Internet/Content/Comon/Anlagen/Broschueren/2005/Verfassungsschutzbericht__2004__de,templateId=raw ,property=publicationFile.pdf/Verfassungsschutzbericht_2004_de. See also "Polizeibericht: 30 Prozent mehr rechte Kriminalitaet," *Hamburger Abendblatt*, January 6, 2006.

3. "In this isolation...," Peter Koedderitzsch and Leo A. Mueller, in *Rechtsextremismus in der DDR*, (Goettingen: Lamuv Verlag, 1990) 13.

4. "Beat clothing...," in an internal Central Committee Agitation and Propaganda department report on April 7, 1966, quoted by Jochen Staadt, in *Die geheime Westpolitik der SED 1960-1970*, (Berlin: Akademie Verlag, 1993) 157.

5. "Wanted to give...," in an internal Central Committee Agitation and Propaganda department report on April 7, 1966, quoted by Staadt, 157.

6. "A massive...," Klaus Farin and Eberhard Seidel in *Skinheads*, (Munich: Verlag C.H. Beck, 1993) 232.

7. "Jewish pigs...," Koedderitzsch and Mueller, 15.

8. Neo-Nazis at the stadium recalled by Vera Wollenberger (Lengsfeld) in *Virus der Heuchler* (Berlin: Elefanten Press 1992), 84.

9. Skinheads in Alexanderplatz reported in a Ministry of State Security, Hauptabteilung VIII, Abteilung 13, report of August 24, 1989. Facsimile reproduced in *Staatssicherheit und Rechtsextremismus*, by Heinrich Sippel and Walter Suess, (Bochum: Universitaetsverlag Dr. N. Brockmeyer, 1994) 105.

10. For an account of denazification, see *The Divided Nation*, by Mary Fulbrook (London: Fontana Press, 1991) 141.

11. Western German neo-Nazi leader Michael Kuehnen, a homosexual who died in 1991 of Aids, wrote an essay, "Homosexuality and National Socialism," which he dedicated to Buegner. Rumors were at one time rife that Kuehnen had chosen "a hero's death" to avoid sullying the neo-Nazi image, according to "Maertyrer und Todfeinde—Die Ideologie des Hasses," *Hamburger Abendblatt*, March 4, 1992.

12. Report by the Verfassungsschutz issued in Cologne December 7, 2001 and published on-line by *Berliner Zeitung* on December 8, 2001.

13. "I have talked…," Joerg Schoenbohm quoted in *Hamburger Abendblatt*, August 3, 2000.

14. "Even in bars…," Fuessenhaeuser quoted by Jutta Kriegler in *Stuttgarter Zeitung*, February 8, 1992.

15. "The identification with…," Walter Friedrich quoted by Andreas Borchers in *Neue Nazis im Osten: Rechtsradikalismus und Auslaenderfeindlichkeit—Hintergruende, Fakten, Perspektiven* (Weinheim: Beltz Verlag, 1992) 189.

16. "In the days and nights…," Rolf Schmidt-Holz in "Von Negern und Menschen," *Stern*, October 2, 1991.

17. "Merely changed a shirt…," Kortus quoted in "Warum griff die Polizei zu spaet ein?" *Hamburger Abendblatt*, August 26, 1992.

18. "Almost all deployed…," Herbert Wessels in "Rostock und die Politiker—Nebel fuers Volk", *Hamburger Abendblatt*, August 29, 1992.

19. "The blame for the…," Hans-Juergen Mueller in "Die Krawalle in Rostock—Gruesse von gestern," *Hamburger Abendblatt*, August 26, 1992.

20. "There are people who…," Helmut Schneider in "Duemmer geht's nimmer," *Schweriner Volkszeitung*, November 2, 1992.

21. Details of this riot vary. See, for example, "Hate Crime in Germany," *International Herald Tribune*, Paris, May 20, 1994; and "All detainees freed after night of street battles in Magdeburg," *dpa*, May 14, 1994.

22. "This is precisely… " Vogel quoted in "All detainees freed after night of street battles in Magdeburg," *dpa* English-language service, May 14, 1994.

23. "Although true enough. . . ," in "Hate Crime in Germany," *International Herald Tribune*, Paris, May 20, 1994. Herzog later did become German president.

24. "Im Himmel gibts…," Wolfgang Metzner and Joachim Rienhardt in "'Keiner hat sie fuer voll genommen'—Der eine Brandstifter von Moelln war ein unzufriedender Auszubildender, der anderer ein Sonderschueler ohne festen Beruf," *Stern*, December 10, 1992.

25. Questioning of Peters by Stroebele quoted in "Ich war immer gegen Gewalt," *Hamburger Abendblatt*, May 18, 1993.

26. "The police come often.... ," Thierse quoted in *Berliner Stimme*, (the SPD magazine for Brandenburg and Berlin) Berlin, April 7, 2000.

27. "The public gallery...," Ulrike Koltermann in *dpa*, date unknown.

28. "Many victims refuse...," same *dpa* report, date unknown..

29. Thierse quoted in *Die Zeit*, Hamburg, July 27, 2000.

30. Cottbus police spokesman Berndt Fleischer said Isaka Kaba was arrested at 5:00 a.m. and held until 1:00 p.m. the next afternoon. See "Polizei liess einen Auslaender stundenlang in Handschellen sitzen," *Berliner Zeitung*, Berlin, February 17, 1999.

31. The case received widespread publicity. This account is based on a number of reports including "Killing Fields", in *Jungle World*, Nr 8 1999; "Hatten Behoerden Vorbeugen Koennen?" in *Rhein-Zeitung*, on-line edition, February 14, 1999; "Wie Guben mit dem Gewaltsamen Tod des Algeriers Omar Ben Noui und dem Prozess gegen elf Jugendliche umgeht," by Wolfgang Kunath in *Berliner Zeitung Brandenburg*, February 15, 1999; *Frankfurter Rundschau*, November 2, 2000; "Gubens Polizei . . Bissel Durcheinander," by Constanze von Bullion, in *taz*, February 17, 1999. Khaled Bensaha, who was badly traumatised in the attack, was later served with a deportation order, as if he had been to blame. It was only after Thierse intervened personally with some tough arm-twisting that the Algerian was allowed to remain. Isaka survived his ordeal only to be attacked once more—on a streetcar in Potsdam. But this time someone did come to his aid and, although badly shaken, he emerged without physical injury. He was granted a provisional work permit and is employed in a Potsdam restaurant.

32. "Lawyers sympathising...," Thierse quoted in *Berliner Stimme*, April 7, 2000.

33. "What was he doing...," Wochatz quoted in *Berliner Zeitung*, Berlin, February 13, 1999. The remark cannot be dismissed as merely a thoughtless slip of the tongue. Wochatz caused a political row in 2004 when his associations with former members of Hitler's SS division, with whom he had fought in France as a young man, drew heavy criticism from both within and without his own CDU party. Wochatz attended meetings of ex SS members where young neo-Nazi extremists were also present. See "Kritik an CDU-Politiker nach Besuch bei SS-Treffen," *Berliner Morgenpost*, June 23, 2004, on-line edition; "CDU-Politiker nach Besuch bei SS-Treffen in der Kritik," *Die Welt*, June 23, 2004, on-line edition; and "Schlacht aus dem Nichts," *Die Zeit*, August 19, 2004, on-line edition.

34. "Minor criminal tendencies..." Ley quoted by Irina Repke, Thilo Thielke and Sonja Volkmann-Schluck, in "Fassungslose Gutmenschen," *Der Spiegel*, February 22, 1999.

35. "It will happen...," Nicette quoted in "Fassungslose Gutmenschen," *Der Spiegel*, February 22, 1999.

36. "Organized death...," Heitmann quoted in *Sueddeutsche Zeitung*, September (date unknown) 1993.

37. "I wonder...," Heitmann quoted in "Rechte Mann, rechte Zeit—Der Ostdeutsche Favorit des Kanzlers fuer die Weizsaecker-Nachfolge ist ein strammer Konservativer," *Der Spiegel*, September 6, 1993.

38. "You're a real...," former prisoner quoted in "Immer nur Missverstaendnisse," *Stern*, October 7, 1993.

11

A SWING TO EXTREMIST PARTIES

PARTS OF SAXONY-ANHALT STATE are scarred with dark moonscapes where bucket-wheel dredges once gouged coal to feed the furnaces of dilapidated, nineteenth century brick factories. The factories closed when the Stalinist economy was blown away as the market economy hurricane struck in 1990.

New industries moved in, but a few high-tech firms were not enough to soak up the unemployment. The state's growth rate remains almost zero. The jobless rate is officially about twenty percent but the real figure is over forty percent.

Here, like much of the East, casual travelers do not sense the despondency, certainly not in hotels or the restaurants, where employees and guests are often Westerners. But Saxony-Anhalt has all the ingredients for political drama.

When, in April 1998, the campaign for the state parliamentary election warmed up, the more depressed areas buzzed with abnormally high levels of discussion, although few were able to say what it meant.

The state was governed by a minority coalition of Social Democrats and Greens that could pass laws only through a toleration deal under which the PDS did not vote against them.

The Christian Democrats were also in opposition. The federal Christian Democrats, led by Chancellor Helmut Kohl, were in power in Berlin. With a general election coming up in September that year, Kohl and his party wanted to drum up support in the East. The Saxony-Anhalt election was part of that plan.

The opinion polls predicted that the Social Democrats in the state would be returned with a sharply improved vote, that the Christian Democrats would lose votes, and that the PDS would again poll about twenty percent. They also said that the neo-Nazi German People's Union (DVU) might sneak into parliament.

Helmut Kohl came along to support his candidate for prime minister, Christoph Bergner. When they appeared together in the shoemaking town of Weissenfels, a heckler hit Bergner with a tomato. When Kohl spoke in the state capital, Magdeburg, he was whistled down. People were not blaming the local Social Democrats government for their problems. They were blaming Kohl and his federal government.

This was not the first time Kohl had received a hot reception in Saxony-Anhalt. He had raised expectations before unification by promising a "a blooming landscape." When this turned out to be a mirage, he might have been statesman enough to rally spirits by making a rousing speech urging people to battle on. But he did not. Instead, he avoided the East. When he did finally go there, it was mid-1991 and hostility towards him was running high. In the industrial city of Halle, someone threw an egg at him—with pinpoint accuracy.[1]

Now, in 1998, the Christian Democrats based their election tactics on a "red-scare" campaign.

As election day neared, surveys showed opinion hardening for the DVU, which seemed likely to poll about six percent. Its campaign was controlled by Gerhard Frey, a Munich publisher with an inherited real-estate fortune who was spending huge amounts of cash and using slogans such as "German jobs for Germans." Frey had increased DVU membership from barely 5,000 in 1976 to 22,000 in 1990.[2] The party's insular appeal was crude: keep the German currency, the mark; reject the European currency, the euro; and blame foreigners for everything.

One DVU poster showed a "foreigner" with greasy, black hair, smoking a cigar and carrying a sack with the label: "Money from drugs, murder, robbery and blackmail."

The DVU candidates did not make public appearances. Frey knew his candidates were best kept out of sight. Instead, his campaign was based on mass mailings, posters, and banners towed by aircraft. He sent out over a million letters and posted 20,000 placards. His total expenditure was said to be three million marks ($1.7 million), far more than any other party.[3]

Polling day arrived. The DVU polled almost thirteen percent overall. In Bitterfeld, Wolfen, and parts of Halle its vote exceeded seventeen percent. In some villages it topped twenty five percent. Not since the days of Hitler had a fascist party polled so well.

The PDS won almost twenty percent of the vote.

A total of 486,000 people—nearly a third of the voters—turned their backs on the established democratic parties in favor of two extreme parties with links to despotism and dictatorships, the DVU and the PDS.

No one had expected this.

Initially it was believed opinion surveys had it wrong because people had refused to admit their voting intentions. But it emerged that several pollsters had either not made available their findings, or deliberately released them late, in an effort to avoid a bandwagon effect.[4]

The neo-Nazi performance drew howls of outrage. One paper said the day was "A Black Sunday...for all democrats."[5] while another said some voters "were clearly hoodwinked by DVU promises."[6] On the Frankfurt Stock Exchange, the main DAX index the next day closed 56 points down, and dealers blamed the election. Businessmen groaned about Germany's image in the world.

One editorial writer insisted that the vote was not a shift toward Nazism.[7] The bulk of the DVU voters were not neo-Nazis but young people without hope, he said.

The Christian Democrat red-scare strategy had badly misfired. It might have worked in middle-class Western electorates where people are anxious to keep their affluence and privileges, but in these deprived industrial regions, a red scare was an irrelevance. The Christian Democrat vote plunged from thirty four percent to twenty two percent.

The DVU won sixteen of the 116 seats in the new assembly.

In the post-election euphoria, the party's prospective parliamentary leader, Helmut Wolf, said,

> In four years time we'll take over the government and will want to provide the prime minister.

But the party was soon bickering with itself. Just a few days later, one candidate pulled out, claiming he had only discovered through the media the sort of people he was associating with.[8] A year later, Wolf was fighting off an attempt to depose him as parliamentary leader. One of the renegades, Torsten Miksch, objected to Frey's tight controls over deputies, saying,

> If a DVU deputy operates like a marionette, he is the best. But when Pinocchio wakes up...the problems begin.[9]

Miksch was sacked from the parliamentary party. Three others deputies abandoned it. Wolf himself lasted barely eighteen months. Then he, too, was out after his own row with Frey.

In the next state election four years later the DVU was in such a mess that it fielded no candidates at all.

The party's big 1998 vote was not just a reaction to high unemployment. A more involved set of forces was at work. Easterners feel overwhelmed by Western arrogance. They see Westerners as a force of carpetbaggers that has dismantled almost the entire old order and substituted a new one, supposedly better in every respect. Western disdain often borders contempt. Eastern resentment is everywhere. In the depressed atmosphere of a drab Quedlinburg bar frequented by morose, card-playing, unemployed Easterners, a long-distance truck driver told me,

> Wessies (Westerners) accuse us of not working. I tell you we had to turn shit into bon bons. We had to improvise because our technology was no good. I had to make repairs on the road, change tires myself. The Wessis just ring the ADAC [motor organization].

Jochen Wolff, himself a Westerner who is editor in chief of *Superillu* magazine, which has a mainly Eastern readership, said, "The West looks down on everything that comes from the East."[10]

That, of course, includes the PDS. The Saxony-Anhalt election was a way of telling Westerners: you ignore the PDS, so we will really give you something to think about and vote neo-Nazi. Another factor was the PDS itself. Its toleration agreement with the state government had eroded some of its image as an opposition force, and thus its potential as a vehicle for protest.

The voters had made their point and bloodied the Western nose. A few months later, in the general election, they deserted the DVU, leaving it with a miserable 3.2 percent.

But a disturbing pattern of protest voting seemed to be setting in, with both the DVU and another neo-Nazi party, the National Democratic Party (NPD) managing sporadic successes in subsequent state elections in the East.

The NPD was founded by a Prussian nobleman, Adolf von Thadden, in 1964. Between 1966 and 1968, it rode into six state assemblies on the back of economic recession, although its electoral successes were all short-lived.

The party became tied up in internal dissent in the late 1960s[11] and faded. After the collapse of East Germany, it emerged in a repackaged form, and was blamed for much of the neo-Nazi violence after unification. An attempt to ban it failed.

NOTES

1. When explanations about the security lapse were sought from the Saxony-Anhalt interior minister, Wolfgang Braun, a member of Kohl's own Christian Democrats, he said nothing for three days. Then he explained that Kohl himself was at fault because his car had stopped sixty meters before it should have and thus had been in an "unprotected zone." See "Schutzlose Zone—Der Magdeburger Innenminister Wolfgang Braun, seit langem wegen seiner DDR-Vergangenheit umstritten, droht nun ueber ein Ei zu sturzen," *Der Spiegel*, May 21, 1991.

2. Statistics from Armin Pfahl-Traughber, in *Rechtsextremismus in der Bundesrepublik*, (Munich: Verlag C.H. Beck, 1999) 28.

3. In a *dpa* report on April 22, Leon Mangasarian quoted German intelligence sources as saying that the DVU's spending was greater than the combined spending of the two main parties, the SPD and the CDU.

4. See "Uebles im Busch—Die Meinungsforscher wussten, dass die DVU in Sachsen-Anhalt ein zweistelliges Ergernis erzielen wuerde," *Der Spiegel*, May 4, 1998.

5. "A Black Day...," *Bild-Zeitung*, April 27, 1998.

6. "Were clearly hoodwinked...," *Saechsische Zeitung*, April 27, 1998.

7. Heinzgeorg Oette, in "Schock und Auftrag", *Magdeburger Volksstimme*, April 27, 1998.

8. The candidate, Eberhard Lehnert, gave various explanations including that he "had not been precisely informed about the nature of the DVU," (*Hamburger Abendblatt*, May 2, 1998); and that he had "health problems," (*Berliner Zeitung*, May 2, 1998.)

9. "If a DVU...," Torsten Miksch quoted by Werner Kolhoff in "Freys Marionetten machen sich selbstaendig—Nach einem Jahr im Landtag von Sachsen-Anhalt versuchen DVU-Abgeordnete sich vom Gaengelband des Muenchener Multimillionaers zu loesen," *Berliner Zeitung*, April 26, 1999.

10. "The West looks down...," Jochen Wolff in "Es berichtet der Korrespondent," an interview with *taz*, November 9, 2004.

11. By the end of 1972, the NPD had been voted out of all state assemblies. Von Thadden retired to the Canary Isles where he sold real estate. He died in 1996.

12

REIGN OF TERROR
IN THE BAROQUE CITY

IF ANYONE BELIEVED NEO-NAZI extremists were merely disparate groups of bored youths striking targets of opportunity, they were rudely awakened in June 1991 when more than 1,500 marched through the baroque city of Dresden in the biggest fascist parade since the end of the Third Reich.

The marchers came from Germany, Austria and the Netherlands. They carried Third Reich battle ensigns and banners saying "Martyr of the Reich." They called "Auslaender raus" ("foreigners out"). Some wore the brown shirts of Hitler's SA organization. Young women wearing uniforms of Hitler's *Bund Deutsche Maedel*, the Nazi girls' organization, marched with them, keeping time to the beats of a big drum as international television teams perched on balconies of buildings lining the route filmed every step.

The marchers vowed to take revenge for the demise of Rainer Sonntag, a neo-Nazi who had been killed in dramatic circumstances two weeks earlier.

Although Sonntag was born in Dresden, he had been to the West, where he drifted in and out of jobs as a pimp and picked up convictions for assault and illegally possessing weapons. He once bragged that "the best job I ever had was as a bouncer in a brothel."[1] He ran unsuccessfully for parliament in the state of Hesse as a member of the *Nationale Sammlung*, a neo-Nazi party founded by a former *Bundeswehr* officer, Michael Kuehnen.

Sonntag returned to Dresden, where he and his followers won a reputation for upholding law and order. It happened this way. Unification brought a sharp increase in crime. The police, recruited from scratch to replace the old force tainted Stasi links, was inexperienced and lacking in confidence. Sonntag hit Dresden's red-light areas and the story got around that he was running a war against the drug dealers who had flooded into East Germany as soon as it became part of the deutsche mark zone in 1990. The story was mostly myth, but enough people believed it to win him both public and police support. The fact was ignored that he was a pimp and extortionist, and that his war on the brothels and his crime fighting had more to do with making money than with moral indignation.

One skinhead, Ingo Hasselbach, remembered that "the local police were very happy with Sonntag's initiative, one so much so that when he was off duty he chauffeured him (Sonntag) around the city out of gratitude."[2] And when neo-Nazis gathered for a demonstration and a journalist suggested the police should do something about people at the main station openly giving Hitler salutes and shouting "Sieg Heil", a policeman replied, "I can't see anyone calling out 'Heil Hitler.'"[3]

Sonntag's big success was against the *Huetchenspieler*. *Huetchenspiel*, literally, the "little hat game," was a simple trick played on the streets by professional gangs that used sleight of hand to deceive people naive enough to take part. The aim was for a passerby to guess which of three inverted matchboxes—each minus the slide cover—hid a little ball. Betting was usually in multiples of 100 marks ($58).

The game was often run by Yugoslavs and Romanians working a beat in teams of four or five. One pretended to be a member of the public who played and ostentatiously "won" to show how easy it was. In Berlin, signs went up warning people against playing. But a test prosecution against a Huetchenspiel gang was defeated in court. In Dresden, neo-Nazis headed by Sonntag the Sheriff drove the gangs off the streets.

But not only the gangs. Parts of the city became deserted at night because of the hostile atmosphere. A Mozambican man, Jorge Gomondai, twenty-eight, died when skinheads threw him off a streetcar. One report said, "Colored people dared not go onto the streets at night; fear of attacks by skinheads pervaded the bars of Dresden's Neustadt. The authorities appeared impotent, the residents silent and powerless."[4]

Sonntag was not smart enough to know his limits. He forgot that, in taking on brothel owners, he was also taking on the underworld.

On the morning of May 31, Sonntag and two sidekicks demanded 50,000 marks ($30,000) in protection money from a brothel known as the Sex-Shopping-Center. The center was partly owned by two men cloaked tastily in frizzy, shoulder-length hair, and silky, perfumed-drenched clothes. Nicolas Simeonidis and Ronny Matz refused to pay.

Just before midnight that night, Simeonidis and Matz left the brothel and were about to drive away in their Mercedes car when a gang of between thirty and forty youths stopped them. Simeonidis stepped out of the car carrying a sawed-off shotgun. Sonntag advanced toward him, daring him to shoot. He did, blowing half Sonntag's head to smithereens.

Sonntag, the neo-Nazi they called the Sheriff of Dresden, was thirty-six when he died.

Seventeen days later, Interpol officers walked into a hotel in Bangkok, arrested Simeonidis and Matz, and flew them back to Germany. Simeonidis, twenty-four, and Matz, twenty-five, appeared before a Dresden superior court charged with murder. The prosecution said that both had sought a confrontation with a band of neo-Nazis and, motivated "by hate and [feelings of] revenge," had murdered the gang leader, Sonntag, before the eyes of his own followers.[5]

The two brothel owners were acquitted on the grounds that they had acted in self defense.[6] But the extreme right wing of the new united Germany had its first martyr, Rainer Sonntag.

Another neo-Nazi, referring to Sonntag, told Hasselbach:

I couldn't...stand the jerk. Now he's dead and he's a martyr as well. That's not bad for a small-time pimp. What more could he want?[7]

The "memorial march" revealed the ineffectiveness of the forces of law and order in Eastern Germany. Dresden's mayor had naively allowed the march to take place because "it would not be a political demonstration."[8] The dangers of a resurgent German nationalism were only reluctantly being learned, as events elsewhere were also making clear.

For nine terror-filled months in 1990, Skinhead HQ Germany was a nondescript gray, four-story apartment near Lichtenberg railway station in East Berlin. In March the *National Alternative* (NA) set up camp on the first floor at 122 Weitling Strasse probably unaware of the irony that the street took its name from a pioneer of the German socialist movement, Wilhelm Weitling, who died in 1871. This was where recruiting was organized, where youths were put in touch with regional neo-Nazi groups. This was where press and television crews went for interviews—which they had to pay for.

This was also where riots were planned and lines of communication set up with battalions of hooligans waiting to be called up for battle. Life was a nightmare for residents, as skinheads and militant left-wingers fought pitched battles up and down the street. An antiterrorist unit raided the house but found little apart from propaganda material. The raid generated such publicity that donations to the extremists increased. Cash rolled in from outside Germany, while income from the almost daily press interviews hit new heights. On New Year's Eve 1990, the occupants of 122 Weitling Strasse smashed the interior of the building for fun and then walked out. Local residents breathed sighs of relief.

One of the Weitling Strasse ringleaders was Hasselbach, who was born in 1967 as Ingo Fuellgrap. His father, a communist and a journalist in West Germany, had defected to the East, where he ran a radio station known as *Stimme der DDR* (The Voice of East Germany). The son grew up with his grandfather and grandmother in Berlin. As a small boy, he came into contact with a hippie commune in the inner suburb of Prenzlauerberg, where at the age of thirteen, he began smoking and drinking. He sniffed glue and gasoline, he stole and drank liquor from supermarkets, he robbed tourists and was arrested by the police. In 1985 he was convicted for being a rowdy, a term covering a multitude of offences, and in 1987 was jailed for publicly demanding that the Berlin Wall must go. At beginning of 1988, he drifted into neo-Nazi circles.

In November 1990 Hasselbach joined up with a party of 600 hooligans and skinheads traveling in hired buses from Berlin to watch a soccer match in Leipzig. On the way, they raided an autobahn filling station and a supermarket. Near Bitterfeld, 500 hooligans from the West joined them. Word went ahead to Leipzig where a waiting police squad fired tear gas and rubber bullets in a bid to prevent them from getting to the stadium. The hooligans stole two cars, halted a bus, forced the passengers out and set the three vehicles on fire. The badly outnumbered police withdrew under a hail of stones. When they returned, they were armed. Again they came under attack. Not used to such situations, they opened fire. One rioter immediately fell to the ground. Mike Polley, eighteen, was dead.

This mindlessness of it all finally affected Hasselbach. In 1993 he caused a shock by leaving the neo-Nazi scene. At the age of twenty-five, he went underground to avoid revenge attacks. He had tired of the neo-Nazi mentality and saw that he was not a victim but an offender. Hasselbach was a member of a lost generation with nowhere to go, who, driven by hate and pumped up on alcohol, had staggered into the militant scene simply because it was there waiting for him, a sort of oasis for the aimless and the angry. He got out because he outgrew the people in it and the crudity of their ideas.[9]

NOTES

1. "The best job...," Sonntag quoted in "Der Unfall mit den Todesschuessen," *ADN/Hamburger Abendblatt*, March 2, 1992.
2. "The local police...," Ingo Hasselbach and Winfried Bonengel in *Die Abrechnung, Ein Neonazi steigt aus*, (Berlin: Aufbau-Verlag, 1993) 113.
3. "I can't see...," Hasselbach, 113.
4. "Colored people..." in "Der Unfall mit den Todesschuessen," *ADN/Hamburger Abendblatt*, March 2, 1992.
5. "By hate...," in "Schlappe fuer Bossi—Anklage im Prozess um Neonazi-Mord," *Hamburger Abendblatt*, March 5, 1992.
6. The acquittals were later overturned. In a retrial, in October and November 1993, Simeonidis was jailed for five years and Matz for ten months.
7. "I couldn't stand...," neo-Nazi quoted in Hasselbach, 114.
8. "It would not be...," Dresden's mayor Herbert Wagner quoted in "Eine Stadt in Angst und Scham—Dresden erlebte am Wochenende das bisher grosste Treffen von Neonazis in Ostdeutschland," *Berliner Zeitung*, June 17, 1991.
9. The Weitling Strasse episode received widespread publicity. This account was partly based on Hasselbach's own version in *Die Abrechnung*.

PART FOUR
THE STASI REPUBLIC

13

VICTIMS FIGHT TO AVOID OBLIVION

A BATTLE TO MANIPULATE HISTORY is being fought out across Eastern Germany. The manipulators want to remove any concept of guilt for the killing of more than a thousand people at the Berlin Wall and the fortified border between the two German states during the Cold War.[1] They say this violence resulted from twelve years of Nazi rule that led to Germany's division into two hostile camps. Subsequent events were a function of this legacy that led, in turn, to the building of the Wall and to the deaths in the no-man's-land there by gunshot, landmines and automatic self-shooting devices. No one is to blame—there are no villains, only victims, runs the argument. The aim is to let the East Berlin regime, and thus its henchmen, off the hook.

Advocates argue that prisoners were not tortured in dungeons, and that the regime did not routinely persecute people for speaking their mind, reading what they wanted, or associating with whom they wanted. No Stasi kidnap or assassination squads were sent to the West to kidnap escapers, they say.[2]

The East German regime did not like the term "Stalinist." But that is what it was. The first party boss, Walter Ulbricht, eliminated his opponents as political forces, including those communists wanting a more humane form of rule, the so-called "Third Way Marxists" (though this term did mean different things to different people). That left the Stalinists unchallenged. From their wartime exile in the Soviet Union, they brought to Germany the concept of Stalinism: one-party rule, no opposition, the use of terror to subdue the population.[3] Thousands fled. To halt the exodus, East Berlin built a ninety-six mile wall around West Berlin and an 838-mile wall-fence along the border between East and West Germany. It stationed armed guards in watchtowers along the death strip behind the wall and ordered them to shoot escapers. A wall without bullets would have deterred no one from leaving.

Many people did escape over the Wall to the West, but many were shot dead, shredded by landmines, or killed by self-shooting devices.[4] Untold numbers were wounded.

The "no-blame" argument is as ludicrous as denying the Holocaust took place under Hitler. "No-blame" advocates are often helped by bureaucratic and political indifference. An inscription in front of a preserved part of the Wall at Berlin's Bernauer Strasse reads, "Memorial to the victims of the Second World War and the division of Germany." A person unfamiliar with events is likely to be left confused—which is the intention of the authors. But, a short walk away at the entrance to the site, a less sanitized dedication reads, "In memory of the division of the city between August 13, 1961, and November 9, 1989, and to remember the victims of communist tyranny."

The second inscription was only set up after a struggle headed by Klaus-Peter Eich. But he failed in an attempt to have the wording arranged in a more logical order so that "victims" were mentioned before "division."[5]

Official coolness was shown when a row broke out over a memorial to the people who were killed trying to escape. In 2004, a forest of more than a thousand black, wooden crosses was erected on a site at the former Checkpoint Charlie. The memorial was unusual in that it was not, like most memorials, over-designed and under-appreciated; but simple, unadorned and brutal. There was nothing nice about it, but there was nothing nice about the killings of a thousand people. Yet some Berlin politicians were irate. Apparently they want tourists to the city to spend money in shiny shopping emporia, safely out of sight of anything that might spoil the taste of their coffee.

One said, "No Disneyland, please."[6] Disneyland? The only Disneyland here is the endless souvenir stalls and stores that have done a roaring trade hawking bogus bits of the Wall and Russian officers' hats since the Wall fell in 1989. The crosses, far from being Disneyland, were a hard-hitting memorial assembled by the founder of the Museum at Checkpoint Charlie, Rainer Hildebrandt, and his wife, Alexandra. Frau Hildebrandt completed the project after her husband died in January 2004. The crosses were forcibly removed by court order in July, 2005.

One aim of the "no-blame" campaign is to erase from public awareness not only those people who were killed or wounded, but also the thousands of people who were imprisoned for "political offences," a loosely defined phrase which meant anything the state deemed it to be.[7] As the human rights organization amnesty international (ai) pointed out, some laws were "so vaguely formulated that almost any form of undesired political activity could lead to incarceration."[8]

The regime dropped the use of the term "political prisoners" in 1951 because the term did not fit in with the regime's concept of itself. Instead, political prisoners were regarded as criminals and treated as such. More than 180,000 people were arrested for political reasons. Their "offenses" included attempting to leave the country without exit permits—known as "fleeing the republic"—or reading or writing or saying the wrong thing. Walls had ears. Stool pigeons infiltrated every walk of life. Suspicion was enough. Once arrested, victims were in effect, already convicted. Most were kept for long periods in solitary confinement, often without access to fresh air or medical aid. The only people they saw were interrogators and guards. In the early days of the state, execution by guillotine was common. Torture was routine. Enforced idleness was aimed at breaking the spirit. No reading matter, no access to radio or television, no writing material. Only their own thoughts. Some did not survive. Others emerged with ruined health.

Ai commented that "blows causing bruising or broken noses; chaining to beds; chicanery liable to drive prisoners to suicide; solitary confinement; and inadequate medical care; were routine in both investigative custody and prisons."[9]

Achim Beyer was one of a group of nineteen Abitur students arrested by the Stasi one night in 1951 as they distributed anti-regime fliers. Beyer, then nineteen, recalled the psychological pressure. The Stasi interrogation room contained whips of different sizes that were tried out on a table as prisoners watched. "The Stasi even went as far as trying to provoke suicide. The walls of the changing room...were full of red flecks. Whether blood or red paint, I don't know. A guard said that many people had ended their own lives here."[10] Beyer was sentenced to eight years' jail but was released in November, 1956.

The regime was so desperate for convertible currency that it arrested people and sold them to West Germany in a controversial project both sides tried to keep secret. The trade was, depending on point of view, either a praiseworthy operation that helped oppressed people, or a sordid business that served to prop up a loathsome regime. East Berlin earned 3.4 billion West marks ($1.9 billion at the 1989 rate) from it over twenty-five years.[11]

Ex-prisoners qualify for a miserly single payment of €300 ($370) for every month in jail—with some variations—and payout has been slow because of attempts by successive governments to cut spending. Guenter Nooke, a former East German civil-rights activist, described the situation as "a complete disgrace."[12] He is a member of the opposition Christian Democrats in the federal parliament, but his remark was not intended to score points at the expense of the governing Social Democrats. His own party was in power for most of the immediate postunification years of the 1990s.

In contrast, former members of the Stasi secret police, as long-serving civil servants, qualify for generous pension payments. Some draw pensions in line with what they would have received had they worked in West Germany and not East Germany. In 2004, the German parliament rejected a proposal for an honorary pension for former political prisoners. A few weeks later, the Constitutional Court handed down a ruling that, in effect, means an increase in pensions for career Stasi officers.[13]

For forty years, the Stasi used terror to help the ruling SED survive. In the words of amnesty international, the party, through the Stasi, "intimidated, terrorised, and imprisoned" people."[14] Now, a Stasi officer who spent a working life systematically cowering an entire population is rewarded while many of the victims scrape for a living. Victims' resentment is understandably high.[15]

The realities of East Germany's sordid history are receding with time. According to Thomas Lukow, himself a former political prisoner, they are cloaked in a "creeping amnesia...a fatal ignorance of German history is apparent in all sections of the German population."[16]

On a visit to Hohenschoenhausen museum prison, I heard a tour guide ask a party of schoolchildren aged about seventeen or eighteen why the Wall was built. They hmmed and haahed, but did not know. I later put the question to several *Gymnasium* (academic high school) pupils due to take their *Abitur* examination for university, and they did not know either. One thought it was to keep Westerners out.

Lukow often speaks to students and tour parties at memorials. He comes across many examples of distortion. He writes of students "exclusively in the East who sometimes come out with the defiant statement: 'Everything was better in East Germany.' After closer questioning, 'better' is replaced by 'simpler.' Sure, many things were uniform and simple. For example, there were no complicated tax returns. But 'simple' does not by a long shot mean 'better'."[17]

Victims of persecution have no lobby strong enough to force their case. Western Germans are not interested. The Western-dominated electronic media show at most a sporadic interest. The result is a distortion of history by neglect. Juergen Aretz and Wolfgang Stock say that, "in some television talk shows these days, a picture of East Germany is shown that excludes essential elements of reality and, in cases where cynical acts of contempt for humans cannot simply be rejected, dismisses them as an [isolated] mistake by an individual person." This trivialization leads to victims being portrayed as "yesterday's people" whose obsession with the past is preventing "internal" unification. But, say Aretz and Stock, the real destroyers of "internal unification" are the defenders of the East German system and those who make it sound better than it was.[18]

The forces of disinformation are contantly at work. A book that states on its back cover it is intended for school pupils and university students, claims to explain, in a question-and-answer form, all about East Germany. One example:

Question: Why were people put in jail for uttering a critical opinion?

Answer: No one was put in jail for [expressing] criticism.[19]

Eich himself nearly became a fatality at the Berlin Wall. On October 12, 1961, two months after the Wall went up, he tried to get through a double wire fence to reach West Berlin. As he lay on his stomach, guards opened fire at him. He was hit in the back, captured, spent two years in an East Berlin hospital, and, when he emerged, was wheelchair-bound.

According to Eich, "many people in East Germany were corrupted by the inhuman system. They accepted the criminal events at the border and found no empathy for the victims of the Wall and the no-go area. Often you would hear: 'It is his own fault. He knew it is forbidden to violate the state border.'"[20] Eich made the comment in 1996 at a parliamentary ceremony in Berlin to mark the 35th anniversary of the building of the Wall.

His speech was delivered in unusual circumstances. The original speakers' list included only politicians. Eich applied to be placed on the list, but was turned down. After strong protests, another former victim, Ilse Leopold, was included, but not Eich. Leopold opened her speech at the ceremony by saying, "Because Klaus-Peter Eich is not being allowed to deliver his speech on behalf of victims and their relatives, I will read it."[21] After a few sentences, she broke off and invited Eich himself, who was in the audience, to continue. He did so, to sustained applause.

Eich might be forgiven for thinking that forces are conspiring against him. In the early 90s, a number of wooden crosses in memory of people who died at the Berlin Wall were erected next to the Reichstag building. Eich told

me that, as he rolled himself past the crosses in his wheelchair, he was star-
tled to see his own name. One of the crosses was in memory of himself.[22]

Prison administrators aimed to demoralize political prisoners and force
them to make confessions. Inmates were often isolated. Tactics included sleep
deprivation—lights on every fifteen minutes, interrogations in the middle of
the night; and enforced mental inactivity. How do you pass the time in a windowless cell with no reading matter, no writing material, no contact with
other people apart from guards and interrogators? Prisoners lost track of
time. They were fed snippets of disinformation designed to bend their minds.
Is the child really ill? Has the wife/husband really remarried? The mental
gnawing begins. No verifiable facts are made available. In a system where no
nosey lawyers or international agencies bothered prison administrations,
Stasi bully boys could work unchallenged.

In the early days prison violence was common. This declined over the
years as the state sought international recognition, and, instead, higher levels
of psychological torture were used. The intention was to intimidate prisoners
so they would be unable to function as "opposition" figures after their release.
But much of the brutality was for its own sake.

The policy of isolation and disorientation was highly refined. One trick
was to take prisoners in a darkened van fitted with tiny, windowless cells, for
long rides to get from A to B. The prisoner finished the journey without knowing that the van had arrived back where it had started from. Yet destination B
might be the block next to starting point A.[23]

Some of the most notorious prisons, Hohenschoenausen, in Berlin, and
Bautzen I and II, both in the town of the same name, have been turned into
museums. The visitor can see padded underground cells designed to conceal
noise and hide violence, cells with ribbed-metal floors and walls where inmates were forced to stand in cold water for days, and cells where no daylight
penetrated. Many guides are themselves ex prisoners willing to describe their
prison treatment. Many have written personal memoirs about life on the inside. But prosecutions of prison staff have been few because of the difficulty of
linking health problems with prison maltreatment, because of the statute of
limitations, and also because of a lack of urgency by prosecutors. When the
balloon went up in 1989, Stasi staff shredded evidence.

Legality did not bother the Stasi. Timo Zilli was a young Italian living in
West Berlin. One day in 1970, he was returning home from a works party. By

his own admittance, he was drunk as he went to change trains at Friedrich Strasse station, which served as a junction. Although the station was on East German territory, it was possible for West Berliners to change trains without having to pass checkpoints and enter East Berlin itself. Zilli was descending a set of steps when he was seen by a Grepo. Here the stories differ. A statement the following day at the police station said Zilli "is under strong suspicion of, in the evening hours of 11.11.1970 in the Western part of the S-Bahn Berlin Friedrichstrasse having carried out agitation hostile to the state and performed resistance to state measures, with the aim of incitement against the social order of the German Democratic Republic"...and "with physical violence," prevented Vopos "from fulfilling their designated tasks."[24]

Zilli says he walked unsteadily down the station steps, and, as he paused to look at himself in a mirror, a Grepo pushed him to the ground, saying, "Piss off, you drunken pig," and hit him with a truncheon. More Grepos came to the scene, and Zilli called them "Nazi pigs." The first Grepo claimed later Zilli had attacked him. Zilli spent over eighteen months in jail, where he was beaten, hung from his wrists from rings so that he could only reach the floor on tip toes. He was suspended from the cell window grating for up to six hours at a time. A guard knocked out a tooth with a set of steel handcuffs.

The case was not quite as accidental as it seemed. Zilli had been involved with the 1968 student movement in West Berlin. His Stasi files show that he had been shadowed before his arrest by the Stasi, who believed he was helping people escape East Germany. It provoked the station incident to arrest him.

He was released in 1972 with ruined wrists and emotional problems. He told organisations in the West how he had been treated, but few people believed him. Christian Pross, of the Center for the Treatment of Torture Victims, said, "Not even amnesty international (wanted to believe him)."[25]

Many ex prisoners suffer from conditions that have no apparent organic explanation. They "are changed into suspicious and reserved loners. They suffer particularly from a lack of understanding by people in Western Germany, who do not believe them. Former Stasi victims are regarded by many doctors as psychopaths, elderly neurotics, or socially abnormal."[26]

Horst Hennig, a former prisoner who is now a doctor, is highly critical of both the medical profession and politicians: "The doctors in this field have no understanding. The time when political prisoners suffered is for them largely unknown territory. Unfortunately this applies equally to politicians."[27]

Siegfried Rataizick is a quietly spoken, gray haired man in his seventies (born in 1931). Looking misty-eyed behind his metal-rimmed spectacles, he becomes almost maudlin as he tells how his mother was imprisoned by the Nazis and how he wanted to ensure that Nazi excesses never happened again. Listening to him speak in a documentary television film[28] is like hearing a retired schoolteacher talk about some bygone mellow lemonade era on the playing fields.

But Rataizick was no schoolteacher. He was a colonel in the Stasi, and the misty days he refers to are when he was in charge of the Stasi Hauptabteilung XIV, which ran prisons. Rataizick was a major part of the machinery that bulldozed over human rights. This is how Hennig described interrogations in prisons such as those run by Rataizick: "A mixture of threats, oppression, blackmail, and raw violence pursuing prisoners as traumatic consequences until the end of their lives."[29]

> Rataizick: I worked forty years for the Stasi, fighting half my life for a good cause, trying everything to improve (the lot of) humanity …and then I had to discover virtually overnight in 1989 that all was lost…I wanted only the best.[30]

Which prompted one film reviewer to retort:

> Because the prison director's relatives died in a concentration camp, he had to torture political prisoners in Hohenschoenhausen. 'The work often was real fun,' was how Rataizick summed it up.[31]

NOTES

1. A total of 1,008 border deaths between 1946 and 1989 had been proved by 2002, according to the Work Group 13 August, an organization headed by Rainer Hildebrandt, based at the Museum at Checkpoint Charlie in Berlin. The toll also includes East Germans killed trying to escape through other countries such as Bulgaria, the former Czechoslovakia, Poland, and Hungary. See Chapter 21—The Death Strip.

2. Cases are widely documented. See Chapter 14—Echoes from the Dungeon, for details about the cases of Walter Thraene and soccer player Lutz Eigendorf. See Chapter 15—The Making of a Police State, for the case of Robert Bialek.

3. See Chapter 15—The Making of a Police State.

4. More than 5,000 people escaped across the fortified border between the building of the Wall in August 1961, and when the Wall came down, on November 9, 1989, according to the Museum at Checkpoint Charlie. For more about the self-shooting devices, see Chapter 24—Gartenschlaeger's Private War.

5. The first inscription, following a persistent campaign to overcome bureaucratic and political resistance, has been removed, leaving only the inscription at the entrance that recognizes the "victims of communist tyranny."

6. "No Disneyland...," Green politician Katrin Goering-Eckardt, quoted in "Rise of new wall fuels Berlin dispute," *FAZ Weekly*, November 12, 2004.

7. See Chapter 17—The People Trade.

8. "So vaguely formulated...," in *Deutsche Demokratische Republik—Rechtsprechung hinter Verschlossenen Tueren*, (Bonn: amnesty international, 1992) 115.

9. "Blows causing...," in *Amnesty International und die DDR: Die Arbeit fuer die Menschenrechte in der DDR von 1961-1989*, (Berlin: amnesty international, 2003) 12.

10. "They went as far...," Beyer quoted in "Justiz/Vorgehen gegen Ausreisewillige," *Enquete-Kommission, Aufarbeitung von Geschichte und Folgen der SED-Diktatur in Deutschland—Recht, Justiz, Polizei IV* (Frankfurt: Suhrkamp Taschenbuch Nomos, 1995) 245.

11. See Chapter 17—The People Trade.

12. "A complete disgrace...," Guenter Nooke in a panel discussion with Guenter Schabowski in Hamburg on April 30, 2002. The author was present.

13. For details of the ruling, see "Offene Verhoehnung," *Der Stacheldraht*, July 22, 2004.

14. "Intimidated, terrorised, and...," in *Amnesty International und die DDR*, 12.

15. See Chapter 14—Echoes from the Dungeon.

16. "Creeping amnesia...," Thomas Lukow in "Schwierigkeiten des Zusammenwachsens," *Der Stacheldraht*, April 30, 2004.

17. "Exclusively in the East...," Lukow in "Schwierigkeiten des Zusammenwachsens."

18. "In some television...," Juergen Aretz and Wolfgang Stock in *Die Vergessenen Opfer der DDR: 13 erschuetternde Berichte mit Original Stasi-Akten* (Bergisch-Gladbach: Bastei-Verlag Gustav H. Lubbe, 1997), 25.

19. "Q: Why were...," *Fragen an die DDR—Alles, was man ueber den deutschen Arbeiter-und-Bauern-Staat wissen muss*, (Berlin: Das Neue Berlin Verlagsgesellschaft, 2003) 105.

20. "Many people in...," Klaus-Peter Eich quoted in "Opfergedenken ohne Opfergedanken," *Der Stacheldraht*, August 26, 1996.

21. "Because Klaus-Peter...," Leopold quoted in "Opfergedenken ohne Opfergedanken."

22. The mistake can probably be put down to erroneous source material. Eich is listed as dead in two German-language books known to the author that deal with victims of the Wall. Eich said he contacted the authors of one of the books, who said they would provide the original source, but did not. In a conversation with Eich on September 21, 2004, I told him that this error had been repeated in an English-language book about the fall of the Wall and that I had sent an e-mail to this effect to the publishers. I received no reply. The English-language book had acknowledged using the German-language book as source material.

23. A description of such an operation at Hohenschoenhausen is related by Robert Ide in *Die Neuen Architekturfuehrer Nr. 43—Gedenkstaette Berlin-Hohenschoenhausen* (Berlin: Stadtwandel Verlag, 2003), 19.

24. Facsimile of the document reproduced in *Folterzelle 36 Berlin-Pankow*, by Timo Zilli (Berlin: Edition Hentrich, 1993), 212.

25. "Not even Amnesty...," Pross writing in Zilli, 7.

26. "Are changed into...," Silvia Schattenfroh in *Frankfurter Allgemeine Zeitung*, September 10, 1991. Reproduced in English in "The suffering of Stasi victims continues," the *German Tribune*, September 22, 1991. Schattenfroh was reporting on the findings of a Cologne specialist, Uwe Henrik Peters, who examined the case histories of thirty Stasi victims in the medical journal *Fortschritte der Neurologie-Psychiatrie*.

27. "The doctors in...," Horst Hennig in "Lebenslang gezeichnet—Folter in politischer Haft 1945-1956, Teil 2," *Der Stacheldraht*, August 25, 2004. The text was excerpted from a contribution to a book, *Zwischen Bautzen und Workuta—Totalitaere Gewaltherrschaft and Haftolgen*, due to be published by Leipziger Universitaetsverlag.

28. Rataizick was speaking on *Alltag einer Behoerde—Das Ministerium fuer Staatssicherheit*, a film by Jan N. Lorenzen and Christian Klemke, a joint *MDR/Arte* e-Motion Picture Baden-Baden 2002.

29. "Mixture of...," Horst Hennig in "Lebenslang gezeichnet—Folter in politischer Haft 1945-1956, Teil 1," *Der Stacheldraht*, July 22, 2004.

30. "I worked forty...," Rataizick on *Alltag einer Behoerde—Das Ministerium fuer Staatssicherheit*.

31. "Because the prison...," Roland Brauckmann in "Opis in Uniform?—Der Dokumentarfilm 'Alltag einer Behoerde'," *Der Stacheldraht*, February 20, 2003.

14

ECHOES FROM THE DUNGEON

Stasi officers worked on the principles of "moral probity; a positive attitude to work—its justification and necessity; honesty; reciprocal trust with, and to one another...and clean living." —former Stasi general Willi Opitz, on *ARTE* television, November 10, 2003

SIGRID RUEHRDANZ AND FORMER Stasi officers have one thing in common—both are trying to come to terms with the past. For both, the past defines the present.

The similarity ends there. The Stasi regards this plump and graying grandmother as a dangerous political agitator. She sees the Stasi as a force driven by evil. The Stasi was once her jailer, and she was its prisoner. And what she has to say makes it difficult for the former jailers to justify their past.

In May 2002 she went to a meeting in Berlin of 200 Stasi generals and other ranks for the presentation of a book, *Die Sicherheit—Zur Abwehrarbeit des MfS* (Security—on the Counter-Intelligence Role of the Ministry of State Security). The book's authors were twenty former Stasi officers, including eleven generals.

One of these ex generals, Wolfgang Schwanitz, was deputy to the Stasi minister himself, Erich Mielke, and thus right at the center of the oppression apparatus. Schwanitz assured the meeting that "there is no need for regrets" about the past. That won him sustained applause. The aim of the two-volume work was to present an "objective picture" to counter the "flood of calumny" about the Stasi, he said.

In other words, the book was an attempt at a whitewash.

One reviewer, Konrad Weiss, wrote:

There are some highly irrelevant books around, and this is one of them. The editors and the twenty named authors are former high-ranking Stasi officers (ranking) from colonel to general...I doubt

that this opus has even the slightest value for the study of contemporary history...All (the authors) were, and remain, not merely counter-intelligence specialists, but also disinformation specialists...they
hide more than they reveal. They continue to deny the injustices
they themselves were responsible for. What long ago was documented and verified—the human-rights violations in East Germany,
the torture in the Stasi prisons, the Stasi subversion efforts, the systematic ruining of people, the surveillance of their own population
—apparently didn't take place at all.[1]

The meeting was meant to be secret. No probing capitalist press was wanted,
no uncomfortable Stasi victims. But word got around. Ruehrdanz and a small
number of other former prisoners turned up, including Herbert Pfaff. Inside
the crowded hall, he found a seat some distance from her.

The gathering was heavy with nostalgia for those who longed for the
heavy-handed days of the Stalinist past—and that was almost everyone. No
filming allowed, photographs only to be taken in the direction of the stage.
The moderator, Klaus Steiniger, announced, generously, "journalists who
have found out about this meeting are allowed in." But a feeling of déjà vu descended when he added, "But not all of them. We have heard—and sometimes
you hear these things—that provocations and organized disruptions by professional anticommunists have been planned."

One woman reporter smuggled in a microphone. When Ruehrdanz
asked why some of the media had been excluded, she was told, "We are not
saying—for good reason."

The hall, which occupies part of a crumbling building near the
Ostbahnhof, is known for obscure reasons as the Blue Salon. It is the former editorial office of the party newspaper, *Neues Deutschland*, and
Steiniger must have felt at home. Before he became editor of a Marx-
ist-Leninist newspaper, *Rotfuchs* (Red Fox), he spent many years as foreign correspondent for *Neues Deutschland*. The paper is different now, but
in the East German days, it served up relentless gray swathes of propaganda.

The meeting this summer evening soon warmed up, and not only because the ancient heating system resisted all effort to control it as it gurgled
away at maximum temperature.

After the audience heard how the state of East Germany was the "greatest success in German history," Ruehrdanz attempted to put some questions. Steiniger retorted, "I take it that the disruption is now beginning. Sit down and shut up!" Ruehrdanz explained that all she wanted was the facts. The audience became restive. When she said that in 1964 as a member of a prison cleaning team she had cleaned out a cell smeared with blood and feces, she was told, "Shut your mouth! Close your trap! Get out!"

A lone voice called, "There was no torture."

Herbert Pfaff, sitting across from Ruehrdanz, stood up and introduced himself as a former prisoner who had been imprisoned twice in the 1950s and 1960s. He had been beaten up in the notorious "submarine" cells at Hohenschoenhausen prison, he said.

"How much are they paying you?" called another lone voice.

Pfaff, a combative type, traded angry insults with a man sitting near him. Two ushers hustled him out of the hall, giving him a push as he went. The other former prisoners followed him out, leaving Ruehrdanz alone with the hostile audience.

Just another "professional victim," explained Steiniger of Pfaff.

Ushers wearing badges identifying them as members of the PDS "reformed communists" ordered Ruehrdanz to leave. She refused. But not even this mob was prepared to manhandle a lone grandmother.

She was determined to speak to Schwanitz. But when she got the chance, he replied, "I am not going to talk to you."[2]

Torsten Ruehrdanz was born in East Berlin on January 27, 1961, seven months before the Berlin Wall was built, with a malformed spine and a defective esophagus. He needed surgery the East could not provide, so his mother, Sigrid Ruehrdanz, took him to Westend hospital in West Berlin for surgery. After he returned home, she was able to obtain medicines and special foods from the West that were unavailable in the East.

But the building of the Berlin Wall stopped the border hopping. Without supplies from the West, Torsten's health declined. One night, he was taken to hospital spitting blood. The duty doctor, Burkhard Schneeweiss, realised that a plastic tube needed to be inserted into the esophagus, an operation that could not be done in the East. Torsten needed to return to Westend hospital, but that was difficult because the East was tied up in red tape. It took

Schneeweiss much behind-the-scenes maneuvring to get around the bureau-cracy and arrange for Torsten to return to Westend.

Sigrid and her husband, Hartmut, applied for exit permits to visit him. It was the beginning of a long struggle with unforeseen consequences. After six long weeks, officials relented and allowed Sigrid to attend Torsten's baptism in the hospital on a one-day pass valid for a matter of hours. She returned to East Berlin.

When the bureaucratic skirmishing resumed, the Ruehrdanzes decided to get out permanently. Hartmut contacted three college students who worked with escape organizers, and opted for a getaway on an established route through Denmark using forged documents. The plans blew apart when the Stasi learned of the plan.

Torsten, still alone in Westend hospital, was now suffering from another condition which was stunting his growth.

One February morning in 1963, the Ruehrdanz misery took a dramatic turn for the worse. It was 15 degrees below zero when, at 7:30 a.m., Sigrid left the Kaulsdorf house and walked across the hardpacked snow to catch a bus. At the corner of Ulmen Strasse and Sadowa Strasse, two men in civilian clothes forced her into the back of a BMW car and drove off. A few minutes later, another team went to the house and took Hartmut away.

Sigrid was taken to a prison cell and interrogated. At 3:30 the next morn-ing after more than nineteen continuous hours of questioning, she was told Hartmut was also in the prison. She did not believe it. She was given a note in his handwriting that said, "Let's break with the past and one day we'll begin again from the beginning. Hartmut."

At 6:00 a.m., after twenty-two solid hours of questioning, she was al-lowed two hours' rest, brought before a judge, and taken by windowless van to another jail.[3] She was placed in solitary confinement, and the questioning went on for fourteen days. The cell light burned all night every night. A guard looked through the spy hole every three minutes. She did not know where she was and neither did anybody else. To the outside world, she had vanished. She was allowed no lawyer and no telephone calls. She had only one means of communication, the age-old system of tapping messages on the cell wall. Somewhere below her, someone tapped back. Another prisoner in solitary be-came known to her as "Joe." "Joe" and "Lie" tapped to each other from April to the middle of July 1963.

Hartmut and Sigrid saw each other again in August, when they went on trial in Rostock. More unpleasant shocks were in store. Instead of being charged with trying "to flee the republic," they were indicted with the more serious count of inciting the three college students to flee. The court sent them both down for four years. The Stasi records show that the sentences had been set in advance. Sigrid went back to the same jail, and, after more than a year, she was told where she was—Hohenschoenhausen in East Berlin. Hartmut was sent to another jail in the town of Bautzen.

The Stasi made Sigrid an offer. She would be released and allowed to visit Torsten. But in return she was to arrange a meeting in a West Berlin park with Michael Hinze, a college student who had been helping people escape to the West. She was to be a decoy for a kidnap squad.

She said "no." They threw her back into solitary.

Sigrid went to work in her trade as a dental mechanic, making crowns and bridges for the prison dentist in a workplace separated by a steel door from two rubber-lined interrogation cells. One day she heard screaming, muffled but unmistakable, from one of the cells. The screams went on day and night. After two weeks, they stopped, and a man was taken out. Later that morning, two blood-soaked items of apparel were brought to the prison laundry: a guard's uniform and a straitjacket. Sigrid was ordered to clean out the cell. It was filthy with blood and feces. The prisoner never came back. He has never been identified.

In August 1964 the West German government paid 80,000 West marks and, after nineteen months in prison, Sigrid and Hartmut were free. But still they were not free to visit Torsten. They had to wait another eight months for that, and by then he had turned four.[4]

Walter Thraene made a guest appearance at the Museum at Checkpoint Charlie in June 1993 in an evening billed as "Number 595 Lives." Among the guests were Sigrid and Hartmut Ruehrdanz.

Thirty one years before, in August 1962, Walter Thraene fled from East Berlin to West Berlin with a girlfriend named Barbara Schoener. Thraene had no trouble passing the checkpoint, because he was a captain in the Stasi's scientific branch. In West Berlin he should have contacted the West German intelligence agency, the BND. Instead, he looked up a Western businessman he had met at the Leipzig trade fair, Manfred Homann. It was a costly mistake. Homann was not only a businessman, he also worked for the Stasi.

Thraene and Schoener reached West Germany. Three weeks later they drove to Austria in the belief that they were keeping one step ahead of a hit squad sent by Stasi minister Erich Mielke. About 22:30 p.m. on September 4 they followed a detour sign near the town of Kremsmuenster, near Linz, and turned off. The sign was a dummy, and they reached a dead end. The car stopped. Thraene recalled, "Suddenly the door was torn open, pistols pointed at us. I was hit over the head, and everything went black."[5]

When he came to, he was back behind the Iron Curtain, in Prague. He was flown to East Berlin, tried in a secret hearing, and sentenced to fifteen years' imprisonment on charges of treachery and desertion. Barbara Schoener was jailed for four years.

To the outside world, Thraene had simply disappeared. No one on either side of the East-West divide, neither friends nor relatives nor former colleagues, knew what had happened to him. He was interned in Hohenschoenhausen, where he was given the number of 595 and placed in solitary confinement. He was often taken to torture cells in the basement of Hohenschoenhausen prison where he was made to stand in cold water for hours at a time. Sometimes he was placed in a darkened cell. Beatings were routine.

Thraene was released in 1973, after nearly eleven years of solitary, and was given a low-paid job in the steel-making city of Eisenhuettenstadt and forced to take an assumed identity.

At the Museum at Checkpoint Charlie, Sigrid Ruehrdanz compared notes with Thraene and realized that, thirty years before, they had tapped messages to one another from one isolation cell to the other at Hohenschoenhausen. Joe and Lie had at last come face to face.

Sigrid Ruehrdanz told me what Thraene had told her:

Whenever they took him down to the (so-called) arrest cells, they beat him. They hit him in the kidneys and liver. He tried to kill himself five times, but the guards controlled him too closely for that. After that decade in solitary, he was released and sent to Eisenhuettenstadt where he was required to live under a false identity. For eighteen years he lived under this identity. Another cruel blow was when he met his parents. They had believed him to be dead and here he was suddenly in front of them. The shock must have been enormous.[6]

Not surprisingly, Thraene's health was bad. Another meeting with Ruehrdanz was arranged, but Thraene could not make it. His years in prison had caught up with him. The beatings and the cold water treatment had caused permanent internal damage and, on November 9, 1993, he died at the age of sixty-seven.[7]

A tiny, dark-haired figure waited at the bottom of the steps, hunched against the wall of the Gruenau S-Bahn station concourse. A few minutes later, with me beside him, Torsten Ruehrdanz was threading his Mercedes through the Saturday afternoon traffic in the weak, late summer sunlight.

We chatted about the communist days and about what Germans euphemistically call the *"Wende,"* the "change" of political and economic systems.

After leaving school, he trained as an electronics technician and worked in a state-run factory that made television sets and medical equipment. When the Eastern economy was privatized in 1990, his factory closed, and like thousands of others, he was pitched out on to the street. He turned to setting up sound systems for concerts.

He swung the Mercedes into the driveway of the chipped cement house at Kaulsdorf and brought it to a halt next to the the seven-meter cabin cruiser built by Hartmut that dominates the back garden.

Hartmut, a cheerful man with graying hair and moustache who is always ready to direct a scornful laugh at the old communist establishment, sees irony in the family's situation. All he and Sigrid wanted to do in 1961 was to visit Torsten, but the state had no official mechanism to arrange approval. It was a bureaucratic disaster that no one was empowered to sort out. What should have been a simple case escalated into catastrophe, he said.

Sigrid, sitting in the modestly furnished living room and clad in an unpretentious dress, is round-faced, earnest and reflective. She lives close to the past. She talks about it freely, repeatedly rolling over her thoughts and ideas in a process that she believes has helped her come to terms with it. Watching her is to see the emotions churning. She is still troubled by the feeling that thirty years ago she might have acted unfairly toward Torsten when she rejected the Stasi offer to betray Michael Hinze. But, in a society where denunciation and betrayal was widespread, she resisted the pressure. "In any case," she says, "how was I to know that they really would have freed me? They could have said anything."

Hinze now works as a journalist in Hamburg. He knew nothing about the danger he had been in until years later. He has met and remains in contact with Sigrid Ruehrdanz, the woman who saved him from execution or imprisonment.[8]

The Ruehrdanz case showed the limits of the Stasi. It had broad powers but remained an arm of the party and reported what the party wanted to hear—that the West was the source of dissent. People like the Ruehrdanzes were classed as enemies of the state instead of what they were—people in trouble because of circumstances beyond their control. Hounding the family was a waste of resources. Yet such cases were no exception.

In the end, the sheer inaccuracy and irrelevance of the information the Stasi accumulated throttled the state. The Stasi helped bring East Germany down. One commentator, Siegfried Suckut, wrote,

> The party had become a prisoner of its own propaganda. The Stasi, with its slavish loyalty to the party, undermined the security of the state. The result was that it involuntarily deceived the leadership. The Western secret services could not have hoped for a greater disinformation success. Similarly to [the workers' revolt in] 1953, the Stasi failed in 1989. But this time the damage was irreversible.[9]

Standing on the green grass of the Buelowplatz in Eastern Berlin is like being in the middle of a football ground. It is surrounded by grandstands: the five-story PDS headquarters, known as Karl-Liebknecht-Haus; the classic lines of the *Volksbuehne* theater; and long, gray apartment buildings. This is a quiet part of town but it was not always so. Buelowplatz looks much the same today as it did on that day seventy years ago when it echoed with the roar of a crowd—not the cheers of a football crowd but the curses and tumult of rioters clashing with police.

Karl-Liebknecht-Haus has been a headquarters of the communists and their successors since the 1920s, except in the Hitler years. In the 1920s, Walter Ulbricht ran the Berlin party from his third floor office.

A pacifist writer, Carl von Ossietzky, wrote in 1931 of Buelowplatz as being the battleground for a sort of civil war where the police acted like troops. "First step, a punch in the ribs and a shout; second step, the club; third step, the revolver." He likened Karl-Liebknecht-Haus to "a series of cellar caves in which masked conspirators meet at midnight and talk in codes...doors without handles are opened by a lever under the table."[10] The communists, he wrote, were breeding a romanticism for revolution that had no basis in reality.

This part of town is known as the Scheunenviertel. It is close to the center of old Berlin and was a destination for waves of migrants from Eastern Europe in the nineteenth and twentieth centuries. It was a cultural melting pot, an area of cafes and bars, of prostitutes and Jewish prayer houses, of shoemakers and street hawkers. It was also a cradle of violence in the turbulent years after World War One with hyperinflation, the Crash, and street fighting between left and right. Fascism was on the way. In 1923, a decade before the Nazis came to power, Jews were a clearly identifiable scapegoat.

A pogrom of Jews has been taking place on the streets of Berlin …the faces distorted with hate that gape at the Jewish specter, the total unity of hostility toward Jews.[11]

On May Day 1929, police opened fire on a mob in the "Red" Wedding neighborhood, so called because of its strong communist following. The official death toll was seven, but the unofficial estimate was three dozen. In January 1930 a communist was shot dead in Joachim Strasse. The communists went looking for revenge. On February 23 they found their victim, Horst Wessel, together with his former prostitute girlfriend in a tenement room, and shot him. Wessel, the twenty-two-year-old leader of a Nazi troop, died the same day.[12] The volatile atmosphere persisted. In August 1931 police shot dead an eighteen-year-old youth, Fritz Auge, during a communist-dominated demonstration. Posters immediately went up saying, "For one worker shot dead, two policemen will die. The Red Front takes revenge."

A few days later, on a hot late-summer afternoon, the Communist Party marched on the Buelowplatz. A squad of police raced to the scene. It included Paul Anlauf, Franz Lenck, both captains, and a sergeant, August Willig, who were known to the demonstrators as "Schweinebacke" (pig face), "Totenkopf" (skull), and "Husar" (hussar). Willig heard someone behind him call out, "You, Husar! You, Schweinebacke! You, the other!" Willig went for his pistol. Shots rang out. Anlauf and Lenck both fell to the ground. Willig kept firing until his magazine was empty. Anlauf died almost immediately. Lenck was dragged to the nearby Babylon cinema, where he died. Willig survived with stomach wounds.[13] Two members of the "self-defense" squad, Erich Mielke, then twenty-three, and Erich Ziemer, a year older, were incriminated. They went to ground.

Two decades later, Mielke was the boss of East Germany's secret police, the Stasi.

Mielke enjoyed watching soccer matches. His club was Berlin Dynamo, and he created it in the image of Moscow Dynamo, the KGB team. He gave it access to the best resources and the pick of the players, with the result that it won the league ten times in a row between 1979 and 1988. Every year, the Dynamo ball was held in East Berlin's huge Palast Hotel. Another Politburo member, Guenter Schabowski, recalled being a reluctant guest. He complained of having to endure music from tired rock bands hired on the cheap from the West and a droning speech by Mielke followed by a round of cheers from the players. The format was the same year after year.[14]

Lutz Eigendorf scored many goals for Dynamo Berlin. In 1979, he traveled with Dynamo to the West for a friendly match against FC Kaiserslautern. When the team returned, Eigendorf was not with it. Mielke was shattered. He canceled engagements and withdrew to smolder. Insider sources said he "became so livid that he planned the footballer's murder…a traffic-accident plan was drawn up."[15]

On March 5, 1983, Eigendorf was on the reserves bench for his new club, Brunswick, which was playing a West German Bundesliga match against Bochum. After the match, he remained in the clubhouse, where eyewitnesses said he drank several glasses of beer. About 11 o'clock that night, Eigendorf was driving his Alfa Romeo just outside Brunswick when it failed to hold a curve and crashed into a tree. He died two days later.

The circumstances surrounding his death remain unclear. He had been put under pressure by the Stasi to return to the East, and the Brunswick club had beforehand received an anonymous letter saying that the brakes of his car should be inspected.

The Berlin suburb of Wedding has strong working-class traditions rooted in the industrial revolution. At the turn of the century, it was a hotbed of left-wing defiance. It was here that Erich Mielke was born in 1907. He joined the communist youth organization in 1921 and became a member of the Communist Party in 1925. He worked as a dispatch clerk in the haulage business and later became a reporter for the party newspaper, the *Rote Fahne*, before being recruited into a hit squad under the command of the local party boss, Walter Ulbricht.

After Mielke shot dead the policemen in 1931, he fled to Spain to fight against Franco in the Spanish civil war. When World War Two ended in 1945, he returned to Germany and, in 1949, at the age of thirty-seven, became chief police inspector in East Germany. In 1957 he took over as state security minister and remained so until the collapse of the state in 1989.

Mielke often wore the uniform of an army general with rows of gleaming medals, yet he had never commanded any sort of army in battle. He claimed that he fought at the front in Spain, but this is widely disputed. He was a short, barrel-chested ex-gunman, brusque, arrogant, loud-mouthed and ruthless, and he trampled on anyone who crossed his path.

But his behavior in the Politburo in 1989 when the crisis was at its height was anything but military. He turned and blamed Honecker for everything —from the shootings at the Wall to illegal telephone tapping. The tough guy was a whining coward, protesting his innocence and blaming others. When a squad of newspaper reporters arrived at the once hermetically sealed Wandlitz settlement, Berlin party boss Guenter Schabowski received a telephone call from a frightened Mielke: "Comrade Schabowski, are they going to beat us to death?"[16]

A psychologist's report quoted Mielke as saying,

> I don't understand any of this. I don't know what people want from me. The whole world is lying and cheating me…I have not done anything wicked, or enriched myself, I didn't even own a car.[17]

He was responsible for a day of pure theater in the *Volkskammer*. He addressed the deputies in November 1989 after he had been already thrown out of the Politburo. When he told them: "We [the party] have an extraordinarily high [level of] contact with all working people, everywhere…," he was interrupted by ripples of laughter. The deputies, no longer in fear of retribution, laughed at him to his face. Mielke turned first toward one part of the chamber and then toward another, desperately looking for allies. He blurted out, "Yes, I love you all, actually. I love you all."

It was the best line ever delivered in that benighted hall, and it brought the house down. The despot had become the village idiot.[18]

A few weeks later, he was arrested. He was under investigation for a string of crimes: killings, telephone tappings, ordering border guards to shoot escapees, installing self-shooting devices at the border, misusing state cash, election rigging. But evidence strong enough to stand up in court was meager. After legal wrangling over the statute of limitations, it was decided to proceed with the 1931 Buelowplatz killings.

One crucial witness for the prosecution was an American journalist, John O. Koehler. He described meeting Mielke at a Soviet reception in Leipzig in 1965 at which functionaries stood drinking iced vodka and eating caviar in a dingy hall stinking of lavatory disinfectant and cheap tobacco. He recalled Mielke as a stocky man with flabby jowls, five-o'clock shadow, and huge bags under his eyes, and he put it to him that he had been involved in the murder of the policemen. Mielke had replied, "You are right; after that, I had to move to the Soviet Union."[19]

The prosecution case was based on evidence taken by police between 1931 and 1933. Mielke was convicted and sentenced to six years in jail. He was released on humanitarian grounds in 1995 after less than two years.

A contemporary described Mielke as being "driven by a morbid compulsion for control and regimentation."[20] One person who remembered him with loathing from the Wandlitz settlement, where the party bosses lived, was Beate Matteoli, daughter of Walter Ulbricht. She recalled Mielke as "the filthiest piece of work...As a child, I instinctively kept out of his way."[21]

He was such a villain, such a symbol of the asinine Stalinist terror that discredited communism, that, after East Germany collapsed, he was rejected by all but a tiny hard core of party faithful. When he died in May 2000, at ninety-two, his wish to be buried in a cemetery reserved for heroes of the socialist movement was refused. His death was kept secret for four days, and the funeral plans were shrouded in secrecy to head off protesters. But within hours of his burial, his grave had been vandalized.

As for the Dynamo soccer club, it changed its name after unification to FC Berlin in an effort to eliminate its past. But its performances on the field, without support in high places, became dismal. It dropped into the lower leagues and now plays in a regional competition alongside such obscure teams as FV Motor Eberswalde and SD Croatia. In 1999 it decided to resurrect the old name of Dynamo Berlin on the grounds that, even its past were grubby, it was at least successful.

BERLIN—The German cabinet on Wednesday approved increased pension payments to former members of East Germany's state security service, the Stasi. —*Frankfurter Allgemeine Zeitung*, December 21, 2000

BERLIN—We look on impotently as the pensions of our former tormentors are increased while our demands for honorary pensions come to nothing.

—Horst Schueler, in "Zusammenstehen," *Stacheldraht*, April 2, 2002 (Schueler was arrested on political grounds in East Germany in 1951 and spent four years in the KGB's Vorkuta prison camp in the Soviet Union.)

NOTES

1. "There are some…," Konrad Weiss, in "Eine Rolle rueckwaerts," *Rheinischer Merkur*, September 19, 2002. This review was taken from the on-line version. Weiss is a former East German civil rights activist.
2. Account of meeting from talks by the author with Sigrid Ruehrdanz and Herbert Pfaff, plus a report by Jutta Schuetz, in "Ex-Stasi ueber Stasi: 'Es gibt keinen Grund zur Reue,'" *dpa*, April 23, 2002. A written account by Ruehrdanz, "Wir Koennen Wieder Sicher Sein," appeared in *Der Stacheldraht*, June 10, 2002.
3. Length of interrogation confirmed in Stasi files.
4. Account based on many conversations the author had with Sigrid, Hartmut and Torsten Ruehrdanz.
5. "Suddenly the door…," Thraene quoted in "'Der schreibt keine Karte mehr'—29 Jahre blieb das Schicksal des abtruennigen Stasi Hauptmann Walter Thraene im ungewissen," *Der Spiegel*, January 27, 1992.
6. "Whenever they took…," Sigrid Ruehrdanz to the author on October 4, 2004.
7. Three of the seven kidnappers were jailed for sentences of up to four years, according to Karl Wilhelm Fricke in "Ein Zeuge wider die Staatssicherheit—Ex-Hauptmann Walter Thraene gestorben," *Der Tagesspiegel*, February 2, 1994. Fricke himself fled from East Germany to West Germany in 1949 aged nineteen and worked as a journalist. His comments annoyed the East Berlin regime so much that they sent a kidnap squad after him. In 1955, he was doped and taken back to East Germany, where he was imprisoned for "slandering the state" and "currency offenses," and later for "crimes" against the constitution. He was released in 1959, and allowed to go to West Berlin. Since then he has written extensively on East Germany.
8. Hinze confirmed his end of the story in a talk with the author in Hamburg in February, 1998.

9. "The party had become…," Siegfried Suckut in "Das Ministerium fuer Staatssicherheit in der DDR-Geschichte," a contribution in *Zehn Jahre Deutsche Einheit* (Opladen: Leske + Budrich 2000), 131.

10. "First step…," Carl von Ossietzky in "Buelow-Platz," *Die Weltbuehne*, August 18, 1931, 242.

11. "A pogrom of Jews…," in "Die Schicksalsstunde des deutschen Judentums," *Judische Rundschau*, November 9, 1923 (cover price: 20 billion marks).

12. For an account of Horst Wessel's life and death, see Imre Lazar's *Der Fall Horst Wessel* (Stuttgart and Zurich: Belser AG fuer Verlagsgesellschaft & Co. KG, 1980) .

13. Willig's account is in the police records of the time. The account of the killings is based on evidence presented to the Berlin State Court at a hearing between June 4 and 19, 1934.

14. "Dynamo annual ball…," Guenter Schabowski in *Das Politbuero* (Reinbek bei Hamburg: Rowohlt Taschenbuch Verlag, 1990), 47.

15. "Became so livid…," Manfred Schell in "Moerder in den Westen geschickt: Mielke liess Fluechtlinge umbringen," *Die Welt*, August 14, 1990.

16. "Comrade Schabowski…, " Mielke quoted in "Genosse, schlagen die uns tot?" *Der Spiegel*, April 30, 1990.

17. "I don't understand…," Mielke quoted by Hans-Juergen Mueller in "Ich moechte in mein Bett zurueck'—Verhandlungsunfaehig oder nicht? Simulant oder schwachsinnig? Mord-Prozess gegen Erich Mielke," *Hamburger Abendblatt*, February 7, 1992.

18. A video tape of Mielke's speech to the Volkskammer, is played at the former Stasi complex in Normannenstrasse, Eastern Berlin, part of which has been converted to a museum.

19. "You are right…," Mielke quoted by John O. Koehler in *Stasi: The Untold Story of the East German Secret Police* (Boulder, Colorado: Westview Press, 1999), 2.

20. "Driven by…," Guenter Schabowski in *Der Absturz* (Reinbek bei Hamburg: Rowohlt Taschenbuch Verlag, 1992), 110.

21. "The filthiest…," Beate Matteoli quoted by Anna Meissner in "Lieber Papa, boese Lotte—Walter Ulbrichts Tochter erinnert sich," *Super*, September 4, 1991.

15

THE MAKING OF A POLICE STATE

NEVER HAD LECTURE HALL 18 AT Karl Marx University in Leipzig been filled to beyond capacity as it was this March evening in 1990. Students waited in the corridors in the hope that space inside would miraculously appear and enable them to see East Germany's most famous nonperson, the man with the name that could never be spoken.

Professor Wolfgang Leonhard, enemy of the working class, traitor to the people, acknowledged the tumultuous applause and could be forgiven for savoring the moment. He had been waiting a long time for this triumph.

Moscow, April 29, 1945: As parties go, it was low key. But an underlying mood of exultation, stoked by modest amounts of vodka, was palpable. A select few German communists who had spent the war years in the Soviet Union were celebrating on the fifth floor of the exiles' home, the Hotel Lux. For them, the Stalinist purges with the late-night raids by the Soviet secret police were a thing of the past. Tomorrow, they would return to Germany.

The men in the apartment of a leading communist, Wilhelm Pieck, were middle aged—except one. With his shock of dark hair framing a high forehead and his boyish, sensitive face, Wolfgang Leonhard, just twenty-four, contrasted sharply with his gnarled colleagues.

The war was reaching a brutal denouement as the armies of Marshal Georgi Zhukov and Marshal Ivan Koniev vied with each other to reach Berlin first. Zhukov had an account to settle. He had defended Leningrad, Moscow, and Stalingrad and his record showed an unbroken series of victories. But the record was wrong. Operation Mars, designed to break the German stranglehold on the Rzhev salient, was fought out in blinding snowstorms in 1942. Zhukov was forced to give up after taking heavy losses. Operation Mars was passed off as a mere setback, but it was a disaster. Zhukov and he badly wanted Berlin as compensation.[1]

Zhukov and his senior officers did not sleep for six nights as they advanced on the capital. They kept themselves going by drinking looted cognac. His forces reached the foot of the Seelow Heights, east of Berlin, where they battled heavy resistance to take the ridge. They lost 30,000 men doing it. The way to Berlin was clear. Zhukov had beaten Koniev to the Big Prize.

Everyone at Pieck's party in Moscow had been hand-picked to resurrect the German Communist Party (KPD) and set up a Soviet-backed administration in Germany. There were three groups. Group Ulbricht was going to the center of Hitler's Reich, Berlin.

Early on the morning after the party, the exiles were driven to the airport with each carrying 1,000 rubles and 2,000 newly minted Reichsmarks in cash and a small suitcase with a minimum of possessions. Moscow's streets were decorated in readiness for May Day, and portraits of Marx, Engels, Lenin and Stalin shone in the early morning sun. The groups flew in Red Army Li-2s, which were Dakotas made available by the Americans that were outfitted like cattle trucks—passengers sat facing each other strapped to crude wooden boards.

Ulbricht's team set up the party Central Committee in a building at Prinzen Allee 80. The most urgent task was to build up the organization in the Western sectors before the Americans, British and French arrived. Ulbricht said the new district councils should have good representations of Social Democrats and middle-class people, but he added, "It must look democratic but we must have everything in our hands."[2]

Leonhard had gone to the Soviet Union with his communist mother in 1935 as a thirteen-year-old. He was sent to board at the Karl Liebknecht School in Moscow together with other children of exiled German communists, and grew to adulthood in the era of the midnight knock on the door.

One day in October 1936 he went to visit his mother, but found her door barricaded. The NKVD[3] secret police had taken her away. In 1938 the NKVD came to the school and, in front of the class, arrested a teacher. The NKVD came again at four in the morning, pulled Leonhard's seventeen-year-old classmate, Rolf Geissler, out of bed and took him away. He was never seen again.

No one was safe. Yesterday's heroes were today's traitors. Russians who had been leading figures of the socialist revolution were arrested as imperialist agents and foreign spies. Germans and other foreign communists who thought they had found a refuge were taken away. Some survived. Almost every day, Leonhard saw the green vehicles carrying prisoners through the city streets. He watched the fear grow, as Muscovites waited for the clump of heavy boots and the click of the rifle bolt. Doubts about the system began to churn in his mind.

In Berlin, Leonhard was put in charge of propaganda and agitation. The official party position was for postwar Germany to become a parliamentary democratic republic, and Leonhard believed it. He did not think the Stalinist excesses of the Soviet Union would be carried over to Germany.

In October 1945 the party unexpectedly declared its intention to merge with the zone Social Democrats, who had far more popular support. The merger was sealed on April 22, 1946. The Soviet-zone Social Democrat chairman, Otto Grotewohl, told 3,000 delegates the new united party, known as the Socialist Unity Party (SED), would follow a democratic path to socialism, and added that no party had a higher regard for human rights. Leonhard believed him. He later recalled,

> This night, I could not know that inside a few years almost half the delegates...would have been kicked out of their jobs, [otherwise] sacked, defamed, or become purge victims.[4]

The Social Democrats were buried by the communists and eliminated as a political force.

Leonhard's idealism was being heavily tested. He had been a beneficiary of the system of privilege that shielded party functionaries from wartime deprivation in the Soviet Union. The apparatchiks knew no shortages. And now that system of privilege was taking root in Berlin's Soviet sector. Pieck, Grotewohl, Ulbricht, and the others lived in villas in a sealed-off area guarded by Soviet troops.

Elitism was emerging everywhere. Leonhard recalled a communist visiting from a Western zone who stormed out of a party canteen in disgust when he learned there were, in fact, different canteens serving meals varying from simple to luxurious, depending on a member's status. The Western visitor objected, "Different (payment) tokens, different meals...but surely we're all comrades?"[5]

Leonhard was unlikely to have been aware of the full extent of Soviet thuggery in the zone. The Soviet Military Administration in Germany (SMAD) had brought its jailers and executioners with it. It took over Nazi prisons and

set up a Stalinist-style Gulag. It filled the cells with anybody decreed to be politically tainted: men, women, judges, doctors, teachers, laborers, juveniles.
High on the target list were Social Democrats who resisted the political
merger. The aim of the purges were ostensibly to wipe out all traces of fascism, but the real aim was to smash the German middle classes.

In August 1947 Leonhard was taken from the agitprop department and
sent to lecture at the propaganda school, the Karl Marx Party Academy. In the
summer of 1948 he was reunited with his mother again in East Berlin. She
had spent nine of the intervening twelve years in a Siberian prison.

Yugoslavia was now rebelling, and Tito was openly criticizing Stalin.
Leonhard visited Yugoslavia in 1947 and was surprised by the freedom of discussion within the party, the openness and enthusiasm in the youth movements, and what he felt was a better quality of party functionary. The
Yugoslavs were "much cleverer [in their methods] than the Russians, much
cleverer than the SED," he wrote.[6] In 1948 Yugoslavia was expelled from the
Cominform, the international communist organization. This breach shattered
what little faith Leonhard still had in Stalin. A colleague at the academy spoke
privately in anger, calling Stalin a "half-educated barbarian."[7] On November
22, 1948, Leonhard read an article in the academy bulletin accusing him of
putting events in Yugoslavia in a positive light. He recalled, "It was a warning
shot."[8]

Leonhard drew up contingency plans.

In March 1949 he was accused of deviating from the party line. He knew
he had to win time by avoiding immediate arrest.

I decided to admit making a few 'errors' and to present myself as being confused. That was the only way I could make sure no immediate steps against me were taken.[9]

When he was told, "The report on your statements hostile to the party and on
today's discussion will be submitted to the Politburo…in a few days, the decision on your case will be issued," he breathed a secret sigh of relief.[10]

A day later, academy students waited in the lecture hall for their lecturer,
Wolfgang Leonhard. He did not come.

Communist insecurity was reinforced in the local all-Berlin election in October 1946, when the new SED party received a miserable 22.7 percent of the
vote and was beaten out of sight by the Social Democrats with 48.7 percent.

The Soviets pulled down the shutters. Ideas about a single German state were forgotten. East-West relations, already in decline, continued to deteriorate. In March 1948 the Red Army's Marshal Vassily Sokolovsky walked out of the Allied Control Commission, the city's four-power coordinating authority. It never met again.

In January 1948 the Soviets began to pull the noose tight around Berlin's Western sectors. They delayed trains, checked freight, examined personal luggage, pored over passports and visas. In March, nighttime interzone freight transport was banned. On April 1 access roads into Berlin were cut.

The U.S. military governor, General Lucius Clay, had already shown he was a man for a tight corner. In 1942, he had solved a supply blockage by untangling congestion at the war-damaged French port of Cherbourg.

When the Berlin garrison ran short of supplies, Clay assembled all the aircraft available and flew essential provisions along three air corridors to the besieged half-city. In June, the Soviets stopped all rail freight for two days. Then they cut river and road access. The West was faced with a dilemma. It could withdraw and leave the city to its fate or it could defy the logistical odds and try to supply it by air. President Harry Truman was convinced the future of Western Europe was at stake in Berlin. "We'll stay in Berlin—come what may,"[11] he wrote in a private note. He later wrote, "We had to face the possibility that Russia might deliberately choose to make Berlin the pretext for war."[12] The military imbalance was extreme. The allies had a total of 6,500 troops in the city. These were surrounded and outnumbered by 18,000 Red Army troops in Berlin and another 300,000 in the German hinterland.

Material differences between the zones were increasing. Women in the Soviet Zone could only look on enviously as U.S. troops brought in the ultimate luxury good and status symbol, the nylon stocking, to the *Fraeulein* of the American sector. Nylons symbolized the divide. The Soviets knew that divide could widen dramatically, and they intended to prevent it.

By the middle of 1948, the turn of events was hardening Germany's division. Toward the middle of June, the ubiquitous black market suddenly dried up. On June 20 a new currency was issued in the West. Ten of the old Reichsmarks were swapped for one new German mark. Then Ludwig Erhard, a Bavarian economics professor working with the occupying forces, freed consumer items from rationing and other controls. Almost everybody thought that was a mistake. Erhard, a round-faced, cigar-chomping Franconian who avidly listened to classical music and read *Kicker* soccer magazine every Monday morning, was called to order by U.S. officials, who pointed out that changing the rationing arrangements was the business of the occupying powers. Erhard retorted, "I haven't changed them. I have abolished them."[13]

The two measures resulted in higher prices and more unemployment, but they also killed off the massive black-market and brought goods back on to shop shelves in the Western sectors. Soon prices came down. So did unemployment.

On June 28 the Americans, backed by the British, began the Berlin Airlift. In the space of 48 hours, 155 aircraft were keeping 2.2 million Berliners supplied by flying round-the-clock along three air corridors into the city. More aircraft were brought in. Accidents were inevitable. A Dakota fully laden with flour and descending in heavy cloud towards Tempelhof, dropped below the cloud cover and hit an apartment building at No. 3 Handjery Strasse. Both pilots were killed.[14]

The Red Army bribed thugs with cigarettes and vodka, and trucked them in to harass Western sector councillors on the joint council that met at the town hall, in the Soviet sector. Western councillors pulled out and from then on met separately in the French sector.

The Soviets produced enough ration cards for the entire city. The official *Neues Deutschland* newspaper said the only blockade in Berlin was by Western councillors who had "forbidden Berliners in the West from shopping in the Soviet sector."[15] But, despite their deprivation, only about 20,000 West Berliners, fewer than 1 percent, accepted the Soviet offer to buy in the East.

Two airports, Tempelhof in the American sector and Gatow in the British sector, were in use but, when a third was needed, a site was found in the French sector. When construction of Tegel was held up by two Soviet radio transmission masts which were unlit and thus a hazard to aircraft, the French asked the Soviets to remove them or fit them with lights. The Soviet ignored repeated requests to act. The French commander, General Jean Ganeval, ordered his engineers to blow them up. Which they did. When the Soviets protested, asking how the French could have done such a thing, Ganeval coolly replied, "With dynamite."[16]

Berliners tried to brighten their lives with diversions. Beer went on sale, ladled from roadside pails. People grew tobacco in flower pots. Bookshop shelves were bare, but a publisher, Ernst Rowohlt, thought up the idea of printing novels in newspaper format. They sold like hot cakes for fifty pfennigs each.

The airlift was a welcome chance for the East to blame others for its economic troubles. A Soviet-zone trade-union leader, Bernhard Goering, said "economic criminals" were diverting textiles to the West and preventing production plans from being met.[17]

Students and staff at the Karl Marx Academy in the Soviet sector listened to the aircraft coming into land at Tempelhof in the American sector. The Dakotas and Skymasters came in as little as forty-five seconds apart. Counting the intervals became a compulsive habit. From the middle of 1948, the noise was perpetual, twenty-four hours a day, day after day, month after month. One academy lecturer said, "The Americans have learned historical materialism better than we have. They understand you have to have the basis of food and help before you can begin party education."

By the time the airlift officially ended on September 30, more than 277,000 flights had brought in more than two million tons of supplies. But the city's divisions were now clearly demarcated. The Western and Soviet sectors had separate administrations and separate currencies.

Wolfgang Leonhard watched these events with some detachment. The day he fled the Karl Marx Academy, he made three short telephone calls in which he used prearranged coded messages. One was to his mother, the second to his girlfriend. Half an hour after the third call, a car arrived at his home. The car took him to the border with Czechoslovakia. Thirteen days later, after a risky journey during which he had to evade police controls, he reached Belgrade, capital of Tito's renegade communist state.[18] No one outside Yugoslavia knew where he was. The mystery was solved on April 22, when a declaration by Leonhard against Cominform's decision to expel Yugoslavia was read out on Radio Belgrade in twelve languages. Four days later, *Neues Deutschland* newspaper announced he had been expelled from the party.

At the age of twenty-eight, his dreams of a moderate form of communism had been shattered and now he saw the economic changes taking place in the West of Germany, where the *Wirtschaftswunder* ("Economic Miracle") was gathering pace. Industry recovered so quickly after currency reform, the introduction of Marshall Plan aid, and the end of rationing that by 1951 the three Western zones—which in 1949 had become West Germany—were exporting more than they were importing. East Berlin was not able to counter the lure of the West. So it had to use strong-arm methods. The border between the two states was cleared of vegetation in 1952, so escapers heading West could be more easily seen and shot at. But the population loss continued: 144,000 in 1959, 200,000 in 1960, and more than 200,000 between the beginning of 1961 and August 13.

BERLIN—The chief Berlin correspondent of the British news agency Reuters suddenly obtained asylum in the Soviet sector today and denounced his past career as "a tool of the American war machine." John Peet, a thirty-four-year-old Londoner, disclosed his decision at a press conference called by East German propaganda chief Gerhart Eisler. Reuters then announced his connection with the agency had ceased. —*International Herald Tribune*, June 12, 1950

The rate in August reached almost 4,000 a day. A total of 2.7 million people left between 1949 and mid August, 1961. Most crossed where it was easiest, in the metropolitan turbulence of Berlin, where there was no field of fire.

The bleeding could not go on indefinitely. Most of those leaving were young and crucial to the economy. There was another factor. The 60,000 people who lived in East Berlin but who worked in the West for Western levels of pay had so much purchasing power that they were aggravating the existing shortages in the East. Speculation about what would be done grew so intense that Ulbricht took the unusual step on June 15, 1961, of holding an international press conference and announcing, "No one has any intention of building a wall."[19]

Construction of a wall around West Berlin began on August 13.

Wolfgang Leonhard made his way from Yugoslavia to West Germany. This exposed him to new risks because East German kidnap gangs could operate more easily there than in Yugoslavia. Other top East Germans had deserted the cause, but most were former SPD members or officials who had spent the war in Germany. Leonhard was different. He was one of the communists' own, educated and indoctrinated in the Soviet Union. He was under no illusions about what would happen if he were caught. He took precautions. He walked on the left-hand side of the road to avoid kidnap vehicles coming from behind him and he stopped drinking beer, cognac, and whisky and, instead, drank wine because he believed wine was less likely to be spiked. He stopped using salt because salt was too easy to poison. Whenever he went to West Berlin, he flew, because he could not risk using the overland route. He changed his address every night.[20]

Kidnapping was a real risk. One high-profile victim was Robert Bialek, who was sacked as *Volkspolizei Generalinspekteur* in 1948. In 1953, went to London, where he worked for the BBC's German-language service. His Wednesday-night broadcast won a large clandestine audience in East Germany and angered the regime.

Bialek returned to West Berlin. In 1956 he went to a birthday party, was given a spiked drink, and was later seen being driven away in a car. He was never seen alive again.[21]

After arriving in the West, Leonhard lectured at Oxford and Yale. He wrote articles, he was widely interviewed. But he could not go to East Germany again until the Wall fell in 1989, forty years after he had fled. He went East Berlin, to Dresden, to Leipzig, to Rostock…He contacted many of his former communist comrades including a dozen of the Politburo members dumped in 1989. He played it carefully, never arranging meetings in West Berlin but always in the East and always in party buildings where his former colleagues would feel less tense. He was generally well received.

There was one major exception. He telephoned a woman he had first met in exile in the Kazakh city of Karaganda in 1941—Charlotte Kuehn, who later married party chief Walter Ulbricht—and suggested they meet. Lotte Ulbricht refused, saying, "I don't see what we could possibly talk about."[22]

NOTES

1. For an account of Operation Mars, see *Zhukov's Greatest Defeat: The Red Army's Epic Disaster in Operation Mars, 1942*, by David M. Glantz (Lawrence, Kansas: University Press of Kansas, 1999).

2. "It must look democratic…, " Ulbricht quoted by Leonhard, in *Die Revolution, enlaesst ihre Kinder* (Cologne: Kiepenheuer & Witsch, 2001), 648.

3. The Soviet secret police was known by several names over the years. In 1917, it was founded as the Cheka. In 1922 the Cheka was replaced by the GPU, which became a subordinate division of the NKVD, which was in charge of the conventional police force. In 1923, the GPU was detached from the NKVD and became the OGPU. In 1934, the OGPU became the GUGB and was again affiliated to the NKVD. The NKVD, which now controlled the conventional police, the border guards, internal troops, and labor camps, be-

came the common name for the secret police. In 1941, another organizational change led to the GUGB being again detached from the NKVD and becoming known as the NKGB. In 1946, both the NKGB and the NKVD became ministries. After another organizational shake-up, the KGB was founded in 1954. (Source: *KGB: The Secret Work of Soviet Secret Agents*, by John Barron (London: Corgi Books, 1975), 443.

4. "This night, I…," Wolfgang Leonhard in *Die Revolution*, 544.

5. "Different (payment) tokens…," Leonhard in *Die Revolution*, 606.

6. "Much cleverer…, " Leonhard in *Die Revolution*, 572.

7. "Half-educated barbarian…," Leonhard in *Die Revolution*, 648.

8. "It was a…," Leonhard in *Spuren Suche*, (Cologne: Kiepenheuer & Witsch, 1994), 225.

9. "I decided to…," Leonhard in *Die Revolution*, 656.

10. "The report on…," Leonhard in *Die Revolution*, 660.

11. "We'll stay in Berlin...," David McCullough in *Truman* (New York: Touchstone, 1992), 647.

12. "We had to face…," McCullough, 647.

13. "I haven't changed them…," Hans Riehl in *Die Mark—die aufregende Geschichte einer Weltwaehrung*, (Hanover: Fackeltraeger-Verlag Schmidt Kuester GmbH, 1978), 122.

14. A plaque commemorating the two aircrew who died marks the spot where the plane crashed.

15. "Forbidden Berliners…, " *Neues Deutschland*, September 15, 1948.

16. Over the years, there have been various versions, all slightly different, of the transmission mast demolition episode. This version is told by Thomas Parrish, in *Berlin in the Balance*, (Reading, Mass: Addison-Wesley, 1998) 277.

17. "Economic criminals," Goering quoted in *Neues Deutschland*, September 15, 1948.

18. Leonhard left Belgrade and went to West Germany in 1950. He later lectured at Oxford University in England and Yale University in the United States. He has published many books dealing with the Soviet Union. He continues to live and work in Germany where he is in great demand as a speaker.

19. "No one has any intention…, " Ulbricht quoted by Curtis Cate, in *Riss durch Berlin—Der 13. August 1961* (Hamburg: Albrecht Knaus Verlag, 1980) 45—original title, *The Ides of August* (New York: M.Evans and Company Inc, 1978).

20. Leonhard told the author of his security measures in May 2002.

21. Bialek died in 1956 in jail in the town of Bautzen. Peter Przybylski, a former East German prosecutor, in *Tatort Politbuero-die Akte Honecker* (Reinbek bei Hamburg: Rowohlt Taschenbuch Verlag, 1992) 75, says "Robert Bialek probably died as a result of inhuman imprisonment conditions, and [the effects of] relentless interrogations. But in which month or day could not even be ascertained after November 9, 1989 [the fall of the Berlin Wall]."

22. "I don't see what we…," Lotte Ulbricht quoted by Leonhard in a conversation with the author, May 2002.

16

THE GULAG

WOLFGANG LEONHARD'S FEARS about the lash of Stalinism were well founded. The Soviets brought their Gulag with them. In their zone of occupation, they imprisoned huge numbers of people on political grounds. They brought them before crude tribunals, pronounced them guilty, and imprisoned or executed them. Hearings lasted minutes, witnesses were seldom called, and no legal representation was allowed. Prosecutions were usually based on denunciation.

People entered prison weakened from wartime deprivation. If they weren't shot in the back of the head, or hanged, they succumbed to tuberculosis, heart attacks or circulation failure. Thousands were sent to Siberia as slave laborers. Some prisoners had committed offences but most were victims of Soviet paranoia.

Prison conditions were bestial. They were designed to kill by attrition. Often, prisoners did not wash for weeks. They received no water, no clothes, no toothbrush. Sores erupted. Toenails and fingernails rotted. Tuberculosis broke out.

In her book, *Gulag*, Anne Applebaum wrote,

In the famine-wracked post-war years, these German camps seem to have been even more lethal than their Soviet counterparts.[1]

She believes about 240,000 mostly political prisoners passed though them in five years and that the death toll was probably 95,000.[2]

"If the lives of Soviet prisoners were never particularly important to the Soviet authorities, the lives of German 'fascists' mattered even less,"[3] Applebaum said. She added that most high-ranking Nazis or proven war criminals were not held in East German camps but taken back to Moscow and interned in Soviet camps.

Horst Wiener is one prisoner who survived. He remembers the crash of heavy boots on concrete floor jerking him out of his sleep at daybreak; the echoing clang of steel doors and the clanking of slop pails coming closer. "We had to work fast," he told me.

> There was just one slop pail. You had to piss and try and shit into it before the guard opened the cell door to take it away. Otherwise you'd have the stench in the cell for the next twenty-four hours.

He was just eighteen years old. It was 1945, and he was in jail in Weimar, a beautiful town, green with parks and steeped in the arts, the city of Goethe and Schiller. But now there were heavy coated Russian soldiers on every street corner.

Wiener continued:

> You had to be careful. If any shit spilled, you had to scrub the floor and the guard would kick you in the arse or toe that filthy cloth in your face. Sometimes you slipped and fell in your own shit. Your clothes were soaked in it.[4]

The most notorious prison was a nineteenth century complex of buildings on the north side of the picturesque town of Bautzen that was known, because of its yellow brick construction, as the Yellow Misery[5]. It was built for 1,350 prisoners but the Soviets packed it with 8,000. In 1990 skeletons were dug up outside the prison on a mound known as the Karnickelberg. The closeness of the remains to each other indicated that this was a mass grave where executed prisoners had been secretly buried. The remains of 248 people were disinterred and reburied with crosses.

Bland words often take on sinister connotations simply by association with awful deeds. "Literally, the word GULAG is an acronym, meaning *Glavnoe upravlenie lagerei*, or Main Camp Administration," wrote Applebaum. She says that the word came to signify the entire system of slave labor and prison camps, and then broadened further to mean the repressive Soviet system itself,

> ...the arrests, the interrogations, the transport in unheated cattle cars, the forced labour, the destruction of families, the years spent in exile, the early and unnecessary deaths.[6]

Early in 1950, the Soviets handed over the zone prison system to the East Germans. Prisoners believed conditions would improve. Guards and prisoners spoke the same language, and both were, after all, compatriots.

They were wrong. The abuse worsened.

Wiener, who was transferred to Bautzen, recalled:

The Germans used the same Stalinist methods as the Russians. The
food got even worse. The sick bays became more crowded. The
death rate rose. The Germans didn't give a damn.[7]

Another former prisoner, Wolfgang Hardegen, remembered that, when the
Germans came,

I made big plans for the summer. After my release I wanted to flee to
the West as quickly as possible...but...it soon became clear that we
had gone from the frying pan to the fire. We couldn't believe it. Our
own people were treating us worse than the Russians.[8]

The disbelief spilled over into anger. The prisoners revolted. The revolt died
out but flared again some days later and was brutally put down.[9]

A letter detailing reasons for the revolt was smuggled out and read out at
the annual conference of the West German Social Democrats in Hamburg. After that, the death rate decreased. Later in the year, several hundred prisoners
were released. For the rest, more misery or death followed.[10]

Some prisoners were taken to a prison in the town of Waldheim to face
secret trials as crude as the Soviet military tribunals. Between 1950 and 1952,
a total of 3,385 hearings were held. Thirty-two people were sentenced to
death and 146 to life imprisonment, 1,829 to between fifteen and twenty-five
years and 916 to between ten and fifteen years. Twenty-four executions were
carried out on the night of November 3-4 1950. Waldheim became a byword
for the rampant insanity of a system out of control.[11]

I met Horst Wiener one late sunny autumn afternoon in 1985 at the
Bahnhof in the old mining academy city of Freiberg. A short, gray-haired man
emerged diffidently from the shadows of the station, his dark eyebrows curled
upwards like question marks. He might have been a railroad booking clerk
heading home after a day shift. He later told me he had nearly refused my request to meet him because he suspected I represented some dark political
force. He could not be blamed for that.

It took a leap of imagination to associate this mild, self-effacing person
with the sort of grainy, black-and-white images of Soviet terror. Like most
other boys, he had been a member of the Hitler Youth. The city of Eisenach
was a target for RAF bombers because of its BMW vehicle factory and Junkers
aircraft works. As a sixteen-year-old, Wiener drove trucks as allied aircraft

made low-level bombing runs against rail and road transport. He was in Dresden when it was hit by the big British bombing raids of February 13 and 14, 1945, but survived with a broken arm. He returned to Eisenach.

In April, 1945, the war was over and the Americans arrived with their Camel and Lucky Strike cigarettes and their casual cheerfulness. They talked loudly and chased girls and handed out cigarettes and chocolate. Wiener and his friends practiced their English with them amid the rubble, the ruins and the bomb craters. Some GIs warned them that the Russians meant trouble. When the U.S. forces pulled back to the pre-arranged borders, the boys should go West before the Russians came, the GIs said. But Wiener and his friends didn't believe them.

The Americans went away. The Soviets brought a threatening silence. People stopped going out at night to avoid the endless controls. People disappeared without explanation.

Wiener was one of them.

The Russians arrested him on a dark, gray winter's afternoon just before Christmas in 1945 as he sat at his desk in the Thueringer Staatsbank in the town of Eisenach. He spent his first night in a cell with no bed, no table and no stool.

The next day he was blindfolded and taken to Weimar, forty miles away, placed in solitary confinement and accused of being a "Werewolf," the name given to bands of youths that, toward the end of the war, attacked Soviet and American forces. There was no trial, no legal representation, no witnesses, no appeal. The accusation was based on unchallenged evidence from a person he had never heard of.

The interrogations were always late at night. The interpreter spoke in broken German. His breath reeked of vodka. And always were the whippings. Death came often in the silence of the night—the muffled sound of a single shot, and then silence.

During the day prisoners were not allowed to lie down and sleep. Exhausted, they were taken away for interrogations the next night. "That's the way it was, night after night for weeks," he said.

On Christmas Eve 1945, Wiener signed a statement in Cyrillic that he could not read in which he admitted being a Werewolf. In a hearing lasting three minutes, he was sentenced to death.

He was taken away to wait in death row to wait for execution by a shot to the back of the head. He waited for four months for the guards to take him away. They didn't.

His sentence was commuted to twenty-five years' imprisonment. He was taken to Fort Zinna prison in Torgau and finally to the infamous Yellow Misery itself, Bautzen.

Wiener was released in 1950. He decided to become a doctor, reasoning that every society needed doctors and doctors were in a position to remain nonpolitical. He put himself through by playing dance music on the piano. From 1963 Wiener worked in a state-run medical practice in the small town of Klingenberg, west of Dresden. Since 1991 he has been in private practice there.[12]

NOTES

1. "In the famine…," Anne Applebaum in *Gulag—A History*, (London: Penguin Books, 2004) 410.

2. Estimates of the numbers vary. According to Moscow Interior Ministry estimates in 1990, 122,671 Germans were interned in special Soviet camps in Germany. Of these 42,889 died and 12,770 taken to the Soviet Union. But according to Western estimates, at least 180,000 people were imprisoned and between 60,000 and 90,000 died. See Martin Pabst, in *Staats-Terrorismus—Theorie und Praxis Kommunistischer Herrschaft*, (Graz: Leopold Stocker Verlag, 1997) 121. By other calculations, a total of 500,000 were arrested immediately the Red Army arrived and deported to hard-labor camps in the Soviet Union. On top of that, at least 140,000 were subsequently arrested and sent to special camps in Germany or deported to Siberia. A total of 53,650 either died or were executed in the special camps in Germany. See *Enquete-Kommission, Aufarbeitung von Geschichte und Folgen der SED-Diktatur in Deutschland—Enquete-Kommission: Antraege, Debatten, Bericht, I* (Frankfurt: Suhrkamp Taschenbuch Nomos, 1995) 355.

3. "If the lives…," Applebaum, 410.

4. "We had to…," Wiener talking to the author in 1995.

5. There were two prisons in Bautzen. "The Yellow Misery," formally known as Bautzen I, was at the edge of the town. From 1950, it was run by the Interior Ministry. Bautzen II, in the middle of town, was the Stasi jail.

6. "The arrests…," Applebaum, 3.

7. "The Germans used…," Wiener to the author in 1995. He believes the death rate rose after the German takeover to between eight and ten a day.

8. "I made big plans…," Wolfgang Hardegen in *Gefangen in Bautzen—Ein Jugendlicher ueberlebt acht Jahre Haft im "Gelben Elend,"* (Berlin: Frieling & Partner, 2000) 167.

9. The prisoners chanted and beat tin utensils against the window bars, they suspended banners made of sheets between windows so they could be seen from the town, and they kept up the din for hour after hour and only tailed off as night approached. They revolted for a

second time on March 31. The first time, the guards had been taken by surprise and were uncertain about what to do. But the second time they were ready. One eye-witness said the revolt began when prisoners transporting an urn containing between 100 and 150 litres of hot soup upturned it over guards climbing the stairs behind them. The ensuing chaos was the signal for pandemonium. The guards came in with dogs and clubs and quickly put the revolt down. Several prisoners died and many on both sides were injured. Some guards went to a sick bay where about 400 patients with tuberculosis and high fever were lying, sprayed them with ice-cold water and left them in their wet beds. See various accounts in *Das Gelbe Elend* and Hardegen.

10. For an eye-witness account of life and death in Bautzen II, see Hans Corbat in "Als Siegfried starb," *Der Stacheldraht*, February 8, 1993.

11. For details of the Waldheim hearings, see Falco Werkentin in "Waldheimer 'Prozesse' der Jahre 1950/52," *Enquete-Kommission, Aufarbeitung von Geschichte und Folgen der SED-Diktatur in Deutschland—Recht, Justiz, Polizei, IV* (Frankfurt: Suhrkamp Taschenbuch Nomos, 1995) 849. See also Eberhard Wendel in *Ulbricht als Richter und Henker—Stalinistische Justiz im Parteiauftrag*, (Berlin: Aufbau-Verlag, 1996).

12. Wiener wrote a book about his time in the German Gulag. *Anklage: Werwolf—Die Gewalt der fruehen Jahre oder Wie ich Stalins Lage ueberlebte*, (Reinbek bei Hamburg: Rowohlt Taschenbuch Verlag, 1991).

17

THE PEOPLE TRADE

Not until the Wall came down did I learn that our country...would throw people in jail just for having another opinion. It hit me then. It really hit me. —Ex-East German ice-skating champion Katarina Witt, quoted by Angus Phillips, *International Herald Tribune*, February 12, 1992

THE PEOPLE TRADE WAS SIMPLE and lucrative. East Berlin arrested people, "tried them," found them guilty, and jailed them. The West German government bought them out. It was supply and demand. The East needed cash. The West wanted the prisoners.

The trade had it origins after the war when church groups in the West used their own welfare organizations to help refugees streaming in from Eastern Europe, people bombed out of their homes, clerics jailed by the Soviets, and soldiers returning from Soviet prison camps. The churches provided building materials, cash, and medicines for the destitute parishes of the East.

For both political and moral reasons, the trade was kept secret. In the West, people objected to paying Ulbricht cash, but the church was driven by a down-to-earth pragmatism. It wanted its people out.

Soon, the operations grew too big for the churches, and the West German government stepped in.

In the 1960s, about 12,000 prisoners were in East German jails on political grounds. In 1963, after behind-the-scenes wrangling, the Bonn minister for all-German Affairs, Rainer Barzel, gave the go-ahead for a buyout. Both sides doubted the good faith of the other, and both were afraid of publicity. The East was afraid the Western press would make political capital, while the West did not want to be caught giving cash to the very pariah regime it was telling the world to avoid.

The contact men in this gray world between political systems were two lawyers, one in West Germany, Juergen Stange, and the other in East Berlin, Wolfgang Vogel. A list of eight prisoners was prepared, and the sum of 340,000 West marks made available. An initial three prisoners were released into the hands of Vogel and passed on to Stange, who took them by S-Bahn to West Berlin. Then the cash had to be paid. This was difficult. It could not be transferred from bank to bank because that would leave a paper trail. So, a Bonn ministry official, Ludwig Rehlinger, was given the 340,000 marks in cash that he placed in a brown paper envelope. He drove with Stange to the Lehrter Stadt Bahnhof, the last station on the Western side. The East-bound train arrived, Stange stepped in. As the doors were about to close, Rehlinger handed him the envelope, and the train pulled out in the direction of the Friedrich Strasse checkpoint in the East.[1]

The five other prisoners were released and goodwill, if that is what it could be called, was established on both sides. Negotiations resumed, and a price of 40,000 marks per head was agreed. More prisoners were released in 1964.

But paying cash was risky. How would the loss of a small fortune inside an envelope be explained? It was decided that all subsequent deals should involve goods.

When Erich Mende took over as minister from Barzel in 1963, he walked into a bombshell. Just as had been feared, the newspapers got wind of what one called this "trade in humans." Mende gave a press conference and tried to be vague. Afterwards, he explained the situation to newspaper editors and arranged a pact of secrecy with them on the grounds that, otherwise, the trade would be jeopardised. Payment was reported in the press to be "coffee, tropical fruit, and butter." According to one report, "Vogel disclosed that discussions could be held about further projects on a similar basis."[2]

The freed prisoners were taken by bus across the border in spy-thriller style. To minimize attention, the buses were fitted with both East German and West German number plates attached to drums that could be rotated at the push of a dashboard button so they would appear to be licensed on one side of the border or the other.[3] The system was changed in 1987 to disperse the releases and make the process less conspicuous.

It took a while before the East Berlin regime realized it was peering into a gold mine. The chief prosecutor in Saxony-Anhalt, Wolfram Klein, discovered that, in the 1970s, many East Germans had applied for exit permits but that the applications lay unprocessed.

> Klein: Suddenly, at the beginning of the 1980s, many of these people were arrested for practically no reason at all, convicted, and shoved across the border in exchange for deutsche marks.[4]

East Berlin now knew the cash was its for the taking.

By this time, the original West German aim of helping people without at the same time propping up the East German economy had long since faded. The plan had gone badly wrong. Commodities such as oil, copper, rubber, silver, and industrial diamonds were being sold directly by East Berlin on the world markets for desperately needed foreign currency. Yet the fiction that only goods were making their way across the divide was maintained, even after East Germany collapsed.

Cash instead of merchandise was flowing East as early as 1966. A central role was played by a firm named Intrac, part of the shady East German KoKo smuggling empire.[5] KoKo deputy chief Manfred Seidel decided in 1970 that goods "should no longer physically come to East Germany but should be put at Intrac's disposal to be traded on international markets."[6] West German firms obtained supplies to order but, instead of taking them across the border, delivered them straight to Intrac. Intrac simply took the goods, sold them at maximum profit wherever it could in the world, and transferred the hard currency earnings to account number 0628 at the *Aussenhandelsbank* in East Berlin. The cash was used to service debt, to buy industrial goods, and to provide Western luxuries for the party leaders.

Suspicions remain that certain people in the West colluded with the East Germans in a pact that, because of inadequate controls in Bonn, was not detected. Too much money was available in cash, and too many people on both sides of the divide were making a splendid living. The apparent ease with which the East Germans turned the trade to their own advantage suggests that the Stasi and not the Bonn government was in control of it.

It was big business—a total of 33,755 prisoners was bought out between 1964 and 1989, while another 250,000 people came to the West under arrangements allowing families to be reunited. The total cost to the West German taxpayer was 3.4 billion West marks ($1.93 billion at the 1989 rate).[7]

The operation reached its nadir when, in 1983, it was discovered that, between 1978 and 1982, 5.6 million marks ($2.5 million at the 1982 rate) had disappeared. A Bonn civil servant, Edgar Hirt, was jailed for three and a half years for misappropriation. Hirt was not accused of using the cash himself, but he was unable to produce the documents to prove the expenditure. Other people might have faced charges as well but for the fears of political fallout if the case had snowballed.

NOTES

1. Cash handover described by Ludwig A. Rehlinger in *Freikauf, Die Geschaefte der DDR mit politisch Verfolgten 1963-1989* (Frankfurt am Main/Berlin: Verlag Ullstein GmbH, 1991), 35.

2. "Vogel disclosed...," in "Haeftlings-Auslöesung—Gegen Suedfruechte," *Der Spiegel*, October 14, 1964.

3. Number plate switchover related in Rehlinger, 82.

4. "Suddenly, at...," Klein quoted in "DDR 'produzierte' bewusst Haeftlinge fuer Freikaeufer," *Hamburger Abendblatt*, September 4, 1992.

5. For details of KoKo's operations, see Chapter 19—From Marauder to Merchant.

6. "Should no longer...," Seidel quoted by Wolfgang Brinkschulte, Hans Joergen Gerlach and Thomas Heise in *Freikauf Gewinnler*, (Frankfurt am Main/Berlin: Verlag Ullstein GmbH, 1993) 113.

7. Cost announced by Rehlinger on *n-tv* on November 15, 1993.

18

FADING HEROES

LEIPZIG, MARCH 21, 2002: SHE FACES the audience with a hint of uncertainty, like a girl who has wandered in unexpectedly to a dance evening in a strange town. But, as she begins talking, and the television camera rolls, the image of vulnerability vanishes.

Vera Lengsfeld tells a joke against herself. It relates to her arch enemy, the PDS "reformed communists." She had written a book, *Virus der Heuchler* (The Virus of the Hypocrites), published in 1992 by Elefanten Press. It suddenly and unaccountably disappeared from book stores.

"This was strange, because sales were running well below the print run," she explains. She got an even bigger surprise when she learned the publisher is partly owned by the PDS. An Elefanten employee told her PDS leader Gregor Gysi read accusations in the book that he had once been a Stasi informer, and had ordered the remaining copies to be withdrawn.

Lengsfeld, her straight blonde hair just touching her shoulders, grins wryly at the recollection, straightens her skirt, picks up her new book—not published by Elefanten Press—and begins reading selected excerpts. The cameraman films her from different angles. She takes questions from the floor.

Then the show is over. People mill around Lengsfeld, asking questions as she signs copies of her new book. In ones and twos, we vanish into Leipzig's descending gloom.

Yesterday's civil rights activists are no longer the heroic figures they once were, when they led a perilous existence, walking a fine line between the arbitrariness of rules set by Stasi commanders. Many went to jail more than once. But now, more than fifteen years since the East German state collapsed, fewer and fewer people recall—or choose to recall—the years of struggle against a totalitarian state. Or care. Some former activists, including Lengsfeld herself, claim they are hated. She says she has received death threats by e-mail and telefax. A member of her staff cut her hand on a razor blade set into an anonymous letter.

Many ex activists themselves are accused of being publicity seekers intolerant of other opinions and intent on keeping the spotlight of history on themselves. Their political value today is not highly regarded. They tend to be pigeonholed as specialists on the issue of German unification.

They have not even been given much credit for bringing down the East German regime. In reality, they were a diverse bunch, with widely differing views that achieved little in specific terms until, in 1989, the protests became a mass movement. One of them, Ehrhart Neubert, describes their achievements during that year: "They used their experience of passive resistance over the years to keep the revolution peaceful; during the month of October, they resisted attempts by the SED to use the politics of dialogue to muzzle the opposition; they forced (the establishment of) the Round Tables (the interim forums that replaced the SED as policymaker) that from the beginning aimed at setting a date for free elections; and they stopped the work of the Stasi and other organs of repression."[1]

But most of that has been forgotten. Certainly they exercised virtually no influence at all over the outcome of the first democratic East German election in March 1990, which was won by a conservative coalition holding out the promise of affluence.

This obscurity and resentment is partly because former civil rightists raise uncomfortable memories for many other Easterners, who are reminded that they spent so much of their lives under a living under a tyranny without protest. But another reason is disappointment by some sections of the old civil-rights movement, who claim that too many of their former colleagues have simply forgotten their old values and sold out to conservative political parties.

One commentator who takes this view is Hanna Behrend, who wrote,

> Many former civil-rights activists and sympathizers were disappointed with the outcome of German unification. They also resented the civil rights movement giving up its uncompromising opposition to infringements on human and civil rights and merely continuing to focus on its former [and now] vanquished enemies...While most of the prominent spokespersons of the former civil-rights movement are now part of the conservative and right-wing establishment, there are others who have not betrayed their vision of a democratically and socially just social system and who remain active.[2]

Lengsfeld herself hit international headlines in 1992 because her personal story aroused such interest, but the fame was fleeting. Now she is just another obscure former civil rightist whose past is fading in public memory as quickly as the events of 1989 and 1990. A spot check at a store in the Alexanderplatz, center of the former East German capital, revealed that not a single copy of her new book was in stock. No demand, the sales assistant told me.

Lengsfeld's father was a Stasi officer. Her parents taught her that privilege and corruption existed only in the other Germany. Vera began doubting the system at an early age. At her East Berlin school she met a girl whose father was a party big shot. Big Shot's apartment was filled with Western luxury items. Big Shot's cellar refrigerator contained lots of bananas, a symbol of exotic luxury for which the demand was as high as the supply was low. These were not distributed to people, but fed to a pet monkey that Big Shot had been presented with during a visit to Vietnam.

By 1972 Vera Lengsfeld was a twenty-year-old student of philosophy and history at Leipzig's Karl-Marx University. She was also seven months pregnant and single, and unable to find a place to live. Leipzig was legendary for its tumbledown housing. She was desperate, and applied for membership of the SED ruling party, thinking this would help her find accommodation. The selection committee asked her why she wanted to join. She should have answered, "To help develop socialism." But out of a mixture of naivete and bravado she said: "To improve socialism." The faces around the table hardened. Why did socialism need to be improved? Because she, like others, had been unable to find accommodation, she replied. The few apartments she had seen were falling apart and damp, and amenities were crude, she said. A woman with a baby needed a home with hot, running water.[3]

Lengsfeld's application was put on the back burner. Some years later, the party did confirm her membership but, by then, she was disillusioned and no longer wanted to join. As a single mother, however, she dared not say so, because she might have lost her job at the Academy of Sciences.

By 1982 she was in the contradictory position of being a member of both the SED and the opposition Pankow Peace Group, in Berlin, which she helped found. The group, which used the Protestant church as its shelter, discussed ecology, disarmament, and women's issues. It talked about retarded mental development among babies in industrial areas; it discussed radioactivity in the uranium mining region of AG Wismut. It was hardly a revolutionary cell, but it aired topics that were not supposed to be discussed—and was therefore suspect.

Vera Lengsfeld married Knud Wollenberger, a poetry-writing mathe-matics graduate she had met at an Academy of Sciences group vacation. Knud was the son of a communist who had fled to the United States in 1937, and who fled again, to Denmark, with his Danish wife in 1952 during the Mc-Carthy-era witch hunts. Knud was born in Denmark, before the family moved to East Germany. He spoke Danish to his mother, English to his father, and German to his sisters. Because he had a Danish passport, he was not pre-vented from leaving East Germany, but he was free to travel as he wanted.

An undated Stasi surveillance photograph shows Knud with Vera at an undisclosed outdoor site. He is thin and gawky, with long, black hair parted in the middle and a huge beard, and he walks knock-kneed, with his arms dan-gling awkwardly as if he does not know what to do with them.

Some years later, Vera and her son, Philipp, aged ten, were among hundreds who turned out with their bicycles for a Pankow Group protest. The event was more picnic than protest. The group carried picnic baskets but no banners. It made no clamor. But the informers had done their work and the *Volkspolizei* arrived and encircled the park, closed in, checked identity papers, and sent the picnickers away one by one.[4]

Vera Wollenberger was a marked woman.

The Stasi cracked down. It set up "Operation Virus" to monitor the Pankow group and reported that it dealt with "vile themes, and propagated free love,"[5] and possessed "hostile-negative" plans.[6] Around this time, reports circulated that Knud Wollenberger had provided the Stasi with information that led to the arrest of some members of East Germany's emerging punk groups. But no hard evidence was offered and Vera thought no more about it. In 1983 the party expelled her because of her Pankow Peace Group work. More accusations against Knud surfaced, but he denied them point-blank.

The big annual parade to mark the murder in 1919 of two pioneers of German communism, Rosa Luxemburg and Karl Liebknecht, took place on Sunday, January 17, 1988. Dissidents planned to turn out showing banners displaying a quote by Luxemburg, "Freedom is always the freedom of people who think differently." Vera Wollenberger and a friend, Herbert Misslitz, walked the few hundred yards between her front door and the parade in the Frankfurter Allee. Vera clutched her furled-up banner displaying a quote from the East German constitution, "Every person…has the right…to express opinions freely and publicly."

They were arrested before they even reached the marchers.

Vera and 120 other dissidents were thrown into jail. She and Misslitz agreed to say in defense that they had not intended to join the demonstration but wanted to go to Misslitz's apartment on the other side of the street. When Vera came for trial before judge Juergen Wetzenstein-Ollenschlaeger, her lawyer, Wolfgang Schnur, called Misslitz as a witness. She recalled the moment:

I considered him a person who was not easily fazed, but when he entered the courtroom with knocking knees, lowered head, and eyes that flitted to every part of the courtroom except where I was, and when he said everything that the judge wanted him to say, I (knew) ...the situation was hopeless.[7]

She was sentenced to six months' jail for "attempted rowdyism."[8]

Complex negotiations followed between Knud, Schnur, and another lawyer, Gregor Gysi, and her sentence was exchanged for an exit visa. She was expelled and went to Britain, where she enrolled at Cambridge University.

Back in East Berlin, Philipp, now sixteen, was in trouble at the Carl von Ossietsky high school. The head teacher, Rainer Forner, set up a version of the Hyde Park speaker's corner in the playground and invited pupils to speak out. This was the era of glasnost in the Soviet Union. Philipp and a friend used the chance to demand an end to the big annual military parade in East Berlin. The pair was expelled.[9]

Lengsfeld believes the speaker's corner idea was a trap organised by Margot Honecker, who was not only the wife of party boss Erich Honecker but also education minister. She believes it was a way of getting back at her. Officials often took revenge on dissidents through their children.

She returned to East Berlin from Britain on the morning of November 9, 1989. Within hours, she was watching on television the Berlin party boss, Guenter Schabowski, address an international press conference. A few hours later, the Berlin Wall was no longer an impediment to travel.

In the revelations that followed, she received one shock after another. Her lawyer, Schnur, was exposed as a Stasi agent; Gysi was suspected of being another. She believes Wetzenstein-Ollenschlaeger and Schnur jointly worked out her court case outcome beforehand.

A total of forty-nine spies had been set on her: academic associates, members of environmental groups, the half brother of her brother-in-law. A neighbour, a spinster of advancing years thought to have been mentally retarded and harmless—her room was filled with dolls and cuddly toys clad in pink—was not merely an informer but a Stasi officer. Her reports were precise and detailed. Lengsfeld recalled meeting the spinster after discovering the truth:

> She turned up...as I was packing. The apartment door was open...she sat down in a chair...I wanted to know who she was giving her reports to now. 'What do you mean?' 'I found your reports in my file. 'Oh, that's why.' She just stood up and left the apartment.[10]

Wollenberger confronted Herbert Misslitz—who had given evidence against her in court—with evidence from his own files, showing that he had cooperated with the Stasi. He denied the accusations, but avoided all further meetings with her.

But the act of treachery that shocked Wollenberger the most was another. In December 1991, a newspaper article named Knud as an informer. Knud said the report was incorrect. In January 1992 Vera saw for the first time her personal Stasi files. The second page contained the information she was dreading: personal details that only Knud could have known about. They had been passed on by an informer with the code name of "Donald"—Knud.

"I cannot describe the condition this left me in," she said. "I would rather have spent years in a Stasi prison than have gone through this."[11]

When Knud was again confronted, he said had wanted to do everything to ensure that Nazism did not return. Vera asked, "What did our private life have to do with the fight against Nazism?"

Knud tried in a television appearance to justify himself. A dark, bushy beard hid the lower half of his thin face, and his eyes twinkled from behind his spectacles as if he were amused. He said he had not been threatened and had received no money. But he was unable to explain. He lapsed into long silences. He said, "It is difficult, once you are in this situation and you are an informer and not in a position to free yourself."

He knew his television performance had been dismal. He must have thought long and hard about it, because two years later he was much better prepared. He told an American writer, Tina Rosenberg, that he had been supplying the Stasi with information in an attempt to change society. No one understood that what he had done was just another path toward reform, he said.[12]

But Knud was reinventing the past. This has become an art form in Eastern Germany. Party members, generals, and Stasi commanders responsible for the persecution had not only done what they were told to, but did so for the the loftiest of motives. They just wanted the best. Informers say their reports harmed no one. But they contrive to present wallowing in a cesspool as a hallowed deed.

Since the revolution, "villains have become victims, order givers have become obedient servants, and fellow travelers have become heroic dissidents," wrote Vera.[13]

Knud made a further attempt to rescue his reputation by issuing an open invitation for people to discuss his informer activities at a public meeting. No one came.

Part of the readiness to help the Stasi can be traced back to the state education system. Lienhard Wawrzyn believes that "kindergarten teachers were the indirect trailblazers for the informer. They bred the informer mentality. They instilled conformity."

Products of such a system seemed unable to have the strength to say "no." Instead, not having learned to settle conflicts, the target of a Stasi recruiting attempt acted in the way he or she had been taught: by fulfilling expectations and saying "yes."[14]

The habit of informing was rife during the Third Reich. In 1939, one observer recalled, "No one in Germany trusted anyone else anymore. Denunciation had become a patriotic duty and was a way of earning respect."[15]

A German who acted as an interpreter for the Russian occupation forces told me about a Red Army major speaking to German civilians in Quedlinburg in 1945. The major said, "We are treated as if we want to lock you all up. But we cannot run anyone in because we don't know anyone. However, you Germans make accusations and we have to react to them." A woman stood up and said, "It is good that you say that. An SS man is living in the apartment above mine. You can come and get him." The major retorted, "See. That's you Germans. That's you Germans."[16]

Rosemarie Gramsch seems to have discovered the secret of resisting Stasi recruiters. She was asked if she could "perform a favor now and again." She mentioned the recruiting attempt to her husband, told the Stasi she had done so, and heard no more of the matter.[17]

Vera Wollenberger immersed herself in the politics of the new Germany. She joined the Greens ecological party, and reverted to her maiden name of Lengsfeld. At unification she entered the all-German parliament as a member of the Alliance 90/Greens political group. But by 1998 she was becoming frustrated with the Greens' pacifism and what she saw as their increasing shoulder-rubbing with the PDS. She accused her party of "creeping rapprochement" with the "reformed communists," and the row came to a head when she suggested that war should not be ruled out as a way of halting the killing in Bosnia.

She and six other rebellious Greens defected to Chancellor Kohl's Christian Democrats.

All faced hostility from fellow Greens, but Vera later recalled that one who gave her comfort was the party's dominating figure, Joschka Fischer, "who personally gave me protection against the attacks from his party."[18] Perhaps Fischer understood. He became foreign minister in the Schroeder coalition government in 1998 and had to ram acceptance of the Kosovo war through a reluctant Greens conference.

One day in 1992 banks of press photographers were waiting outside the Berlin court hearing murder charges against former Stasi chief Erich Mielke. When Mielke's attorney, the silver-haired Wetzenstein-Ollenschlaeger, emerged, a woman walked up, flailed at him, tore at his tie, and screamed, "You pig. One day we'll get even with you." Kornelia Voigt, aged thirty, said Wetzenstein-Ollenschlaeger sentenced her to sixteen months' imprisonment in 1977 for taking part in a demonstration in the Alexanderplatz. She had been picked out of the crowd and sentenced after a hearing lasting ten minutes, she said. She was just sixteen at the time.[19]

Wetzenstein-Ollenschlaeger, the "judge" whose courtroom in East Berlin had a direct telephone line to the Stasi's Abteilung IX,[20] was born Juergen Glass in Coburg, in West Germany. He went to East Germany in 1960, the year before the Berlin Wall was built, worked in the book-printing industry and studied law. His rise was rapid and he soon became a judge.

He was one of more than 2,500 former East German judges and lawyers under investigation for perversion of justice. One of the cases under scrutiny was Wollenberger's. Wetzenstein-Ollenschlaeger said later he considered Wollenberger's six-month sentence lenient. "The maximum was three years. I made it six months, two months less than...demanded (by the prosecution)...If I'd made it any less, it would have cost me my head."[21] Some time later he told Wollenberger he had had some sympathy for her. But sympathy is not a quality that she associates with him. She told me, "My impression was that he was a conscientiously efficient Stasi judge who did his job without the slightest trace of human feeling."[22]

Eastern lawyers are allowed to practice in the united Germany but, because Wetzenstein-Ollenschlaeger had realized that few of East Germany's Stasi judges would be allowed to practice, he had himself reclassified as a lawyer.[23]

Wetzenstein-Ollenschlaeger was suspected of having misused state money through a firm, Dr G. Forgber GmbH, which was involved with the KoKo state smuggling network. The head of the firm, Forgber himself, was in custody. The suspicions revolved round a sum of seventeen million marks paid into a private Austrian bank account.

One Friday early in 1992, a warrant was issued for the arrest of Wetzenstein-Ollenschlaeger. It was too late, by some hours. He was gone. Neither he nor the seventeen million marks has been seen since.[24]

On April 22, 1999, three men entered the Gries & Heissel bank in Berlin with a case containing over 3,300 securities with a face value of twenty-six million marks ($22 million). Bank employees suspected the papers were forged and rang the police.[25] Wolfgang Schnur, the man who "defended" Vera Lengsfeld, was arrested for trying to deal in forged securities.

When East Germany collapsed a decade earlier, Schnur entered politics and was touted as a future cabinet minister under a postcommunist administration. The chancellor, Helmut Kohl, became his political ideal. The two appeared side-by-side at public meetings.

His decline began when evidence of Stasi involvement emerged. Wilting under the pressure, Schnur was taken to hospital. On March 14, 1990, two politicians visited him. They demanded his resignation. Schnur said: "Why didn't you just bring a pistol for me?"[26]

He quit in bed.

NOTES

1. "They used their...," Ehrhart Neubert in *Zehn Jahre Deutsche Einheit—Eine Bilanz* (Opladen, Germany: Leske + Budrich, 2000), 239.

2. "Many former...," Hanna Behrend in "The Rise and Fall of the East German Civil Rights Movement," *New Politics*, Vol. 6, No. 3, 1997. This excerpt was taken from the on-line version. Behrend is a former senior lecturer in English literature at Humboldt University (1969-87), in East Berlin, and is widely published in both German and English. Her publications include *German Unification: The Destruction of an Economy*, (London: Pluto Press, 1995).

3. Episode related by Lengsfeld in *Mein Weg zur Freiheit—von Nun Ging's Bergauf* (Munich: Langen Mueller, 2002) 78.

4. Episode related by Lengsfeld in Lengsfeld, 142.

5. "Vile themes…," Vera Wollenberger (Lengsfeld), in *Virus der Heuchler* (Berlin: Elefanten Press, 1992), 33.

6. "Hostile-negative" plans…, Wollenberger (Lengsfeld), 34.

7. "I considered him…," Vera Wollenberger in "Eine Zweite Vergewaltigung," a contribution to *Aktenkundig*, edited by Hans Joachim Schaedlich (Berlin: Rowohlt-Berlin Verlag, 1992) 158.

8. Episode related in Wollenberger (Lengsfeld), 94.

9. For an account of the extraordinary events at the Ossietzky school, see Marc Fisher's *After the Wall* (New York: Simon & Schuster, 1995), 107.

10. "She turned up…," Wollenberger (Lengsfeld), 24.

11. "I cannot describe…," Wollenberger (Lengsfeld), back cover.

12. Knud Wollenberger interviewed by Tina Rosenberg in *The Haunted Land—Facing Europe's Ghosts After Communism* (London: Vintage, Random House, 1995), xiii.

13. "Villains have become…," Wollenberger (Lengsfeld), 151.

14. "Kindergarten teachers…," Lienhard Wawrzyn in *Der Blaue—Das Spitzelsystem der DDR* (Berlin: Verlag Klaus Wagenbach, 1990), 23.

15. "No one in Germany…," Max von der Gruen in *Howl Like the Wolves—Growing Up in Nazi Germany* (New York: William Morrow and Company, 1980), 180.

16. Episode told to the author by the translator, Heinz Mueller, who was an eyewitness.

17. "Perform a favor…," Rosemarie Gramsch, in a letter to the author, August 1, 1997.

18. "Who personally…," Lengsfeld, 386.

19. "You pig…," Kornelia Voigt quoted by Joachim Rogge in "'Rote Socken' in schwarzen Roben," *General-Anzeiger Bonn*, February 14, 1992.

20. See Peter Przybylski, in *Tatort Politbuero*, vol. 2 (Berlin: Rowohlt Berlin Verlag GmbH, 1992), 296. Przybylski was an East German public prosecutor.

21. "The maximum . . .," Wetzenstein-Ollenschlaeger quoted in "Mit kalter Hoeflichkeit und der Stasi im Ruecken," *Berliner Zeitung*, February 13, 1992.

22. "My impression…," Lengsfeld in a letter to the author, January 22, 1998.

23. See Dieter Staecker in "Streit um Ex-DDR Richter—Der Verteidiger Mielkes hat in SED-Zeiten Demonstranten verurteilt," *Bremer Nachrichten*, February 13, 1992.

24. Wetzenstein-Ollenschlaeger is thought to have gone to Cuba. There have also been reports that, a decade later, after the statutes of limitation came into force, he had returned to Germany.

25. See "Ex-Anwalt Schnur festgenommen—Versuchter Millionenbetrug," *Berliner Zeitung*, April 23, 1999.

26. "Why didn't you…," Tatjana Doenhoff and Heiko Gebhardt, in "Die Lebensbeichte des Wolfgang Schnurs—Fuer Gott und die Stasi," *Stern*, April 5, 1990.

19

FROM MARAUDER TO MERCHANT

THE VILLAS IN THE FORESTED HILLS surrounding Tegernsee have a panoramic view down to where yachts with painted sails move slowly across the lake. This is an elite address in southern Bavaria. One former resident was Ludwig Erhard, who was credited with getting West Germany's postwar economic recovery off the ground in 1948.

Tegernsee has since gained a more notorious resident, a man with the cumbersome name of Alexander Schalck-Golodkowski. Schalck, as he is known, is one of the few East Germans who profited mightily in the days of communist rule. He was in a position to know that East Germany was in a hopeless financial situation, and he knew the end would come sooner or later. When it did come, he was well-prepared. These days, as a businessman in his own right, he is one of the few Easterners doing very well.

Schalck was East Germany's smuggling boss. He ran an organization known as KoKo (Kommerzielle Koordinierung) that was set up to deal world-wide in any commodity that would earn foreign currency for a chronically cash-strapped country. It sold political prisoners to West Germany, it broke embargoes by smuggling arms to warring states, it illegally acquired high-tech products for industry and for the Stasi, it broke East Germany's own laws on exporting works of art, it provided luxuries for the party bosses. It stole, it lied, it forged, it bullied.

One observer said: "In the Honecker era, the most important issue of culture policy was whether Schalck-Golodkowski could scrape together enough works of art and antiques to sell in the West."[1]

Schalck was unknown in the West, apart from by a few people in high places. He was also unknown inside East Germany, and not even the Soviet Union knew of him.[2] The fact was that "KoKo needed to be kept out of the glare of publicity because (in order to) obtain foreign currency Schalck-Golodkowski...became more and more involved in dubious dealings—weapons and drugs trading, illegal acquisition of embargoed goods."[3]

When Schalck's activities emerged late in 1989 and 1990, they caused revulsion. Easterners knew they had been duped all down the line by the Stalinists, and now this huge, fat man seemed to personify the corruption of a discredited regime that had enriched itself at the expense of the very workers it claimed to represent. Now that the game was up and Schalck's dealings were in the open, he would get his comeuppance. After all, the justice system of the democratic Germany was efficient and fair. Yes, Schalck would be tried for breaking East German laws and sentenced. So Easterners thought. But a decade and a half after unification, Schalck has reason to be satisfied about his life. The new Germany has treated him well.

Eastern hostility toward him was captured by a church minister, Friedrich Schorlemmer, who said,

> The faith of many Eastern Germans in the constitutional state is deeply shaken…while Schalck-Golodkowski resides in a villa and lives from the fruit of his opaque foreign-currency business…To him, when it came to money, there was no difference between pigs and people. He had discreet business partners right up to the highest levels of government…very discreet.[4]

Soon Easterners turned much of their contempt from Schalck himself to what they saw as the pathetic attempts to call him to account for his life of crime. They wondered, with reason, if he was being protected because of friends in high places.

Their resentment was redirected towards the new united Germany.

Frank Kempe's art business looks over the *Hofgarten*, the royal gardens in Munich. The street-long building once housed the House of Wittelsbach royal art gallery but is now let to art dealers. One heavyweight dealer was sitting in his empty store reading a book as I entered and asked the way to Kempe's. He looked at me wearily, heaved himself to his feet, and said in a whining tone, "I'm here to sell paintings, not to give tourist information."

Kempe has no walk-in trade. Appointment is strictly by telephone.

This fresh-faced, casually dressed man in a roll-necked jersey and exuding an easy geniality, was known as "dog" to the Dresden Stasi because he often took his dog for a walk.

The Kempe story dates back to the war years. In the 1930s, the German arts and antiques business was centered on the Schoenhauser Allee, an elegant Berlin shopping street. After the war the street became part of the Soviet sector and slid into decay, smothered under the lumpish menace of great-coated Red Army controls. By the mid 1950s, no art dealers were left in the Schoenhauser Allee as small private traders—storekeepers and tradesmen —gave up in the face of trumped-up tax-evasion charges and increased state quotas. By the early 1970s, only about sixty private art dealers remained in the entire country, most of them in Leipzig and Dresden. One survivor was Kempe's father, Horst Kempe.

Then came change. The regime realized the futility of allowing communist dogma to destroy a potentially lucrative source of foreign exchange from the sale of artworks, so it founded Kunst und Antiqitaeten GmbH as a subsidiary of the state smuggling organization, Kommerzielle Koordinierung —KoKo. In a country strangled by red tape and bureaucratic incompetence, it was a shining example of efficiency. Kunst und Antiqitaeten hijacked the arts market. It collected works of art and exported them to the West for huge profits. Exporting works of art was illegal, but Kunst und Antiquaeten GmbH operated above the law. It plundered artworks from private collections and public museums and, in the words of one commentator, "year after year…reaped millions in foreign currency…[in] one of the saddest chapters in the history of art in East Germany."[5]

The system was the height of communist hypocrisy. As border guards searched private cars to prevent works of art disappearing to the West, Schalck's trucks steamed across the border, taking paintings; antique childrens' dolls and musical instruments; and Nazi memorabilia to the collectors' markets of the capitalist world. One KoKo subsidiary known as VEB (K) Antikhandel Pirna handled much of the smuggling business.

As the state-sponsored robbers trawled the country for booty, some items survived only because people hid them. After an historic and notorious old bar in East Berlin, the Mulackritze, closed in 1963, its entire interior was removed by a transvestite, Lothar Berfelde, alias Charlotte von Mahlsdorf, who stored it in the basement of a disused building. Von Mahlsdorf shielded the collection from the plunderers for more than twenty-five years. Later, the reconstructed bar became a museum.[6]

One of Kunst und Antiqitaeten's first ventures into the art market brought it into contact with Horst Kempe's dealership in Dresden's cynically named Strasse der Befreiung (Street of Liberation).

The troubles began in 1972 when Horst Kempe's wife fell ill on a visit to the West, overstayed her visa, and remained rather than return and face prosecution. Horst Kempe, whose health also was not good, opted to join her.[7] But a few days before he was due to leave in 1974, he was arrested, accused of evading taxes on private heirlooms he had packed to take with him, and jailed for nine months. He was allowed to go to the West only after signing a blank paper that was later filled in with an admission that he owed a quarter of a million East marks in back taxes.

Horst's son, Frank, then ran into trouble. Frank had hired lawyer Wolfgang Vogel to help prevent the heirlooms from being impounded to pay the tax bill. Vogel, a key figure in the sale of political prisoners to the West for hard currency,[8] had told Frank about the prisoner project. It was supposed to be secret, but Frank Kempe talked about it openly. He believes this was why, in 1975, when he set off for Czechoslovakia, he was stopped at the border and forced to surrender his identity papers.

Frank had by now had enough. He told Vogel he wanted to go to the West. Arrangements were put in place. Some heirlooms were sold, and the tax claim against Horst Kempe was settled. The rest of the items were packed into fourteen cases, which he wanted to take with them. After being forced to hand the family house over at no charge, Frank and his sister, Freia, were given exit visas. But when they traveled to Munich on November 13, 1975, they were unable to take the cases.

Some time later, Kempe visited an antiques exhibition in West Berlin, and was shocked to see familiar items of baroque furniture and Meissner porcelain, part of a consignment he had sold to Kunst und Antiquitaeten GmbH to pay off his father's tax "debt." Now, in violation of East German laws, they were being offered for sale in the West.

Kempe contacted an East German dealer, Lothar Oesterreich, who said he was a founder of Kunst und Antiquitaeten GmbH, that he personally knew both KoKo boss Schalck and his deputy, Manfred Seidel, and would help bring out the fourteen cases. But not only would Kempe have to pay a purchase price, he would have to pay kickbacks to Oesterreich himself, Seidel and Schalck.

They were forcing him to buy back his own property.

Terms were arranged. Kempe was to bring the fourteen cases to a central point to be collected by a Kunst und Antiquitaeten GmbH vehicle. He entered East Berlin at the Friedrich Strasse checkpoint,[9] hired a Lada car, and drove to Dresden.

What happened that day was not fully explained until years later. The Stasi knew exactly what he was doing. They picked up his trail outside

Dresden and gave chase. Although he shook them off, they knew where he was headed and picked up his trail again. After another high speed chase, Kempe abandoned his plan and drove back to East Berlin. By now, he knew he would be arrested at the checkpoint. He felt physically sick.

Kempe handed back the Lada in East Berlin and returned to the Friedrich Strasse checkpoint. Then, for the first time that day, luck swung his way. When confusion arose in the lines of people waiting to have their papers checked, a guard trying to restore order absentmindedly handed Kempe's papers back to him before they had been scrutinized, and waved him through. Kempe boarded the S-Bahn train and returned to the West.

The last Stasi entry detailing the pursuit that day ended with the observation, "Dog was last seen crossing the Alexanderplatz."[10]

Frank Kempe only realized what had happened after he read his Stasi files and discovered that thirteen informers, including relatives, had spied on him for the Stasi. He never saw his cases again.

The Kempe story was not unique. A parliamentary commission set up to probe the Schalck empire found that the tax claims made on dealers such as Kempe were "probably a systematically executed plan by KoKo operators to dispossess private owners of antiques with the aim of selling them in the West." Western dealers were suspected of complicity so that Schalck's men would seize items "to order."[11] The case of one East German furniture restorer, Werner Schwarz, almost brought this sleazy East-West trade to a halt. Schwarz had put together a collection of antique coins, furniture, and household implements. In December 1981, he was given a demand for back taxes of about two million East marks, an amount set by Kunst und Antiquitaeten. Schwarz was later charged and sentenced to five years' jail for tax evasion. He was bought out under the prisoner buyout scheme and taken to West Germany. Like Kempe, he discovered items from his collection were being sold in the West. In 1987 he took legal action in West Berlin, and a judge ruled that the entire East German process had been "merely a pretext to confiscate [Schwarz's] property."[12]

This ruling was significant because "Western art dealers were no longer able to deny [knowledge of] the criminal background to their trade with East German items" and could no longer claim they had accepted items "in good faith."[13]

Schalck's secret career took off in the 1960s when the centrally planned East German economy blundered from one disaster to another. Everything was in short supply. The basic dilemma was either to invest in industry and deprive the consumer or fill store shelves and allow industry to decline. Both could not be done. The first was certain to cause social unrest, which was dangerous, and the second was a recipe for economic disaster.

Brutal measures were needed. In the 1960s, an experiment in decentralizing controls was tried, but the bumbledom of central planning soon reasserted itself. In 1966 the state set up KoKo to handle cash paid by the West German government to buy out political prisoners, but its function quickly broadened. KoKo was nominally part of the Foreign Trade Ministry and was run by Schalck.

Two developments vastly increased his powers: he became a colonel in the Stasi; and he was handed what was, in effect, a pirate's license by being declared a "special-operations officer" (OibE). This made him virtually untouchable except at the very top. The longer he ran KoKo, the more independent both he and KoKo became. By the 1970s, Schalck had virtually a free hand as long as he delivered. KoKo deputy chief Manfred Seidel admitted in 1990 that "my task was to use all available means to obtain foreign currency...In doing so, there were no legal provisions to worry about."[14] Schalck answered only to Honecker himself, to industry secretary Guenter Mittag and to Stasi minister Erich Mielke. Schalck claims to have been merely an obedient servant of his state, but that is poppycock. A former party Central Committee member, Manfred Uschner, told an inquiry that in later years, the Politburo had ceased to exist as a decision-making body. Decisions were taken by Honecker before meetings even took place. Only two people had unhindered access to Honecker at all times, Uschner said. They were Mielke and Schalck.[15]

Many of KoKo's front firms were in West Germany. His dealings with the West necessarily had to involve West Germans. Schalck admitted that two West German meat dealers, A. Moksel AG and Gebr. Maerz AG, both based in the southern state of Bavaria, had paid KoKo 1.2 million West marks a year in commission for the right to import cheap East German meat. Profit from the meat trade amounting to sixteen million West marks a year was partly used to buy luxury limousines for the party leadership, he said.

The meat trading case was closely connected with Franz-Josef Strauss, the Bavarian prime minister of the time, who headed the conservative Christian Social Union (CSU). Schalck rated his links with Strauss so highly that he restricted the meat sales to Bavaria, although every other state in West Germany wanted a slice of the action. Schalck believed the trade was in reality a source of money for the CSU.[16] But this has never been confirmed.

Not surprisingly, the exports worsened the existing East German meat shortages. Markus Wolf, head of the foreign espionage service, said, "It was because of this connection that steaks and other choice cuts of beef remained scarce for East Germans. The best cuts all went at dumping prices to Strauss's friend, Maerz."[17]

But that was not Schalck's concern.

Strauss negotiated with Schalck-Golodkowski to arrange a deal in 1983 under which a consortium of Western banks made available to the East one billion West marks in credit. Strauss, who had his own political grounds for setting up the deal, used Josef Maerz, head of the meat company, as intermediary. Maerz had sound commercial reasons for visiting the East and talking with officials, while Strauss himself did not. If an inkling of what was taking place had emerged, the deal would have fallen through because of CSU grassroots protest.

The agreement was finally tied up on June 30, 1983. Spy chief Wolf recalled: "The negotiations with Strauss were so discreet that our sources in Bonn discovered nothing about them. I cannot answer the question as to why, of all people, the Bavarian prime minister wanted to save East Germany from insolvency. The background to the trade remains Mielke's and Schalck's secret."[18]

The gains extracted by Strauss became apparent in September, when East Berlin began dismantling the 54,000 self-shooting devices installed along the 838-mile border between the two states. The behavior of Eastern border officials, usually rude and arrogant toward Western visitors, improved.

KoKo stole Western technology for both the decrepit Eastern industrial complexes and for the Hauptverwaltung Aufklaerung (HVA), the Stasi department that ran spies in West Germany. Access to this technology was blocked by a NATO blacklist known as Cocom, which banned the transfer to the East Bloc of any item with a potential military use.

Schalck got around the blacklist by buying into or setting up firms in the West that he put under the control of front men. He established lines of ownership through third countries, using intermediaries. These firms were able to arrange purchase of forbidden technology for bogus buyers and use circuitous routes to deliver it back to East Germany. Sometimes business was done more directly. The Japanese firm of Toshiba had no scruples about breaking the Cocom ban. One KoKo official went to Japan and recalled that the Japanese "made no secret of their great sympathy toward Germany, regardless of (whether) East or West."[19]

The tentacles spread to anything that made money. KoKo dealt in people, in weapons, in antiques. It set up convoluted channels to ferry weapons to the Middle East from Britain, West Germany, the Soviet Union, other European countries, and the United States. It demanded, and received, commissions from Western companies for arranging commercial deals through normal channels with East Germany.[20] During the Iran-Iraq war, KoKo arranged for arms to be sent to Iran, which was then diplomatically isolated. From December 1980, Iran Air Boeing-747 aircraft landed at night in East Berlin, were loaded with weapons and took off again before daybreak. From 1982 deliveries to Iran were made from the port of Rostock along convoluted sea and land routes.[21]

The Palestinian terrorist group headed by Abu Nidal ran a front company called Zibado Company for Trading and Consulting Ltd in East Berlin. Bank records show that, through a KoKo company known as IMES, Zibado bought thousands of machine guns with a million rounds of ammunition.[22] The armaments were intended for Libyan leader Moammer Qaddafi. "The shipment went via Poland to hide its origin, and Qaddafi paid the equivalent of more than $470,500 in hard currency. Abu Nidal acted as middleman and was paid a substantial commission by the East Germans,"[23] wrote John O. Koehler, a former Associated Press journalist, who specialized in investigating the Stasi.

Koko even provided arms for the CIA. Its contact was a man who moved easily between the world of secret services and private arms dealing, Samuel Cummings. Cummings ran a company known as the International Armament Corporation, or Interarms, that he set up in 1953.[24] "The CIA people were clearly especially good customers of the comrades. At least four times between 1982 and 1985, aircraft chartered from the CIA shell firm, St Lucia Airways, were loaded up at Berlin Schoenefeld [airport] with East German military equipment."[25]

The amount of hard currency raised by KoKo kept increasing, but the original purpose of the cash became forgotten. Less and less of it went where it should have been going—to the collapsing, rusting industrial complexes. Instead, it was used to keep The Great Gravy Train on the rails. It maintained the flow of Western goods, the cars, the television sets and video recorders

—and that symbol of exotic luxury, the banana—to the party leaders and senior functionaries. As the flow of luxuries increased, so did Schalck's value.

Most of the income was paid into three accounts at the state foreign-trade bank in East Berlin, the Deutsche Aussenhandelsbank: numbers 0528, 0628, and 0584. In December 1989, when the regime was falling apart, account 0628 had a balance of more than two billion West marks—2,105,781,064 marks and 92 pfennigs.[26]

When East Germany was in its death throes, a massive money laundering operation went into full swing. Documents were shredded by the ton to destroy the trail as cash was placed by circuitous means in accounts throughout the world. By this time some East German officials were as adept at big money crime as any white-collared villains in the capitalist world. They falsified trade figures of state-owned companies to bolster accounts so the assets could be revalued in West marks. No one knows how much money was siphoned off or simply "invented" to be converted into West marks. One guess of twenty-six billion marks is widely regarded as conservative. By 2003 investigators had recovered a miserly three billion marks (present-day worth: €1.5 billion).

The existence of Schalck and KoKo came to light only when East German investigators went to question Schalck about the misuse of state funds, only to find he had fled to the West and turned himself in. West Germany refused a request to send him back, ostensibly because of a plot to assassinate him. He was the man who knew too much. West German investigators placed him in custody, interrogated him, and, five weeks later, let him go.

East Germany collapsed, and several former KoKo companies in Western Germany slid "quietly and quickly into the hands of new owners, without the Treuhand [privatising agency] knowing anything about it."[27] The newsmagazine *Der Spiegel* said Schalck "has so far survived the collapse of East Germany brilliantly unscathed...Justice officials are searching for 22 billion marks from his economic empire."[28] When questions were raised about how Schalck was able to finance a lavish lifestyle, he said his income was from work as an adviser. But one investigator thought differently: "If I had fifty million in a Swiss account, I would also find people to lend me [money]. Schalck just sits tight. He doesn't make mistakes. He just needs to wait until the statute of limitations applies."[29]

Parliamentary investigations into Schalck's business ran into walls of silence. Former civil-rights advocate Ulrike Poppe, herself jailed by the Stasi in

1983, wrote, "An unholy alliance of the Stasi old boys network and sharp Western profiteers have caused losses of many millions...and, finally, Schalck-Golodkowski: after the Bundestag committee of inquiry spent a legislative period examining the criminal transactions of the KoKo business, a stopper of secrecy protection was slammed on...This all suggests that clarification is being blocked as soon as the involvement of West German politicians in this state criminal organization shows."[30]

Gregor Gysi, a lawyer in East Germany and the dominant figure in the PDS, said cynically that Schalck-Golodkowski would never be brought before a court of law. "He knows too much about top Western politicians. They only bring people to court who pose no danger to them."[31]

Gysi was wrong. But not by much. Schalck did come for trial in 1995, and the next year was given a suspended one-year jail sentence on charges of importing into East Germany firearms and night-vision equipment. Yet the charges, brought under a 1949 allied military government law governing the terms of trade between the two German states, barely touched on the activities of KoKo. The reasons can only be guessed at.

The trial was interrupted to allow Schalck to travel to China as an adviser to a group of German businessmen—so much for the charge of "winner's justice" that East German party hacks complain about every time one of them is prosecuted. (At no time were more party officials in custody on charges of abuse of power and misappropriation of state money than in the last days of East Germany itself. The state, in its dying days, was trying to deal with the corruption and privilege in order to survive.) He appealed against his conviction, and although he lost, he went back to commercial life and set up a company, Dr Schalck & Co, dealing in "merchandise of all categories."

Schalck made a television appearance in May 1991 on an *RTL-plus* channel program, *Explosiv*, in which he was confronted by four questioners including Social Democrat politician Peter Struck and a Stasi files investigator, Hans Schwenke. The interview had its fiery moments. Here is an excerpt in which the argument rages round the supposed amount of KoKo's fluid assets at the time of monetary union:

> Struck: Tell me here and now where the missing twenty-two billion marks is, that is being talked about.
>
> Schalck: I beg your pardon, with all due respect. Do you know at all how many zeros twenty-two billion has?
>
> Struck: Yes, I know. I am a financial politician...

Schalck: Just imagine it: twenty-two billion! For that much I could have bought West Germany! (Thunderous laughter in the studio.)

Schwenke: For a start, it became known shortly after the revolution that this amount had been placed in foreign bank accounts.

Schalck: Twenty-two billion. You really don't know what you are talking about!

Schwenke: The money...is meant to be security, I suggest, to secure you credit of 420,000 marks...

Schalck (angered): That is bare-faced impudence! I have to tell you that this sort of discussion will not lead to a coming together of the two German states...

Moderator Ulrich Meyer, in schoolmasterly tone: "Oh, oh, oh, Herr Schalck."[32]

NOTES

1. "In the Honecker era...," Manfred Jaeger giving evidence on May 4, 1993, in Berlin, to the *Enquete-Kommission, Aufarbeitung von Geschichte und Folgen der SED-Diktatur in Deutschland—Ideologie, Integration und Disziplinierung*, III,1 (Frankfurt: Suhrkamp Taschenbuch Nomos, 1995), 432.

2. When it came to trade, East Germany played its cards close to its chest, especially "in the fields of high tech and trade with the West, half of which was between the two German states," according to Professor Dr. Harry Maier, called as an expert witness in Berlin on February 5, 1993, to the *Enquete-Kommission, Aufarbeitung von Geschichte und Folgen der SED-Diktatur in Deutschland—Macht, Entscheidung, Verantwortung*, II,1 (Frankfurt: Suhrkamp Taschenbuch Nomos, 1995), 665. Maier continued, "The [Soviet] ambassador at the time in Bonn, Yuli Kivitzinsky, complained in his memoirs...that they [the Soviets] had practically no insight into trade between the two German states. This might have partly accounted for the conspiratorial nature of an institution such as KoKo, which, with its monopoly over supply and demand, generally controlled this intra-German trade."

3. "KoKo needed...," Arnold Seul giving evidence in Bonn on January 15, 1993, to *Enquete-Kommission, Aufarbeitung von Geschichte und Folgen der SED-Diktatur in Deutschland—Staatssicherheit, Seilschaften*, VIII (Frankfurt: Suhrkamp Taschenbuch Nomos, 1995), 576.

4. "The faith of...," Friedrich Schorlemmer in *Deutschland Ungleich Vaterland* (Hamburg: Sternbuch im Verlag Gruner + Jahr AG & Co, 1991), 37.

5. "Year after year...," in "Raub in grossem Stil—Die Geschaefte von Schalck-Golodkowski," *Frankfurter Allgemeine Zeitung*, July 14, 1990.

6. A detailed account of the operation as well as a description of the once-lively but now-desolate district where the Mulackritze was appears in Charlotte von Mahlsdorf's book, *Charlotte von Mahlsdorf: Ich bin meine eigene Frau* (Munich: Deutsche Taschenbuch Verlag, 1995).

7. The state did not object to the old and the ill leaving because that saved welfare costs.

8. See Chapter 17—The People Trade.

9. This caused problems. Kempe, as a former East German, was not allowed back into East Germany. So he tried a bluff. He registered as a West Berliner—who were subject to a different set of regulations—went to the Friedrich Strasse Bahnhof checkpoint, and was admitted.

10. "Dog was last…," quote from Kempe's Stasi file.

11. "Probably a systematically…," parliamentary committee finding quoted by Holger Schmale, in "West-Kunsthaendler dealten mit Schalck—Antiquitaetenhaendler mussten vermeintliche Steuerschulden mit Kunststuecken begleichen," *Luebecker Nachrichten*, February 21, 1992.

12. "Merely a pretext…," judge's comments quoted by Schmale, in "West-Kunsthaendler dealten mit Schalck."

13. "Western art dealers…," judge's comments quoted by Schmale, in "West-Kunsthaendler dealten mit Schalck."

14. "My task was…," Seidel quoted by Peter Przybylski, a former East German public prosecutor, in his book, *Tatort Politbuero*, vol. 1: *Die Akte Honecker* (Reinbek bei Hamburg: Rowohlt Taschenbuch Verlag, 1992), 132.

15. Uschner was giving evidence on January 26, 1993, in Berlin to the government-sponsored committee investigating East Germany. See *Enquete-Kommission, Aufarbeitung von Geschichte und Folgen der SED-Diktatur in Deutschland—Macht, Entscheidung, Verantwortung* II,1 (Frankfurt: Suhrkamp Taschenbuch Nomos, 1995), 484.

16. Schalck said some years later in a letter to Stasi boss Erich Mielke on October 27, 1988, "The position of the Maerz business remains unchanged as a hidden source of revenue for the CSU," in Przybylski's *Tatort Politbuero*, vol. 2: *Honecker, Mittag und Schalck-Golodkowski* (Berlin: Rowohlt Verlag, 1992), 280.

17. "It was because…," Wolf in *Spionage Chef im Geheimen Krieg—Erinnerungen* (Munich: List Verlag, 1997), 190. This book is an extended and reworked edition of the original, which appeared in English, *The Man Without A Face* (New York: Time Books, Random House, 1997).

18. "The negotiations with…," Wolf, 192.

19. "Made no secret…," Toshiba officials quoted by Gerhardt Ronneberger, in *Deckname "Saale"—High-Tech Smuggler unter Schalck-Golodkowski* (Berlin: Karl Dietz Verlag, 1999), 165.

20. KoKo made up to sixty million marks a year by charging Western firms as much as ten percent commission, according to a report in the weekly magazine, *Focus*, October 11, 1993. After the end of the communist era, many firms stopped paying agreed commissions. A Western law firm followed up and chased defaulters, many of whom paid up unquestioningly, probably because they were afraid that, otherwise, the truth about their deals with East Germany would emerge.

21. In the Iran-Iraq war, both sides fought with weapons that had come through East Germany. The weapons were made in both East Bloc and Western countries. Sometimes the Western supplier firms did not know where their weapons were going to. But only sometimes. According to a report, "Niklas, Hoelle und Kalle—Die DDR diente internationale Konzernen als geheime Drehscheibe fuer den Waffenhandel," in *Der Spiegel*, September

30, 1991, a cartel of European explosives manufacturers arranged business through Schalck. It describes a delivery method used by one of the twenty manufacturers, the Swedish Bofors, which delivered to Dynamite Nobel in Vienna. The cargo was sold on to a Finnish firm but did not go to Finland. It was taken through Bavaria to East Germany and then transported to Iran. In the 1980s, East Germany received permission from the Soviet Union to manufacture one of the Kalashnikov rifles, the AK 74 automatic—but with a condition that it must not be exported. The Soviets wanted to keep that profitable right for themselves. A KoKo company made slight modifications, called the weapon the STGK 90, and exported it, according to the magazine *International Waffenmagazin*, quoted in "Tricks mit schwerem Geschuetz—Wie DDR-Devisenbeschaffer Schalck-Golodkowskis Firma 'Imes' Sowjet-Waffen nachbauen liess und gegen Moskaus Willen auf dem Weltmarkt verschob," *Stern*, December 18, 1991, 162.

22. Abu Nidal purchases reported by Peter-Ferdinand Koch, in *Das Schalck Imperium—Deutschland wird gekauft* (Munich: R. Piper GmbH, 1992), 137.

23. "The shipment went...," John O. Koehler, in *Stasi: The Untold Story of the East German Secret Police* (Boulder, Colorado: Westview Press, 1999), 381.

24. According to Brian Wood and Johan Peleman, in *The Arms Fixers—Controlling the Brokers and the Shipping Agents* (London: A Joint Report by BASIC, NISAT, and PRIO, Basic Research Report Nr. 99.3, 1999—available online; no longer available in a paper edition), Chapter 1, Cummings began buying and selling small arms at the age of twenty-six. He later started subsidiaries in Britain, Canada, and elsewhere. He bought World War Two surplus weapons in Europe and sold them to the newly independent states of Africa, Latin America, and the Far East. By 1960 Cummings was the most important private arms dealer in the world. He claimed that, within twenty-four hours, he could arm half a million men. Between 1953 and 1968, he bought more than 4.5 million guns and 500 million rounds of ammunition from European stocks. His sales generated a turnover estimated at $80 million a year.

25. "The CIA people were...," in "Gute Kunden von der CIA—DDR war bis zu ihrem Untergang Drehscheibe des WeltweitenWaffenhandels," *Der Spiegel*, May 4, 1992.

26. Method of payment described by Przybylski, vol. 2, 264.

27. "Quietly and quickly...," in "Der macht keinen Fehler," *Der Spiegel*, May 9, 1991.

28. "Has so far survived...," in "Der macht keinen Fehler."

29. "If I had...," unnamed investigator quoted in "Der macht keinen Fehler."

30. "An unholy alliance...," Ulrike Poppe in "Gesperrt fuer saemtlichen Reiseverkehr bis zum 31.12.1999," in *Eine Revolution und ihre Folgen—14 Buergerrechtler ziehen Bilanz*, edited by Eckhard Jesse (Berlin: Christoph Links Verlag, 2001), 216.

31. "He knows too much...," Gregor Gysi quoted in "Quittung nicht ueblich—Der Millionenschatz der mysteriosen Ost-Berliner KoKo ist verschwunden, ihr Chef Schalck-Golodkowski noch immer auf freiem Fuss—warum?" *Der Spiegel*, November 19, 1990.

32. This account excerpted from a transcript of the program published in *Die Schalck Papiere: DDR Mafia zwischen Ost und West—Die Beweise*, by Wolfgang Seiffert and Norbert Treutwein (Rastatt/Munich: Verlags Union Erich Pabel-Arthur Moeweg/Quick Verlag, 1991), 80.

20

AWKWARD QUESTIONS
FOR THE CHURCH

PASTOR ALFRED SCHARNWEBER PUT it this way: when, in the communist era, schoolboys saw him walking past a school, they would take a fiendish delight in calling out to him, "Pastor, when can we come to church?" They knew that would anger the teachers. These days when boys see him, they mockingly call, "Hallelujah."

Things have changed for the church. Under the communists, it was not part of the establishment. Now it is. Under the communists, the church flourished. Since reunification, it has lost both members and influence. But a far more painful issue is being probed. It deals with the fundamental question of how the church survived inside a hostile Stalinist society. Some of the answers are not reassuring.

The church in East Germany usually meant the Protestant church with its various Lutheran/Evangelical denominations: the stout figure of Martin Luther, the Augustinian monk who began the Reformation in the sixteenth century, cast a heavy, uncomfortable shadow across the atheist state. Of East Germany's 16.7 million people, 7.7 million were nominally Protestant and only 1.2 million Catholic. Maps of some areas read like a tour of Luther country—Eisleben, Erfurt, Eisenach, Wittenberg.

At the end of World War Two, the prewar Catholic and Protestant dioceses were spread-eagled across the new East-West divide, which did nothing to dispel the Soviet view that both were tools of the Western powers. Luther was declared an enemy of the people. But the new Stalinist state of East Germany did not choke the life out of the churches. The reason was self-interest. As long as they did not preach insurrection, the churches were tolerated. The party wanted social peace and it saw big economic advantages in allowing the churches to perform grassroots social work—helping the old and the handicapped, building social centers. The cash to do this came from the West. Throttling the churches would have stopped the flow of cash.

It was an uneasy coexistence. Compromises had to be made. In 1969, the Eastern church cut administrative links with the Western church and formed its own administration. The contradictions between church and state were glossed over in a relationship formalized in 1978 when the church agreed to work not against the state but within it. This was known as "The Church in Socialism." The party thought that by allowing the church to publish its literature with greater freedom and letting people meet and discuss issues at church centers, a less dissatisfied population would result. Increased happiness would have an economic spin-off. Industrial production would increase. The theory was hopelessly wrong.

But as a result of this policy, people were able to meet in Evangelical church rooms and discuss disarmament and the environment, usually without being harassed. They were spied on, of course. All groups had their stool pigeon. But they were also outlets for intellectual forces being smothered in schools, universities and clubs.

The Eastern peace movement developed from these groups. In 1979 the uneasy truce came under heavy pressure when NATO decided to station medium-range nuclear missiles in Western Europe as a response to Soviet missiles already in place. Protests broke out on both sides of the border. The official party line was that peace must be armed but that the arms must all be on the Eastern side of the Iron Curtain. This clashed with the Eastern peace movement, which opposed all weapons where they were stationed. The term *Schwerter zu Pflugscharen* (Swords to Plowshares: "...and they shall beat their swords into plowshares and their spears into pruninghooks..." —Micah 4:3) became the movement's slogan. The movement was banned.

In 1983, the 500th anniversary of Luther's birth, the party did an about turn by rehabilitating him. It declared him "a forerunner of Marx, who had mobilized forces against papal exploitation." The change was not prompted by soft-hearted liberalism but by hard political considerations. It enabled East Germany to deepen its historical roots in its own eyes and strengthen its claims for recognition as THE German nation.

The explosion at the Chernobyl nuclear power reactor in 1986 drew the disparate elements of protest together and concentrated minds on the environmental dangers of both nuclear power and sulfur-rich brown coal—with its polluting brown smoke—as well as on the larger issue of political power. Access to Western media, especially television, showed Easterners how desperately little information their own state media was giving them about Chernobyl.

The church offered these strands of opposition both a refuge and a debating forum. By 1988 more than fifty local church environmental groups were holding meetings and their numbers and influence were increasing. Church meetings in Leipzig that began as discussions on the environment grew until they became the historic Monday demonstrations that gave Leipzig the name of the Heroic City and that proved to be the battering ram that brought down the party.

On October 9, 1989, services were held at three churches in Leipzig, after which tens of thousands of people spilled out on to the streets to confront a massive presence of soldiers and police. Back in East Berlin, Bishop Gottfried Forck appealed to the party to begin forming a democratic constitutional state. Two days later, the party issued a statement saying it was prepared to talk. Manfred Stolpe, the senior lay figure in the church, remarked, "For the first time, a process of discussion [will be taking place] in this country." The regime was tottering.

Yet more than a decade after these events, the role of the churches remains far from clear. Scharnweber, a man in his late forties with short-cropped hair and metal spectacles, is pastor in the northern town of Boizenburg. He talked to me in his roomy, book-lined workroom in the old half-timbered vicarage. In the communist days, the church had no money for repairs and depended on help from churches in the West. The West marks were not sent directly but were exchanged in East Berlin for East marks at a rate of one for one. That was the deal. The party got its foreign exchange, and the church got its bricks and mortar.

The church had to work deals to survive. It wanted the elbow room to function as a church and it wanted to help people. In a totalitarian state, it had little option but to deal with that state. That meant dealing with the Stasi. The interface was in a sort of twilight world in which few knew what was happening. The church's role was controversial. At what stage did negotiation become cooperation? Were the churches partners or opponents of the state?

One man who moved in this area was consistorial president Stolpe himself, a man with a ready smile and a gravelly voice. Stolpe says he talked to the

Stasi about issues big and small: repairs to churches, the release of political prisoners, helping a student gain admission to a university, arranging trips to the West. Among Easterners, he is a highly popular politician. But sections of the Western press and some former hard-line dissidents believe that he was far too conciliatory in dealing with the Stasi. They say his role as a go-between branded him as a fellow traveler of the ruling party.

Scharnweber said Stolpe had gone too far in the tightrope walk with the Stasi. "They used him, and he let them use him. Stolpe was playing with power."

But Werner Bley, deacon of St. Servatius church in Quedlinburg, disagrees. His is the majority view. "It is preposterous to make accusations against Stolpe," Bley told me in his office at the foot of the old church, "How else could he have done what he did other than by talking with the Stasi?"

The allegations against Stolpe reflect the charges against the church itself. Did his contacts with the Stasi help the Stasi more than the church? How far did the church's accommodation with the state really go? How much information did Stolpe give the Stasi? Was anyone harmed by this information? Evidence from the Stasi files link Stolpe's name with an informer known as "Sekretaer," but Stolpe says that if he was listed as an informer, it was without his knowledge.

One pastor summed up the situation after reading his own Stasi files by saying, "I know that no one sized up the church so accurately as the Stasi."[1]

Another pastor, Ehrhart Neubert, said the task of informers was to split the church into factions, to influence decisions, to secure the promotion of people loyal to the state, and to demoralize critics. He added,

> The church cannot exist in any way other than as an institution. The destruction of the church begins at that point where, individually, people privately exploit it as an institution. That was the aim (of the regime) and it was partly achieved.[2]

The case of Gerhard Lotz, a member of the Protestant Church High Consistory who was hired by the Stasi in 1955 under the code name of "Karl," went much further than mere cooperation. According to Clemens Vollnhals, an expert witness at a government hearing, Lotz,

> ...delivered to the Stasi all the...information it was in his power to acquire...he passed on personal-political internal information of all

types, as well as information about those ministers and High Consistory members who had had Nazi links…he also personally took part in an action to secretly search the work room of Bishop Mitzenheim.

Lotz's work involved "considerable criminal energy," Vollnhals added.[3]

Although the Catholic church was less in the firing line because it was so much smaller, its role too has been criticized.[4]

In a society in which people became used to living under relentless pressure, lighter moments were rare. When they did occur, they called for some careful treading. In 1980 Scharnweber attended a public event to mark the 725th anniversary of Boizenburg's founding. As a pastor, he was normally not invited to such an event attended party officials, Stasi employees, and civil dignitaries. This was an exception.

He was asked to make a speech, which he did in Plattdeutsch, low-German dialect. He told a joke about a postman, a railway worker, and a soldier, all people in uniform. Everybody laughed at the punch line. Suddenly, the laughter gave way to an embarrassed silence. His audience had been carried away because he had spoken in dialect and they had forgotten for a moment that representatives of the state, especially those in uniform, were not to be made fun of.

NOTES

1. "I know that…," Christoph Wonneberger quoted by Matthias Gretzschel in "Der Mythos von der Kirche im Widerstand," *Hamburger Abendblatt*, December 4, 1991.

2. "The church cannot…," Ehrhart Neubert giving evidence on December 13, 1993 in Erfurt to the 56th session of the *Enquete-Kommission, Aufarbeitung von Geschichte und Folgen der SED-Diktatur in Deutschland—Kirchen in der SED-Diktatur, VI,1* (Frankfurt: Suhrkamp Taschenbuch Nomos, 1995), 130.

3. "Delivered to the…," Clemens Vollnhals giving evidence on December 13, 1993 in Erfurt to the 56th session of the *Enquete-Kommission*, 116

4. The relationship between the Catholic Church in East Germany and the Stasi is dealt with in *Kirche im Visier—SED, Staatssicherheit und katholische Kirche in der DDR* (Leipzig: Benno Verlag, 1998).

PART FIVE
THE WALL

21

THE DEATH STRIP

ONE FORMER BORDER GUARD reacted with scorn when I asked him in 1990 if there had been a written order to shoot inside no-man's-land, "Of course there was!" It was a crucial question because officers and apparatchiks in command of border guards were claiming in their legal defense that no order to shoot existed—which was more or less saying guards shot intending escapers because they wanted to.

I met the ex-guard as I was taking a photograph of a dilapidated half-timbered house in a rural Mecklenburg street close to the former border. It was at a time when many Westerners were laying claim to property under the restitution program, and feeling was running high among Easterners worried about being evicted. He did not look pleased as he approached me. Afterwards, he said he thought I might have been a lawyer. He had not seen my Hamburg-registered car parked further down the street: Hamburg lawyers do not drive dented, unwashed eight-year-old Ford Fiestas with clumps of last week's mud caked to the body.

His initial suspicion soon vanished and he offered to show me round the area where he had spent the past twenty-five years. We spent most of the afternoon in his newly acquired Citroen, bouncing over cobbled and pot-holed roads and negotiating obscure forest tracks that were once inside the designated border zone inaccessible to outsiders.

The great fear of the guards was that they might have to shoot. He was lucky. He didn't have to. His part of the border ran through the middle of the Schaalsee, a lake forty minutes' drive from Hamburg. The first time he saw canned beer was when West German border police tried to tempt Eastern guards to defect by floating dozens of the new-fangled things across on the tide. One warm summer's night, a naked woman was rowed out to the center of the lake in a boat. Guards were urged over a loud hailer to provide the lady with some company—and to come to the West.

He had taken an agricultural degree from the university at the northern city of Rostock before being posted as a border guard in the 1960s. "I was a convinced communist," he said. As part of his propaganda training, he was told that people trying to leave East Germany directly through the border fence were breaking normal courtesies. You didn't visit a neighbor without first knocking. During the afternoon, he made no attempt to excuse or justify. In speaking with me, he was straightforward. The admission that it all had been wrong was implicit.

After being discharged from the military, he remained in the area and went to work on the land. After 1989, agriculture in the East collapsed in the face of Western competition, and he lost his job. So he found work in a warehouse in a city he had never been able to visit because it was on the wrong side of the Wall—Hamburg.

His views contrast sharply with some of his former superiors. Former Deputy East German defence minister and head of the border guards, Klaus-Dieter Baumgarten, told the Thirty-sixth Criminal Court in Berlin in 1996 that the West used people killed at the Wall for propaganda purposes. Baumgarten was facing charges connected with deaths at the Wall and needed to construct a defense.

One of the cases before the court was that of eighteen-year-old Peter Fechter who died in 1962. Early on the afternoon of August 17, Fechter and another eighteen-year-old, Helmut Kulbeik, attempted to get over the barrier of bricks and barbed wire in Zimmer Strasse, 300 yards east of Checkpoint Charlie. As Kulbeik reached the top of the Wall, which was then much lower than it later was, the guards opened fire without warning. Kulbeik came down on the Western side. He was alive and suffered nothing worse than a torn shirt. But Fechter, following behind, was hit several times and fell back on the Eastern side. His mother, waiting in the West, watched, just a few yards away, as he lay for more than an hour bleeding badly. Two Western policemen climbed the Wall and threw some bandages to him, but he was too weak to help himself. An American patrol was told not to interfere. The guards in the East did nothing. They let him bleed to death.

The same day, an Eastern border guard commander, Colonel Tschitschke, said in a report that guards were afraid that Western police would have opened fire if they had gone to Fechter's aid. So they laid a smokescreen to rescue him, Tschitschke said. But photographs only show guards taking Fechter's body away. There was no smoke.

When Baumgarten took the stand thirty-four years later, he said he presumed no one from the Western side had gone to help Fechter because it was better for propaganda purposes that he continue to remain where he was, dying and unaided.

"A corpse damaged East Germany more than a wounded person," he said. In a speech lasting five and a quarter hours, Baumgarten, sixty-five, explained that because the state prosecution had not understood the important points about border security,

> It goes very much against the grain with me to have to produce further facts to rebut the incompetent statements of the state prosecution.

At that, the eyebrows of young prosecutor Klaus-Jochen Schmidt rose slightly.[1] Baumgarten was jailed for six and a half years.

Work on improving and modifying border fortifications along the death strip in Berlin and at the German-German border never stopped. The fence—in some places it was a concrete wall—snaked across the landscape, up hill and down dale, ranging left and then right, mile after mile after mile, a silent and lethal monument to political division and human incapacity to deal with it.

In 1958 border units were issued with armoured cars. In 1960 trip wires attached to flares were installed and 1,000 dogs were deployed in places where the topography made observation difficult. From 1961, around 1.3 million mines were laid. They came in many versions. Most were Russian PMN and PPN-2 models shaped like tin cans, between 5.3 cm and 6.5 cm high, filled with up to 200 grams of explosive and planted like potatoes in furrows. Seven kilograms of pressure was enough to set them off. Most were plastic but some were encased in wood. Others were camouflaged and suspended by wire above ground so that when they were set off by trip wire, they inflicted the maximum mayhem. Guards carried a variant of the AKM 70 Kalashnikov rifle with a muzzle velocity of 770 yards a second. Later came a shorter-barreled version of the AK 74 rifle that spat out 5.45 millimeter bullets with air pockets built into the casing so that when they hit soft human flesh, they did not simply penetrate and exit but yawed and danced and blasted out a gaping wound. Few people wounded by an AK 74 slug lived to tell the story.

In some places, as many as five fences were built behind each other. They were made of cut-resistant, zinc-plated mesh drawn too fine for finger purchase. The East could not make the mesh. So West German firms, in a cynical example of German-German cold-war cooperation, supplied three million pieces, each 2.4 meters by 1.10 meters and costing twenty East marks.[2] On the Eastern side of the fence, electric wires carried low-tension power to signaling devices. The electric circuit was cut by the merest brush of a hand or foot, not enough for the person doing it to notice, but sufficient to send the giveaway signal back to the tower. In other places, trip wires attached to lights or signal rockets were hidden in long grass.

Guards kept watch from octagonal observation posts perched on top of tube-shaped towers. These towers were gradually replaced by more stable, squat, bunker-like blocks. Twin concrete tracks allowed motor vehicles to traverse the death strip and reach the towers.

The Berlin Wall—the outer wall—achieved its final appearance in 1979 when the old Wall of bricks and concrete blocks was replaced by prefabricated slabs of high-density asbestos concrete 3.6 meters high and 1.20 meters wide, each weighing 2.6 tons and capped with smooth-surfaced tubing designed to cause groping hands to slide off.

Between 1949 and 1989, more than one thousand people died along the death strip surrounding East Germany.[3] They were shot dead or they drowned; they were blown up by self-shooting devices; and they were mangled by land mines.[4] The toll keeps mounting as information comes to light about previously unknown victims dying, often in remote locations, often late at night, their corpses dragged away out of sight of prying eyes in the West and taken to morgues where doctors would falsify certificates to hide the cause of death. The statistics were compiled in the West.

At least 140 people died trying to escape by sea, a report by the ZERV investigating agency said. Between 1961 and 1989, about 700 people escaped across the Baltic Sea, while 2,300 others did not make it. There were no limits to the ingenuity of intending escapees. One man in the southern town of Kahla constructed a collapsible submarine, which he tested in inland waters and modified with the aim of transporting it to the Baltic and sailing to the West. But the vessel was discovered. Informers had done their job and the local Stasi knew exactly where to look. In May 1989, two brothers each flew ultralight aircraft wrapped in Russian camouflage into East Berlin. One landed and picked up a third brother as the other circled and kept watch. The first ultralight took off again and both crossed back to the West and landed on the open area in front of the Reichstag building. Former border guards boss Baumgarten has a more conservative version of border fatalities. Only 24 people were wounded and 17 killed, he said in 2005, nine years after being sentenced by the Criminal Court in Berlin in 1996. Baumgarten gives no source at all, just plucking this figure from the sky.

MAGDEBURG—About 750,000 West Germans secretly applied between 1949 and 1989 to move to East Germany, Stasi files official Edda Ahrberg said on Monday. Few applicants were accepted because East Germany suspected that most were saboteurs or spies. —*EPD / Frankfurter Allgemeine Zeitung*, October 17, 2000

The casualties were neither intended nor wanted, he said. He adds, in an astonishing example of hypocrisy, that he offers his "deep, sincere sympathy to all affected."[5]

When, after unification, former generals and their political chiefs were charged over killings at the border, they claimed that no order to shoot existed. This claim contradicted the low-ranking border guards who, when brought to trial, said they were indeed obeying an order to shoot. Logic dictates that guards were not going to shoot unless someone had told them to. The truth is that an order to shoot not only existed, it had to exist. It was the most important order any East German military unit had ever received.

West Germany used trade concessions to negotiate the removal from no-man's-land the self-shooting devices and many land mines. But the West could not negotiate away the order to shoot. Without it, there would have been a mass exodus. The Wall alone would not have stopped more than the aged and the infirm and perhaps not even those. The order existed because the East German state would have been finished without it.

The border guards were, in legal terms, the most accessible part of the chain of command. They were the ones who pulled the triggers. Once their names had been ascertained, prosecution was relatively easy, even if moral justification was not. The guards were under orders. Cracking down on what the Germans call *Schreibtischtaeter* (desk criminals) was tougher. Written orders to shoot were hard to come by. Deserting soldiers might have taken copies to the West. This created a gap between real guilt and prosecutable guilt. No one could seriously believe that East Germany's leaders did not know what everyone else knew: that people were being shot dead at the border between the two German states. Because the prosecution could find no written order, the very existence of the order was disputed. But border troops were expected to shoot and a bounty of 150 East marks and other perks were usually distributed whenever they did prevent an escape by use of firearms.

One retired border guard colonel Guenter Bazyli cut through the haze of argument by stating that an order to shoot did exist. He angered his ex-colleagues when he came for trial on death charges in 1998 and identified the order as number 101, which came straight from the Politburo. Bazyli, sixty-four, who was given a two-year suspended sentence, was abused outside the courtroom as "a traitor" and a "scabby rat" who had "sold out the honor of the officers' corps."

Bazyli earlier told one interviewer that no one would have had to die if 20,000 troops had been deployed along the border. He meant that this would have been a way of preventing escape attempts before they began. But Honecker had rejected this solution as too expensive and instead had opted for the alternative that "we knew would mean corpses," Bazyli said. The sole aim of the Wall was to "keep a bankrupt SED (the ruling party) in power."[6]

If the penalties imposed on border guards have been mild—most of those convicted have received suspended sentences—the treatment of the responsible East German elite has been scandalously lenient. The generals and party apparatchiks who have been convicted are sent to low-security jails or open prisons. They are often released ahead of time, if they are convicted at all. Often their trials have been discontinued because of ill health.

Those responsible for East German state terror quickly began to bluster as soon as they realized nothing would happen to them. Now they sound off about "victor's justice" and grin secretly over the lameness of the constitutional state.
—Stefan Wolle, *Berliner Zeitung*, January 15, 2000

NOTES

1. "It goes...," report of court case by Verena Schmitt, in *Hamburger Abendblatt*, August 14, 1996.

2. A person living in the East close to the border was quoted as saying about the wire mesh from the West, "You don't get that sort of quality over here," in "DDR Grenze—Wie warme Semmeln—Findige Geschaeftsleute aus West und Ost schlachten die deutsch-deutsche Grenze aus: Wachtuerme, Stacheldraht und Zaeune finden reissenden Absatz," *Der Spiegel*, April 19, 1990. Some of the bullets used by East German border guards were also made in West Germany and smuggled in via Austria. For details of this trade, see "Niklas, Hoelle und Kalle—Die DDR diente internationale Konzernen als geheime Drehscheibe fuer den Waffenhandel," *Der Spiegel*, September 30, 1991.

3. The total keeps increasing, as previously unknown cases come to light. A total of 1,008 border deaths between 1946 and 1989 had been proved by 2002, according to the Work Group 13 August, an organization headed by Rainer Hildebrandt, based at the Museum at Checkpoint Charlie in Berlin.

4. A former East German military doctor told a Berlin court that "the term 'mines' was not wanted" in documents relating to people who died after being blown up by landmines or shot by automatic shooting devices. He added that the cause of death was coded by the use of numbers. The death certificates in these cases would simply refer to "injury...through legal measures." The court was hearing charges related to deaths at the Wall against former East German defense minister Heinz Kessler, his deputy, Fritz Streletz, and a regional party boss, Hans Albrecht. In "Die Vertuschung—DDR Aerzte faelschten Totenscheine bei Minen-Opfern an der Grenze," *Hamburger Abendblatt*, April 6, 1993.

5. Baumgarten was writing in *Die Grenzen der DDR—Geschichte, Fakten, Hintergruend*, edited by himself and a former East German colonel, Peter Freitag (Berlin: Das Neue Berlin Verlagsgesellschaft, 2005) 227.

6. "We knew would mean...," Bazyli quoted in an interview with Gerald Praschl in *Super Illu* magazine, December 4, 1997.

22

COLD WAR CAMERA

THE YOUNG, EARNEST PHOTOGRAPHER with the thinning, brushed-back hair, was on the spot in the East Berlin of the Cold War. He was there in 1959 when Soviet leader Nikita Krushchev, standing in an open limousine and waving his hat, was driven through the streets.

The photographer was at Schoenefeld airport in 1960 as Krushchev returned to Moscow from a later visit to East Berlin. He was there as the faithful marched through East Berlin touting huge photographs of party leaders. He was there as uniformed children of the mass "Pioneer" organization marched, beating drums and blowing trumpets.

He photographed party officials speaking to rent-a-crowds. He photographed a father with his small children holding flags at a demonstration. He photographed the slogans: "Socialism Will Win"; "The German Democratic Republic—Savior of Peace."

No one could work that close to the scene without official sanction. Hans-Joachim Helwig-Wilson and his camera were watched by the Stasi, but he was allowed free movement. He was part of the propaganda machine, taking photographs and passing them on to Western media. The photographs showed life in East Germany as it was meant to be, with eager people actively supporting a benevolent and peace-loving regime. Mostly.

Helwig-Wilson did not see his job the way party apparatchiks saw it. He took photographs as and where he wanted. Signs of protest: a row of propaganda posters with the faces of party leaders torn out. Suggestions of shortages: empty shop windows.

Although Helwig-Wilson lived in West Berlin, he grew up in East Berlin and knew the terrain and the people. His photographs were in demand in the West.[1] But his success was also his downfall. His career ended in dramatic fashion in 1961, the year the Berlin Wall was built.

When this slightly built man with a lean face and a white, short-trimmed, old-time preacher-style beard without mustache, shakes hands, you feel the bent, paralyzed fingers. He walks with the aid of a cane.

He would have been a far different story to tell had he not met Heinz Lippmann. Lippmann, born into a Jewish industrialist family in Berlin in 1921, survived both Auschwitz and Buchenwald under the Nazis. Many other members of his family did not. After the war, the twenty-three-year-old was grateful to the communists—whom he believed were responsible for his survival—so he joined the Communist Party and helped set up in East Germany a state branch of the mass Free German Youth (FDJ) movement. In 1952, he became the FDJ deputy head, junior only to the chairman, Erich Honecker.

But Lippmann came under the influence of Franz Dahlem, a veteran who opposed the Stalinist course the party was taking under Walter Ulbricht. In May 1953, Dahlem was thrown out of the Central Committee and relieved of all party posts.

In June 1953, building workers in the Stalin Allee led a workers' revolt that brought Soviet tanks onto the streets. The revolt ended, state security minister Zaisser was sacked for activities "hostile to the party" and a purge began. Lippmann was among the many suspects. He knew it was time to go.

On September 29, he was being taken by car to Schoenefeld airport to fly to a Komsomol (state youth organization) camp in Bulgaria. At Friedrich Strasse station, he told the driver to stop, jumped out of the car, saying, "I just want to fetch cigarettes,"[2] and vanished into the station. He took the S-Bahn to West Berlin and caught a plane to West Germany. He was carrying with him 300,000 West marks, cash from FDJ funds set aside to pay for a promotion drive in the West. And so began one of the more colorful adventures in the history of East Germany.

As arrest warrants were issued in both East and West, Lippmann went to Frankfurt where he threw off the straitjacket of communist reserve with the flamboyance of a man who had won a lottery. He took the name of Heinz Berger, moved into a luxury apartment, and took to driving a turquoise-colored Cadillac. With his start-up capital, he went into business, one after the other as each failed. After less than a year he was arrested and charged with trying to bribe a policeman to obtain new identity papers and of misappropriating the FDJ money.

After four court cases and six months in investigative custody, he was given a nine-month jail sentence and fined 5,000 marks. The sentence was suspended for four years with the court observing as an ameliorating factor that the misappropriated money had originally "been intended for illegal subversive activities."

In 1959, Lippmann began his own newspaper, *Der Dritte Weg* (The Third Way), a name that indicated a political and economic system that was neither capitalist nor Stalinist-type communist. *Der Dritte Weg* was smuggled into East Germany. The paper could not exist from advertising revenue and the FDJ funds were by now depleted. Lippmann was secretive about where he was getting the cash from. In 1959, when Lippmann was in Vienna, he met Michael "Pit" Gromnica, a West Berliner who offered his services to *Der Dritte Weg*. Lippmann accepted.

Helwig-Wilson came into Lippmann's ambit in 1960. A decade before, Helwig-Wilson, then aged twenty, had worked for the East German state rail company and, at the same time, had written reports for *Der Telegraf*, a Western-based newspaper ideologically close to the Social Democrats. *Der Telegraf* circulated small-format supplements designed to be secreted in coat pockets—about twelve pages the size of a paperback book. In the days before the Wall was built, *Der Telegraf* staff fanned out along the border and distributed copies to commuting Easterners at railway stations and other points.

Rationing was still in force, and black-market trading and corruption were widespread in the East. Helwig-Wilson wrote about how potatoes collected by "workers' representatives" had "disappeared" into the black market. His reports irritated the party and he got word through unofficial channels to leave the East in a hurry. He did, leaving behind his mother. He was just in time. Two days later, the police came to arrest him.

He did not risk returning to the East but, in 1958, Western intelligence sources gave him the all clear. So he went with a party of about twenty reporters accompanying a group to a wreath-laying ceremony at the former Nazi concentration camp at Auschwitz, now in Poland. He completed the assignment without incident. It was to be the first of many. Among his employers was the London-based Paul Popper photographic agency, which accredited him on New Year's Day, 1961.

Western publications often hired Lippmann to obtain stories and photographs from the East. In 1961 he commissioned Helwig-Wilson to go to Leipzig to trace Walter Ulbricht's estranged first wife, Martha Schmellinsky, and to photograph the house. He did.

On August 13, 1961, construction began on the Berlin Wall. On Monday, August 28, Helwig-Wilson entered East Berlin by S-Bahn to visit Dieter Wilms, head of the East Berlin information service. A car was sent to take him to the editorial offices of *Neues Deutschland*, the party newspaper. When he climbed out of the car he was inside the grounds of the Stasi headquarters in Normannen Strasse. He was a prisoner.

He would not have gone to the East if he had known two crucial items of information: the first was that Lippmann's paper, *Der Dritte Weg*, was no product of reform-oriented communists based in the West but was being financed by the West German counterespionage agency, the *Verfassungsschutz*. The second was that Lippmann's colleague, Gromnica, was a Stasi spy.[3] Neither did Helwig-Wilson know that, the day before, Gromnica had been ordered back to East Berlin.

The Stasi based its case against Helwig-Wilson on information passed on by Gromnica and other informers. He was taken to an underground cell, beaten up and accused of being a Verfassungsschutz agent who used the codename of "Linse." He was convinced that his arrest was a matter of mistaken identity. Walter Linse was a West Berlin human-rights lawyer who had been kidnapped in 1952, and his fate at the time was unknown in the West. (Linse was taken to East Berlin where he was tortured and handed over to the Soviet Union. He was tried and sentenced to death for spying and executed by firing squad in Moscow.)[4]

On August 29, after fifteen hours of initial interrogation, Helwig-Wilson was taken on the ten-minute drive to the same Hohenschoenhausen prison where Linse had been taken a decade before. It was a dark, subterranean world where interrogators worked in teams, abusing and beating prisoners. On the fourth day, Helwig-Wilson collapsed in an interrogation room and was taken back to his cell. When he came round, sharp pains were stabbing into his back. No doctor was brought. He was held in a cell with no light. He lost track of time. He was taken out to the interrogation rooms and brought back again. He was woken at thirty-minute intervals. He had no idea where he was. He had no contact with the outside world. No one on the outside knew where he was.

Jailers' contempt for prisoners had no limits. When he asked his interrogator, Oberleutnant Guenter Liebewirth, why he was being punished by being kept in a darkened cell, he was told, "Darkened cell? Where are there darkened cells? Someone has been playing a joke on you. They put you in the broom cupboard."

Liebewirth was obsessed with Helwig-Wilson's photographs. One showed an election placard in which someone had torn out the head of party boss Walter Ulbricht.[5] Helwig-Wilson protested that not only had he been given permission to take photographs but he had not ripped the poster. "The people did that. That was their opinion. If it showed the state in a negative light, then that was another issue." Another photograph was of a May Day parade of tanks rolling along Marx-Engels Platz in East Berlin with a banner in the background carrying the contradictory message: "Gegen militarismus —fuer Frieden, Einheit and Voelkerverstaendigung" (against militarism—for peace, unity and understanding between peoples). Liebewirth said he should have whitened the banner out. Because he didn't, he was a spy.

Oberleutnant Liebewirth was not open to other points of view.[6]

After fourteen days, Helwig-Wilson "confessed."

The Stasi sent a letter to Helwig-Wilson's mother, who was still living in East Berlin, telling her that her son was in custody. She contacted Wolfgang Vogel, an East Berlin lawyer who was gaining renown as a specialist in political cases.[7]

Gromnica, meanwhile, was brought before a carefully orchestrated press conference in East Berlin, where he was billed as a West Berlin journalist and SPD official who had changed sides. The state-controlled *Berliner Zeitung* newspaper published a four-part series in which Gromnica told how West German Chancellor Willy Brandt employed a system of spies to "terrorize the West German working class" and to try to liquidate opposition figures. *Der Dritte Weg* had been set up as an espionage agency to act as a cover for West German spies, he said.[8]

The day before his trial was due to begin, Helwig-Wilson believes Liebewirth tried to poison him with doctored coffee. But his stomach, raw from the rough prison diet, rejected the drink and he vomited the poison out.

Helwig-Wilson was sentenced in 1962 to thirteen years' imprisonment at Frankfurt an der Oder and was admitted to the clinic at Leipzig prison. He was given an injection to help his back pains. The contents of the syringe cannot even be guessed at, but it was a venomous mixture that caused one leg to stiffen and remain that way. When his fingers also became stiff and bent, a prison doctor cut the tendon of a little finger in an attempt to straighten it, but the incision was unsuccessful and the finger remained bent.

Helwig-Wilson's health continued to decline. It was so bad that when lawyer Vogel arrived, he hardly recognized the cripple in front of him. He was surprised his client was even alive, he told me.[9]

In May 1965 Helwig-Wilson was back at Hohenschoenhausen, when the Stasi told him he was to be released that same day. They offered him a job in the East. He declined. Helwig-Wilson had been bought out of jail by the West German government and he was accompanied back to West Berlin by Vogel. Helwig-Wilson's children, aged five and three when he was abducted, did not recognize the gaunt stranger with the close-shaven skull who stepped out of a car that May day nearly four years after going missing. He was a physical and emotional wreck and was immediately admitted to hospital. When he did feel capable of writing again, he was unable to tell his story because of an unofficial pact between newspapers and the government. Publicity would jeopardise future buyouts of political prisoners.

When Hans-Joachim Helwig-Wilson was debriefed, the *Verfassungsschutz* counterespionage agency, told him it was astonished at his "recklessness" in heading East when he did. Lippmann had been working for the agency and it presumed Helwig-Wilson knew this. One specialist, Michael Herms, has evidence that Helwig-Wilson was being used without his knowledge as a *Verfassungsschutz* agent under the code name of "Linse"—which would account for the interrogators' use of the name.[10] Helwig-Wilson denies he was an agent. His former counsel, Vogel, told me he did not believe his client had been a spy. The *Verfassungsschutz* has refused Helwig-Wilson access to its files.

These days, Helwig-Wilson is an honorary judge in a labor-disputes tribunal and he campaigns for the rights for victims of the East German justice system. He shows parties of schoolchildren and tourists round his old prison, Hohenschoenhausen, which has been turned into a museum.

He is also trying to nail his Stasi persecutors. He has run into problems in an unexpected place—in the Berlin legal system. He traced Liebewirth, the man who he suspected tried to poison him, to Eastern Berlin and sought to have him prosecuted. But a West Berlin prosecutor pointed out that Helwig-Wilson had admitted in a signed confession to being a spy. Helwig-Wilson feels it remarkable that he had to explain to a lawyer trained in a democratic country the significance of a confession made under duress. He told one reporter it was "a scandal" that judges and prosecutors who worked on cases such as his remained free and, in some cases, were even employed by the state.[11] That was in 1992. Since then, little has changed.

NOTES

1. A selection of Helwig-Wilson's photographs has been published in a book, *Der Staatsfeindliche Blick—Fotos aus der DDR von Hans-Joachim Helwig-Wilson*, edited by Elena Demke, (Berlin: be.bra verlag, 2004).

2. "I just want to fetch…," Lippmann quoted by Michael Herms in *Heinz Lippmann—Portraet eines Stellvertreters* (Berlin: Dietz Verlag, 1996), 156.

3. Michael Herms says Gromnica was hired in Moscow in 1957. Herms, in his book, *Heinz Lippmann—Portraet eines Stellvertreters*, refers on page 228 to a report of Stasi Hauptabteilung V/2 of September 11, 1959, confirming this. Helwig-Wilson himself saw from his own Stasi files that not only Gromnica but also Gromnica's wife had been informers against both himself and Lippmann.

4. For more on the Linse case, see John O. Koehler in *Stasi: The Untold Story of the East German Secret Police* (Boulder, Colorado: Westview Press, 1999), 138.

5. This photograph, which shows a line of posters in which the faces of not only Ulbricht but also of East German prime minister Otto Grotewohl and Moscow party boss Nikita Krushchev have been torn out, can be seen in a collection of Helwig-Wilson's photographs, *Der Staatsfeindliche Blick—Fotos aus der DDR von Hans-Joachim Helwig-Wilson*, edited by Elena Demke, (Berlin: be.bra verlag, 2004) 55.

6. Liebewirth's zeal paid off. He later graduated from the Stasi Law School and reached the rank of colonel, according to Karin Hartewig in *Das Auge der Partei—Fotografie und Staatssicherheit* (Berlin: Christoph Link Verlag, 2004) 145. For his thesis, he and nine other "specialists of violence" wrote "The Characterization of Political-Operational Work of the Ministry of State Security in Preventative Forestallment and Combatting of Political Underground Activity directed against the State and the Societal Order of East Germany."

7. Helwig-Wilson was allowed to write every month to his wife. But when he gained access to his Stasi files in 1993, he discovered that the great majority of his letters had not been sent. Instead, they had simply been placed in the files. See Demke, 95.

8. The series was billed as "exclusive interviews with West Berlin journalist Michael Gromnica who has defected to East Germany," *Berliner Zeitung*, December 21 ("Das Spitzelsystem Brandts"), December 24 ("Erfundene 'Geheimberichte'"), December 28 ("Agentur 'Dritter Weg'") and December 29 ("Spitzel des Ostbueros"), 1961.

9. Poisoning was a common practice in prisons. Whenever it happened, the doctors diagnosed "heart attack," Helwig-Wilson said. The cause of death would have been put like this: "Because of the serious crimes he committed against the workers' and peasants' state, he laid a heavy onus of blame on himself. The ensuing stress eventually caused a heart attack," he said.

10. Herms, in *Heinz Lippmann—Portraet eines Stellvertreters*, 231.

11. "A scandal…," Helwig-Wilson quoted in "Verfolgt, gedemuetigt, gefoltert—Die Haeftlinger der Stasi. Einer schildert, wie es war in der Hoelle von Hohenschoenhausen," *Hamburger Abendblatt*, March 3, 1992.

23

THE BAR AT THE END OF THE WORLD

ONE SATURDAY NIGHT IN AUGUST 1961, the Heidelberger Krug, on the corner of Elsen Strasse and Heidelberger Strasse, was just another street corner bar in Berlin. That changed a few minutes after midnight when forty helmeted border police carrying sub-machineguns with fixed bayonets leapt from trucks and formed a jagged line of steel across Elsen and along the center of Heidelberger.

People trying to enter the Soviet sector were stopped by a row of glinting bayonets. The bar emptied and the drinkers joined a jostling crowd outside on this warm, late summer evening. They watched, anger growing, as uniformed East German work teams trucked in behind the border police rolled out barbed wire along Heidelberger Strasse.

Many in the crowd were both angry and drunk. "Communist pigs!" someone screamed. "Just wait until the Amis come!" yelled another. But the Americans did not come.[1]

The next day, Hans-Joachim Helwig-Wilson arrived with his camera. He stood outside the Heidelberger Krug watching workmen erect a makeshift wire mesh fence in front of a tall apartment building.

A party agitator stood in front of the fence, tie flashing from under an open white trenchcoat, eyes smouldering beneath a newsboy cap. He snarled at Helwig-Wilson, telling him to leave, and added a few words in Russian. It was just the scene Helwig-Wilson wanted. He photographed the man.

It was Sunday, August 13, and construction of the Berlin Wall was beginning. The agitator was one of many sent to the border to harangue Westerners and deflect any hostile comments made to border police or construction teams.

Over the following days, a brick wall topped with wire replaced the mesh fence along Heidelberger Strasse. People living on the upper stories of the apartment building could no longer visit the Heidelberger Krug. They could look down at its lights and listen to juke-box music drifting upwards whenever the corner door opened.

Houses lining the Soviet side of Heidelberger Strasse were demolished to create an open expanse of no-man's land between the main wall and a second, inner, wall. This gave Grepos a clear field of fire in case anyone made a run for it.

Teams dug escape tunnels beneath the border. On March 25, 1962, an East Berliner, Peter Wuestenhagen, was taken to a tunnel entrance hidden by old furniture in the basement of the Elsen Strasse apartment building. But, as he and his contact descended the stairs, they heard someone chopping wood in the basement. Wuestenhagen was taken to a nearby bar to wait. He drank a few beers, and when the all clear was given some hours later, "I was fired up, euphoric."[2] He crawled on all fours in the pitch dark of the tunnel and came out in a another basement, this time on the Western side of Heidelberger Strasse. One of the tunnelers was Heinz Jercha, who helped twenty five people escape.

Two days after Wuestenhagen escaped, a resident of the apartment building, Bernd Kolberg, heard a number of bangs that sounded like balloons bursting. He discovered later they were not balloons but rifle shots coming from the basement. Grepos had discovered the tunnel. Jercha, inside the tunnel, was hit in the chest by a richochet. He managed to stumble back through the tunnel to the West, vomiting blood from his ruptured lungs, but died in hospital.

It was Kolberg who, two days before, had been chopping firewood in the basement. He recalled the night he heard the shots, "Twenty minutes after the bangs, our doorbell rang. They stood at the door holding handcuffs."[3] "They" were the Stasi. Kolberg, twenty-two, and his parents were arrested and interrogated in investigative custody for two months on suspicion of involvement in the escape plan.

The brick wall, just eight paces from the Heidelberger Krug's corner doorway, was demolished and, in its place came a more sophisticated construction, a 12-foot wall of prefabricated concrete slabs with a tubular top designed to make groping hands slip off.

The Wall glowered through every window of the bar like a huge Russian bear. The Heidelberger Krug was the bar at the end of the Western world. The other side of that wall was as remote as the other side of the moon—over there were dark, heavy, inaccessible places places like Warsaw, Sofia, Moscow.

The years passed. This half street became a forgotten corner of the divided city. I first went there in the 1980s, as the tarmacadam surface was becoming cracked and discolored. The Wall had become a target for grafiti artists, a sort of log book of history. The colors faded as the seasons rotated and ice, snow and sunshine alternately clawed at the surface. From the bar stool in the Heidelberger Krug, I looked at the bleached signature of "Kevin" and a more recent autograph, "Adem," and wondered who they were. There was more graffiti: a skull worn away by the weather; a street, symbolically optimistic, running through the Wall.

The bar changed ownership and became known as the Elsner Treff.

On November 9, 1989, the Wall fell. Work teams arrived and demolished it. Kevin's and Adem's footnotes to history vanished in clouds of dust, and the regulars at the Elsner Treff were given back their unimpeded view of the apartment house forty yards away.

The bar changed owners again, and became known as the Sweigel. There is no longer a Soviet sector and there is no longer an American sector. Heidelberger Strasse has been restored to its full width. A thin metal plate set into a double line of cobblestones in the road traces the line of the Wall.

On Elsen, a steel plaque records the death of Heinz Jercha. The death strip behind the Wall is now a wasteland of knee-high Bermuda grass and white cardamine flowers. It looks as innocuous as an uncultivated back garden.

It is as if nothing much had ever happened at the corner of Elsen Strasse and Heidelberger Strasse.

NOTES

1. For an account of events outside the Heidelberger Krug on the night of August 12-13, 1961, see *Riss Durch Berlin—Der 13. August 1961*, by Curtis Cate, (Hamburg: Albert Knaus Verlag, 1980), 146. The book originally appeared in English as *The Ides of August*, (London: Weidenfeld & Nicholson, 1978).

2. "I was fired up...," Peter Wuestenhagen quoted by Peter Brock and Elmar Schuetze in "Acht Tage spaeter wurde da einer erschossen: Peter Wuestenhagen robbte 1962 von Treptow in den Westen," *Berliner Zeitung*, November 8, 2004.

3. "Twenty minutes after...," Bernd Kolberg quoted by Elmar Schuetze in "Der Holzhacker aus dem Keller," *Berliner Zeitung*, November 16, 2004.

24

GARTENSCHLAEGER'S PRIVATE WAR

IT WAS NO PLACE TO BE IN THE middle of the night, this dark Sahara of heathland and opaque forests where the slightest sound raced away to the moon. Nothing here except the faint filigree gleam of a wire-mesh palisade emerging out of the nothingness.

The three men were alone; or just maybe they weren't.

Gartenschlaeger stood by the open car trunk, checked the 7.65mm Espana Star pistol in his pocket, took a can of boot polish, blackened his face and hands, and passed the can to the other two. He took out a shotgun and tossed it to Uebe, who caught it uncertainly and held it as if it were a dead cat. Suddenly, this adventure was not what he had imagined.

Lienicke checked his own 7.65mm Bernadelli pistol and told Uebe, "Don't worry. You won't need it."

Gartenschlaeger slurped down a coca-cola, threw the empty bottle into the trunk, and slammed the trunk door with a detonation that must have been heard for miles.

"Idiot!" hissed Lienicke. He clenched his teeth to stop them chattering.

They marched along the forest path until they found a ladder they had hidden in the forest. Gartenschlaeger suddenly stopped and vomited.

It was 10:30 p.m. when they reached the forest edge, forty yards from the silvery fence. The last forty yards of the Western world. From somewhere, a metallic crash sounded.

"Hear that!" said Lienicke in a loud whisper.

Gartenschlaeger did not answer.

Uebe said, "I heard it!"

"You're both bullshitting," said Gartenschlaeger. "Maybe a fat crow landed on top of the fence."

On other nights, a light had shone at this part of the border. Tonight it wasn't, Lienicke noticed. Something was wrong.

The unrelenting gloom of the Stalinist state drove people to dream, especially the young. Building socialism was okay, but only between Monday and Friday. The weekend was the time for action, when the dazzling lights of the West of the city beckoned like a temptress promising the forbidden. If this was capitalist exploitation, a couple of days couldn't hurt.

For Michael Gartenschlaeger, seventeen, and Gerd-Peter Riedige, eighteen, the stairway to the stars was lined by luminaries like James Dean, Elvis Presley, and a German Elvis imitator, Ted Herold. The youths delved in West Berlin's record stores, and slumped in movie theaters, and they read *Bravo*, a Western music publication condemned in the East as subversive.

Back in East Berlin, the two joined forces with Gerd Resag, Karl-Heinz Lehmann and Juergen Hoepfner to set up a dream factory, the "Ted Herold Fan Club." The club was not much to look at, just a wooden shack and a rickety door. The five sat round staring at *Bravo* posters on the walls, guzzling beer, identifying with James Dean's *Rebel Without a Cause*, listening to Ted Herold gargling up and down the scales, and wishing they were living someplace else.

The club violated Ulbricht's rules simply by existing. In a society obsessed with conformity, leisure activity was controlled through obeisant party organizations such as the FDJ mass youth movement. Individualism was frowned on. The Ted Herold Fan Club teetered at the edge of the precipice.

It plummeted over the side in 1960.

The fault was Gartenchlaeger's. When he placed a small advertisement in *Bravo* telling the world that East Germany had its very own Ted Herold Fan Club, Herold fans in the West swamped him with mail. Informers told the police, the police visited the club and closed it for being "under negative Western influences."

One hot summer's Saturday morning in August 1961, Gartenchlaeger and Riedige pedaled their bicycles to the local S-Bahn train station, and rode to the West to take in a few hours of exploitation.

This day, an unusually high number of people were doing the same thing, and many were being turned back. As the two wandered the streets of West Berlin, alternately biking and walking, East German party boss Walter Ulbricht was ordering changes that would change their lives.

When they returned to the sector border at Clara-Zetkin-Strasse at nearly 10:00 that evening, the usually quiet check point was buzzing with activity. Uniformed officers lined the Eastern side, closely checking people lining up to go to the West. Gartenschlaeger and Riedige were uncertain. If they had known Ulbricht had ordered "security measures," they might have remained in the West. Instead, they pushed through the crowd and re-entered East Berlin.

When they woke up the next day, Sunday, August 13, the border between the two halves of the city was closed. "Security measures" were socialist speak for the building of the Berlin Wall. The escape hatch was shut. No more James Dean, no more Elvis Presley, no more Ted Herold, no more *Bravo*.

The dejected five sang the mournful "Hang down your head, Tom Dooley /Hang down your head and cry." Dejection turned to anger. They smeared a wall of a housing block with paint. They painted signs on shed doors and walls, saying "Open the Gate" and "Free Elections." They set fire to a shack.

The Stasi arrested them and charged them with forming "a counterrevolutionary group." The prosecutor called for the death penalty for Gartenschlaeger and Resag, but revised this to life imprisonment because of their age.[1]

A commentator for a state-controlled newspaper, wrote, "The case showed me with terrible clarity, how craftily the West German madmen, the warmongers of NATO and their cronies, spread their net that caught, among others, these accused."[2]

Resag and Gartenschlaeger were sentenced to life, while the others got between six and fifteen years.

In June 1971, after serving almost ten years, the West German government paid 40,000 West marks each for Gartenschlaeger and Resag under a prisoner buyout program[3] and they were free. Both went to Hamburg. Gartenschlaeger teamed up with another East German he had met in jail, Lothar Lienicke.

Smuggling people out of the East developed into an art form. Escape groups never stopped dreaming up ingenious ideas, and Gartenschlaeger saw it as his duty to smuggle out as many people as he could.

On the afternoon of December 24, 1972, he and Lienicke set off from Hamburg along the transit route to Berlin driving separate cars. They crossed into East Germany as light snow fell. Close to 5:00 p.m. they pulled up outside a restaurant near the village of Quitzow, where a group of other travelers, Westerners from their dress and demeanor, drank coffee. One man sat alone: Gartenschlaeger established brief eye contact with him. This was their man, Peter Fuchs.

Lienicke badly wanted a drink to calm his nerves, but, thinking of East Germany's absolute ban on drinking and driving, settled for a cigarette. Outside, snowflakes drifted silently around a dull street light.

The other Westerners moved to leave. Gartenschlaeger and Lienicke took their cue, and rose as well. Fuchs walked out with them all into the falling snow. Any observer waiting outside would have simply seen a group of people, heads pulled down away from the snow, emerge from the restaurant and disperse into a number of cars.

Fuchs climbed into Gartenchlaeger's car. Lienicke and Gartenschlaeger drove for some time before halting and adjusting the distributor of one car to disable the motor. Fuchs then climbed into a gap prepared behind the back seat of the other car, and hid himself. Lienicke, with Fuchs secreted behind him, towed Gartenschlaeger in the second, disabled, car. Gartenschlaeger believed no border guard would suspect a fugitive of trying to escape in a slow-moving vehicle towing a broken-down car.

They slowly drove the remaining twelve miles to the West Berlin border. The cars pulled in at the checkpoint and Lienicke switched off the motor and wound down his window. The strains of "Silent Night. Holy Night" came from somewhere behind—there were some things even the atheist state could not change. The duty guard, buoyed by the Christmas spirit, commiserated with Lienicke at the fix he was in. He gave the papers of the two drivers a cursory examination, and waved them through. Lienicke, hands shaking, stalled the motor twice before he drove off.

When the two cars stopped at a secluded parking spot on the Western side of the border. Fuchs emerged warily from under a blanket, refusing to believe they were in the West. Then he saw an advertisement for Coca-Cola.

The three of them danced in the falling snow like kids at a party.[4]

In 1973 Gartenschlaeger and Lienicke broadened the focus of escapes to the East Bloc, often using Turkey as a conduit. Gartenschlaeger seemed completely without fear and ratcheted up the level of risk. One on occasion when arrested at the Romanian border as he tried to take a refugee into Yugoslavia, he stepped on the gas and crashed the vehicle through the barriers. He was arrested in Yugoslavia and jailed but he escaped with the help of a guard and reached Austria.[5]

Gartenschlaeger and Lienicke jointly helped thirty-one people escape on various routes, but they knew the Stasi was on to them.

In its obsession with stopping refugees, the regime began installing a nasty piece of equipment, self-shooting devices, known as SM-70s, along the border in 1971. The SM-70 was developed by the Nazis, and refinements were added by East German scientists. The weapon was used along about 240 miles of border, where it was fixed at heights of eighteen inches, four and a half feet, and twelve feet from the ground and set ten yards apart on the metal mesh fence. It consisted a cone-shaped barrel with a charge of 100 grams of TNT placed behind a payload of ninety 4mm steel projectiles designed to tear a human body to shreds. After operating on one victim, a surgeon remarked on the difficulty of sewing up the shredded remains of deep-seated blood vessels.[6]

The detonator was electric powered and was set off when a detonation cable secured to the fence was disturbed. By 1976, 26,000 of them had been installed. Their installation had continued despite the Helsinki Final Act in 1975, an international human-rights treaty that East Germany signed along with thirty-four other countries. But East Berlin didn't give a hoot for obligations. When East German foreign minister Oskar Fischer was confronted in 1976 with the evidence of self-shooting devices, he dismissed it by saying the devices were "dummies designed to deter."[7]

Gartenschlaeger knew this was hogwash. He was determined to act. He took to going close to the border fence, hiding in long grass, and using field glasses to observe teams install, remove, and maintain the devices. But watching wasn't enough. He needed to go a step further.

Then a crazy idea hit him. He would steal one.

He discovered they were screwed to the fence on the Western side, which made access easier. But the cables were a problem. He had to decide which was the detonator cable and which carried electricity. He found the devices were mounted in threes, and all three had to be decommissioned at the same time. The wires had to be cut in the correct order. The detonator could be unscrewed.

Just after midnight on March 28, 1976, a cloudy but dry night, he and Lienicke drove to the border in Gartenschlaeger's BMW car. Lienicke gave cover as Gartenchlaeger crept to the fence and, using a system of hooks and wires, detonated one device. The blast was massive. Lights came on in observation tower a few hundred yards away, but there was no immediate reaction. Neither Gartenschlaeger nor Lienicke knew at this time that about 1,000 accidental detonations a year were caused by wild animals, technical faults, or lightning, so a mere explosion did not necessarily arouse guards' suspicions. Instead, on this occasion, a Trabant car drove slowly past some hours later, and a work team arrived about 8:00 a.m. to replace the device.

The same night, the 28th, both men returned to observe any changes. The next day, on the night of the 29th, both men plus a third person, Jochen Stener, returned to the same area about one and a half miles further north, at a point where the fence took a right-angled turn, at border post 231. It was almost midnight as they moved through drifting patches of fog to the fence. Gartenschlaeger climbed a ladder as the other two took up sentry positions behind him. He worked swiftly and surely and, after a few minutes, triumphantly held an arm aloft in the night sky. His hand held a trophy—a dismantled SM-70. If the operation was a feat requiring some educated guesswork and the nerves to carry it out, Gartenschlaeger showed even more mettle by getting the others to photograph him. He then deliberately made a noise in the hope of attracting the guards, so he could photograph them as well. But none came.

In April he dismantled another device. The BND West German espionage agency first accused him of the theft, and then offered to pay him if he would give it to them. He refused. Instead he went to *Der Spiegel* newsmagazine, which published the story.[8]

Lothar Lienicke has the sparse face and the lean bearing of a combat colonel. I caught up with him the former Stasi headquarters in the city of Magdeburg, where he had come with Franz Bludau to read excerpts from their book about Gartenschlaeger, *Todesautomatik* (The Death Machine). Over the years, Lienicke has thought about little else, and both men spent years digging into files and fighting bureaucratic obstinacy to get to the truth.

The moment everyone had been waiting for arrived. Bludau rose to his feet and held up a piece of apparatus that resembled an innocuous agricultural implement, a couple of feet long, painted green, and consisting of a cone-shaped funnel attached to a metal bar. This was Gartenschlaeger's nasty little trophy, the body shredder officially known as the SM-70.

As Lienicke's mind went back to that night of April 30 1976 under the full moon with Gartenschlaeger and Uebe, his face took on an aura of grim reflection; the colonel recollecting a suicidal combat mission.

The night of April 30 was cool with a full moon as Gartenschlaeger, Lienicke and another former East German prisoner, Wolf-Dieter Uebe, set off for the border to dismantle a third SM-70. Uebe had come in at the last minute and was not fully aware of Gartenschlaeger's intentions. They parked the car near close to a forest track that would take them to the border fence. In the moonshine the trees lining the path shone a dull crystalline.

As they reached the fence, Lienicke saw that a light that had been burning the last time they were here was no longer burning. He and Uebe sensed something was wrong and said so. For once, the headstrong Gartenschlaeger gave in.

But, as they walked back through the forest toward the car, Gartenschlaeger kept muttering like a spoiled child denied a toy. He said, "I'm going to detonate one of them things. It'll be quick. I want to let 'em know I was here. Either you both come, or I do it alone."

He wanted to go to the corner, to border post 231.

"There's a light there. I won't have to fiddle around so much."

Lienicke felt a line of ants creeping across his skin.

They reached border post 231 at a quarter to twelve.

All was quiet.

Lienicke and Uebe took up lookout positions forty yards apart. Gartenschlaeger tapped Lienicke on the chest, turned, crept across the shaven turf, and vanished. Lienicke clenched his jaw to stop his teeth chattering. He had the sudden feeling the three of them were not alone.

In that instant, the dark sky exploded into light with a sound like a million thunderclaps, and he saw Gartenschlaeger silhouetted sharply against the brightness. Lienicke thought Gartenschlaeger had detonated three or four devices at once.

But then he knew the noise was gunfire.

Gartenschlaeger was dead.

Lienicke, Bludau and I adjourned to the bar of the InterCity Hotel, and I asked Lienicke why he and Gartenschlaeger had persisted in returning to the same part of the border in an apparently senseless act.

"He was stubborn. Michael wanted to let the East Germans know it was him, and not anyone else. He wanted there to be no misunderstandings about that."

After the trauma of that night, Lienicke threw himself into discovering the full story behind the ambush and, as part of his plan, allowed himself to be recruited as a spy for both East German and West German intelligence agencies. As a double agent, he led both side on a merry chase.[9]

Lienicke and Bludau discovered that, on the fatal night, the three men had walked into a trap. The Stasi minister himself, Erich Mielke, had ordered Gartenschlaeger's liquidation. An East German unit using night-vision equipment had been lying in wait, and knew every move he made.[10]

The West German BSG border force had made it easy for the Stasi. It knew Gartenschlaeger was active in the area at night, had discussed his movements by radio, and must have known that the Stasi might have picked up uncoded discussions. They had.[11] Two other aces were in the Stasi's hand—information from planted informers, as well as Gartenschlaeger's own mule-headedness.

East German tiny minded vindictiveness knew no bounds.

Gartenschlaeger was buried as "an unidentified water corpse."

In 1999, three former border guards came for trial on charges linked with the death. The guards claimed Gartenschlaeger had shot first and they had acted in self-defense, in spite of a lack of forensic evidence for the claim. East German records reveal that no traces of smoke had been found on Gartenschlaeger's hands, as would be expected if he had pulled the trigger. A total of 120 shots was fired at Gartenschlaeger. The defense claim that a word used in Mielke's orders to "liquidate" Gartenschlaeger did not mean "to kill" but something less, defies belief. But the court believed the evidence was insufficient and dismissed the charges.[12]

NOTES

1. Call for death penalty related in *Todesautomatik*, by Lothar Lienicke and Franz Bludau, (Kiel: Stamp Media, 2001), 51. One of Germany's major publishers, Fischer Verlag, subsequently issued a paperback edition. A television documentary about Gartenschlaeger's life and death, *Gegen die Grenze*, by Alex Dittner and Ben Kempas, was produced for Rundfunk Berlin-Brandenburg in 2004. Lienicke and Bludau were advisers.

2. "The case...," Otto Pfeiffer in "Vom RIAS-Hoerer und Herold-Fan zum Staatsverbrecher, " in *Deutsche Lehrerzeitung*, September 9, 1961.

3. For account of prisoner buyout program see Chapter 17—The People Trade.

4. Account of escape in Lienicke and Bludau, 127.

5. Lienicke and Bludau, 135.

6. According to Rainer Hildebrandt, founder of the Museum at Checkpoint Charlie, the surgeon, Werner Stoll, wrote after unsuccessfully trying to save the life of one victim, "The blood vessels deep in the left thigh...had been so mutilated by the irregularly shaped, sharp-edged and jagged shrapnel from the device—they can be compared with dum-dum shells or even worse—that they were extremely difficult to sew." See Lienicke and Bludau, 7.

7. "...dummies designed to deter...," Fischer quoted at a press conference in Helsinki in 1976, in Lienicke and Bludau, 151.

8. Accounts of the SM-70 in "Schnell das Ding vom Zaun," *Der Spiegel*, April 12, 1976; "Toedliche Wuerfel," *Der Spiegel*, April 26, 1976; and "Verrechnet! Bursche!", *Der Spiegel*, May 17, 1976.

9. An account of his sometimes amusing and often confusing activities which left neither secret service knowing what he was up to is related in "Spiel mit heissen Eisen," *Der Spiegel*, April 24, 1995, and in Lienicke and Bludau, 297.

10. The East German order to kill was elaborated in a secret border unit document, CVS-Nr.: G/400678, dated June 4, 1976.

11. East German documents published in Lienicke and Bludau (201-203) reveal an unbelievable disregard for radio security by the BSG.

12. The court cases are dealt with at length in Lienicke and Bludau, 301. The West German Bundestag (parliament) discussed Gartenschlaeger's death on May 5. See "Verhandlung des Deutschen Bundestages, 7. Wahlperiode, Stenographische Bericht, Band 98, 16,577-16,584." Stasi documents show that a special operation was mounted to kill Gartenschlaeger. See a communication dated April 26, 1976 and written by Oberstleutnant Heckel and signed by Generalleutnant Kleinjung, head of Hauptabteilung I, responsible for border forces and border defenses; and a document dated June 4, 1976, after the killing, (GVS-Nr.: G/400678) which refers to Order 32/76 issued on May 3 1976 by both Mielke's deputy and the head of the border troops that any "Provokateure" making "attacks on border security installations" "will be liquidated." Copies of all are in the hands of the author. Dismantling of the SM-70s began in 1983 after a line of credit was made available to East Berlin. See Chapter 19—From Marauder to Merchant.

25

THE SERGEANT AND THE SINGER

HIGH UP THE SLOPES, LIGHT SUMMER breezes brushed tall fir trees. Down below, in the Bavarian town of Kipfenberg, Conrad Schumann and his family sat in their garden on this June day in 1998. As the shadows slowly lengthened across the lawn, everyone went indoors except Conrad. Shortly afterwards, his body was found hanging from a tree in the garden. There were no suspicious circumstances. Personal problems were said to be the reason for his suicide. Schumann was fifty-six.

A tousle-haired twenty-year-old arrived in New York on January 24, 1961, and, guitar slung over one shoulder, trudged through the flurries of snow to a café in Greenwich Village. Soon, the café resounded to the drawl of a new voice in entertainment. On the other side of the world at a camp at Potsdam, near Berlin, a nineteen-year-old policeman was being drilled that icy winter for promotion to *Unteroffizier* (sergeant) in the East German Interior Ministry police—the force used to smash civil unrest.

Both men were protesters in their own different ways. The folk singer's talent was immediately obvious. In July, he took part in a twelve-hour marathon radio broadcast from the Riverside Church in Manhattan.

In August, the police transferred the sergeant to East Berlin for a special operation. He was relaxing in his barracks on a sultry late summer Saturday night, August 12, when the camp siren wailed. The men tumbled outside, fumbling with buttons, and scrambled aboard trucks. They had no idea where they were being taken to or why. They arrived at the city center and saw that the Soviet sector border was lined with rolls of barbed wire. The sergeant was posted to Bernauer Strasse at a point near Arkonaplatz, where his job was to stop people leaping the knee-high wire and fleeing to the West.

Dawn revealed the awful truth. The entire Soviet sector was cut off by *Volksarmee* soldiers and *Grepos*, border police. Work teams arrived by truck and threw off more barbed wire. Berlin was physically divided. Guards used mirrors to dazzle photographers and cameramen who had rushed to the scene on the Western side.

Panic and anger took hold, as families and friends were separated by the wire and patrolling soldiers. Thousands of East Berliners went to Friedrich Strasse station in an attempt to reach West Berlin, but black-uniformed transport police had surrounded the station. American radio reporter Robert Lochner recalled "a timid old woman with the typical pitiful cardboard box with probably all her belongings" asking a policeman about the next train to the West. "Sneeringly, he answered, 'None of that any more, grandma. You're all caught in a mousetrap'. "[1] On the Monday, the 60,000 Easterners and 10,000 Westerners who traveled to work on the other side could only look on.

On Tuesday, August 15, construction teams began building the Wall proper. Little girls presented posies of flowers to guards. In streets where buildings formed the sector border, bricklayers sealed off West-facing doors and windows. The chatter of pneumatic drills gouging holes for fence posts echoed off the tall, brick buildings. The public mood swung between anger and anxiety. Loudspeaker trucks on both sides blasted out grating propaganda.

Twenty-eight years and eighty-eight days later, a West Berliner leaning out of his ground-floor balcony in Bernauer Strasse at a point near Arkonaplatz watched East Germans marching out through a break in the Wall. He told me what he had seen all those years ago from that same ground-floor window: a border guard just a few yards away on the other side of the barbed-wire entanglements becoming increasing fidgety as the afternoon wore on. Other people on the Western side had also noticed a chain-smoking guard whose body language indicated he was unsettled. Word spread. Press photographers arrived. One was an agency photographer, Peter Leibing.

About 4:00 p.m. Conrad Schumann, the newly promoted sergeant from Potsdam, suddenly sprinted toward the wire, threw away his rifle, and leapt. Shutters clicked. Leibing's photograph froze Schumann in full flight, and that is how readers all round the noncommunist world saw him on newspaper front pages the next day.

A few weeks later, the *New York Times* published an article by Robert Shelton that praised "a bright new face in folk music...it matters less where he has been than where he is going, and that would seem to be straight up."[2] And so he was. Bob Dylan was on his way to becoming a household name.

Then Dylan himself went East. But whereas Schumann left in a blaze of publicity, Dylan's entry was surreptitious. A flourishing underground market always existed in the East for items in short supply. Western popular music was always in demand but it was banned. So the black market met some of the demand. Banned records were played throughout East Germany and the rest of the Soviet empire: Bob Dylan, the Beatles and the Rolling Stones built up a huge illicit audience behind the iron curtain.

Schumann went to live in the southern state of Bavaria under an assumed name and, although the photograph of his leap was often published, few people knew his real identity. He never found peace of mind and was haunted by the thought that secret police assassination squads would hunt him down and kill him. That had happened to others. Manfred Smolka, a border guard lieutenant who fled, was kidnapped in 1959, taken back across the border, convicted of spying and executed by guillotine.

For twenty-eight years, Schumann was unable to visit his parents near Dresden. Then the Wall came down, East Germany collapsed, and he did return, and discovered that, even after all that time, some of his former police colleagues resented him because of his escape. The pressure must have continued to build, driving Schumann to kill himself.

In their different ways, both Dylan and Schumann captured the spirit of the age. Schumann was an instant hero, the man who at the height of the Cold War thumbed his nose at the tyranny of communism with a single crazy act of bravado. It struck a chord worldwide at a time when a cold anger burned at the sheer madness of the Wall. Yet, he was quickly forgotten. By contrast, the popularity of Dylan's music not only did not wane, it was like a finger-wagging memorandum to the communist leaders. Forty years later, Dylan's lyrics are still big sellers.

NOTES

1. "A timid old woman…," Lochner in an interview with the CNN television network, in a Perspectives Series entitled "Cold War, Episode 9: The Wall—Teaching JFK German—President's Interpreter Remembers Murrow visit, famous 'Berliner' speech." (An online series: http://cnn.com/SPECIALS/cold.war/EPISODES/09/reflections/.)

2. See Robert Shelton in "Bob Dylan: A Distinctive Stylist," the *New York Times*, September 29, 1961.

26

GORBACHEV GIVES HIS ANSWER

"Mr. Gorbachev, tear down this wall!" —United States President
Ronald Reagan, at the Berlin Wall, June 12, 1987

MICHAEL SOBOTTA AND ANDREAS SCHULZ were both caught up in the
blast furnace of the revolution as events spun out of control. People knew
from the West German media that reforms were taking place under Mikhail
Gorbachev in the Soviet Union. They wanted change in East Germany as well,
or they wanted out.

Sobotta, a stocky man with the gruff friendliness an up-country stock-
man, these days travels the greater Dresden region installing heating systems.
His cell phone is seldom silent. It rang constantly as he took me down memory lane, along the route he marched with the demonstrators in 1989.

We ended the tour at a café in the broad concrete Prager Strasse,
where the worst riots of the East German revolution took place. We were
joined by the athletic figure of Schulz. Tall and straight-backed, Schulz
was once an East German sports star, a member of the coxed fours that
won the silver rowing medal at the summer Olympic Games in Montreal in
1976. The Soviet boat finished 2.48 seconds faster to win the gold. Third
were the West Germans.

The escape hatch slipped open in May 1989 when Hungary removed the
barbed wire from the fence along its border with Austria. East Germans went
to Hungary "on holiday" in the hope of getting to Austria. Hungarian border
guards looked the other way as little groups slipped across the border. Hundreds more East Germans took refuge in West German diplomatic missions
in Prague, Budapest, and Warsaw in the hope of being given free passage out.

Back on the streets of East Germany itself, demonstrators were becoming more audacious.

In August, the government of Solidarity activist Tadeusz Mazowiecki took office in Poland and allowed refugees to stay with sympathetic residents in and around Warsaw. Then 150 East Germans occupied the grounds of the West German embassy in Budapest. On August 8, the West German permanent diplomatic representation in East Berlin closed its doors because of crowds pushing to get in. On August 13, its embassy in Budapest did the same. On August 19, a gate in the fence separating Austria and Hungary was opened for a few hours as a symbolic gesture to allow people living close to the border on either side to visit each other. Hundreds of East Germans walked across to Austria. The Hungarian guards did nothing.

The Politburo under Honecker was paralyzed. Insiders said later that the exodus was hardly talked about. "The silence became agonizing…" one Politburo member, Guenter Schabowski, recalled.[1]

On August 22 the West German embassy in Prague closed its gates because of overcrowding—140 Easterners were inside the grounds. That did not stop people coming. Television pictures of babies being passed over the high wrought-iron fence into the compound were shown round the world. Easterners saw the scenes on Western television. On August 24, the Hungarians again shrugged their shoulders as 108 refugees left the embassy grounds in Budapest and traveled via Vienna to West Germany. Over the month, about 3,000 used this route to reach the West.

Among those in the Prague embassy grounds were Andreas Schulz and his wife, Gabriele. They had driven to Czechoslovakia for a holiday with no intention of staying, but changed their mind, abandoned their car, walked to the embassy, and climbed over the iron railings. Inside the grounds, there was still room to move about. But within a few days, even the broad stairs inside the embassy itself had become makeshift sleeping quarters. More than 1,000 had now taken refuge in the grounds. Some were accommodated in tents. Lines for bathrooms became longer, and the levels of hygiene declined dramatically. Rain turned the grounds to sludge.

In Hungary, refugee tent cities sprang up.

The escape hatch became a gaping hole in the early hours of September 11, when Hungary again opened the barrier at the Austrian border and this time left it open. Within three days, 15,000 people had poured through to Austria. East Germany bitterly criticized Hungary with the *ADN* news agency blaming it for assisting a "trade in humans."

Not everybody was leaving for the same reason. Tommy, a motor mechanic near Leipzig who had spent all his working life repairing Trabants and Wartburgs, one day had the chance to drive a Mercedes belonging to a Western visitor. Tommy had never ridden in a Mercedes, let alone driven one. The effect was electric. If this was the West, he wanted more of it. Tommy sold his possessions, took his money and flew to Budapest. He took a taxi to the border. There was a tense moment when a border guard with a Kalashnikov approached the car, but the guard just pulled open the big gate, the taxi went through into Austria, and Tommy was out.[2]

Hungary was in a dilemma. It wanted to keep its agreements with its fellow socialist countries by refusing exit to people not holding proper permits but it also wanted to normalize relations with the capitalist countries of Western Europe. Its government was divided between liberals and conservatives, and the West was tightening the screws. President George Bush visited in June. He offered dollars and trade preferences. The liberals won the day. Hungary's foreign minister was Gyula Horn, a progressive communist who saw what others like him throughout the East Bloc had also seen—that the communist system was leading to ruin. Changes were needed. A key to the new order was links with the West, and that meant, in the first instance, West Germany.[3]

In East Berlin the party persisted in avoiding the issue. Schabowski described its sessions as being like a theater of the absurd. "While the people were leaving, we practiced the art of social projections. For example, we decided how we would honour the pioneer achievements of (aviator) Otto Lilienthal in (the town of) Anklam in 1991."[4]

The mood simmered on the nation's ramshackle streets. The biggest turnouts were in the two southern cities of Leipzig and Dresden. In Dresden, protesters turned up at the eighteenth-century Kreuzkirche. They came by car and train and carried candles and chanted "no violence." The huge human column jammed the streets as it went on a two-mile circuit past the city's great buildings, the baroque splendor of the Glockenspiel Pavilion, the high-renaissance Semper Opera House, the Kathedrale, across the River Elbe over the Augustus Bridge and back over the Carolina Bridge. And when the marchers saw residents looking down from apartment windows lining the route, the refrain went up, "Away from the window, down on to the streets. Join in."

The sheer weight of numbers must have terrified the police. Controlling a crowd of thousands was a job for the army. The march passed the police station with a crescendo of whistling and catcalls. The windows were shut tight and in darkness and some marchers placed candles on the building's window ledges. Among the marchers every week was Michael Sobotta, who worked in his father's saxophone reed works in Freital, west of the city.

West German foreign minister, Hans-Dietrich Genscher, himself raised in the Eastern city of Halle, discussed the crisis with Soviet foreign minister Eduard Shevardnadze, who was worried about the high number of children in the camps. In New York on September 27 Genscher negotiated with East German foreign minister Oskar Fischer and they agreed that about 6,800 refugees from the embassies in Prague and Warsaw would be taken to the West by train. The trains would be from the East German Reichsbahn and would travel across East Germany so it could be claimed that the refugees were being expelled for "betraying their homeland." As if anybody would believe that.

Genscher flew to Prague on September 30, where by now 5,000 people had crammed into the embassy. By the time he appeared on the embassy balcony high above the dense sea of refugees waiting expectantly, it was dark and it was difficult to pick him out in the weak lighting. His voice boomed over the loudspeaker, "I have to tell you that your exit…"

He didn't get the sentence finished. The roar that erupted was like a football crowd's.[5]

Genscher later recalled:

This was the hour when I realised…this is the end of East Germany. This is fundamentally the collapse of East Germany from inside and from below. The end of the (Berlin) Wall comes into sight.[6]

The first of the trains packed with refugees passed through Dresden early on the morning of October 1 with little incident. Then the atmosphere deteriorated sharply. With less than a week before the nation was to celebrate its fortieth birthday, the worst violence since the workers' revolt of 1953 broke out in the city. Rumors swept the country that the Czech border was to be closed, and crowds swarmed to the Hauptbahnhof hoping to get to Prague by rail or to jump on the refugee trains as they passed through to the West. Elsewhere the mood was also getting nastier: on October 2, not far away in Leipzig, police baton-charged 25,000 demonstrators in the city center.

Tuesday, October 3, dawned darkly as a thunderstorm lashed the Dresden region. The weather cleared and thousands turned up again at the Hauptbahnhof. After being prevented from entering Czechoslovakia they were angry. They threw bottles at police. Dresden's mayor, Wolfgang Berghofer, spoke late that afternoon to a local party official and was told that "because of the complicated nature of the situation," Dresden party boss Hans Modrow had "assumed control of all measures to maintain order and security." The official told Berghofer bluntly that he should "keep out of it" and instead make preparations for the birthday party.[7] Shortly before 10:00 p.m., when an empty train heading for Prague to pick up refugees pulled in at platform 5, the crowd surged towards it, stampeding past security forces. Fists flew and truncheons flailed, and the battle went on until the early hours.

The next day, Wednesday, police and troop reinforcements were brought in. By around 8:00 p.m., 2,500 people had pushed their way into the Hauptbahnhof concourse, and the security forces sealed off the platform area. Michael Sobotta was at home in Freital, west of Dresden, when word of what was happening reached him. He went to Freital station to catch the train to Dresden but no trains were running. Neither could he find a taxi. He was given a ride in a private car. It was a clear night, but cold, and Sobotta wore his thick leather flying jacket, something he was later thankful for.

Outside the Dresden Hauptbahnhof, the crowd continued to build up, and, when the anger spilled over, the phalanx surged toward the station concourse. A wedge of protesters broke away, overturned a police patrol car and set it alight. Riot police advanced behind their shields, the front line crouched, the second line standing, white helmets gleaming in the weak station lighting. High above, a huge illuminated sign across the arched station window advertised Radeberger beer. Stones torn from the cobbled streets and thrown at the advancing riot squad bounced off the shields, and then the high-pressure water cannon opened up.

Sobotta was let off in Dresden shortly before 10:00 p.m. He joined the crowd making its way along Prager Strasse toward the stone-and-steel Hauptbahnhof. Ahead of him blue lights flashed and staccato voices barked from loudhailers. An overturned car burned. Police, riot squad and Stasi special units were deployed in tight circles so no one could get either in or out of the station. Cobblestones crashed on riot shields. The pushing and shoving and the noise increased the nearer the station they got. In the distance, the chant of "Gorby! Gorby!" and "We're staying here!" rose above the tumult. A policeman yelled at Sobotta: "What are you doing?"

"I want to go home on the train."

"Take a taxi!"

"I can't get to the taxi stand."

Someone pushed Sobotta's head forward and pinioned his arms behind him, and he was forced toward the station. Truncheon blows crunched down on his neck and back and legs, but his flying jacket absorbed much of the force. The ground was wet with water from the cannon. An icy jet of water struck him. Then he was inside the station, in a badly lit, dark-gray, chipped corridor where police dogs growled. People lay on the ground. Some were bleeding. Others stood facing the wall, arms raised, legs spread. Sobotta was pushed to a wall and ordered not to move, not to speak. He was searched and his belongings removed. About 11.30 p.m. he was put on to a truck and taken away to police barracks at the Kurt Fischer Allee where the prisoners were made to stand in rows with hands behind heads.

One riot squad conscript later recalled his feelings as his unit moved toward the advancing crowd that Wednesday night,

> We felt only fear. Stones rattled off our shields. In front of us, Molotov cocktails and acid bottles clattered onto the asphalt. Two of our men collapsed. The stones had smashed their visors...our officers, the police, and the Stasi remained a safe distance away...I felt for the first and only time in my life the fear of death...Behind us the officers and in front of us this infuriated mass of humanity...What we in the middle did, we did out of fear and simply out of a will to survive...I ask you for one thing: pray for me and forgive me, if you can.[8]

Shortly after midnight, the second of the refugee trains from Prague approached Dresden Hauptbahnhof. On board were Andreas and Gabriele Schulz, unaware of the drama taking place just yards away. Inside the station, five thousand people ran through the station toward the platform. The train slowed but did not stop and the centrally locked doors prevented anyone from climbing aboard.

By the early hours, fire, missiles, and water cannon had reduced the station to a saturated shell of smashed windows and broken glass overhung with the stench of burnt rubber and plastic. At the Kurt Fischer Allee barracks,

Sobotta was still standing with his hands behind his head as, hour after hour, trucks continued to arrive from the Hauptbahnhof, bringing in more prisoners.

On Thursday October 5, Andreas and Gabriele Schulz arrived in the West to a welcome of brass band music, a sausage, and a plate of soup. At the Fischer barracks, Sobotta still had not been allowed to use a telephone. He was taken and questioned. In the evening, the nightly battle at the Hauptbahnhof resumed, and the trucks resumed their shuttle run, bringing more arrested protesters.

At 2 a.m. on Friday, October 6, some twenty-eight hours after being pulled in, Sobotta was shoved out the door of the barracks on to the street. He stood in the dark, alone, and he felt a raw hatred.[9]

Friday, October 6: Soviet president Mikhail Gorbachev came to town for the state's fortieth birthday party. He swept into Berlin from Schoenefeld airport in a motorcade of stretched black limousines past crowds calling "Gorby! Gorby!" Throughout the country, the pressure from below was increasing.

The confidence of the protesters was directly linked to Gorbachev. On Saturday, the day of the birthday party, Honecker and Gorbachev stood on the rostrum as dutiful crowds lined up beneath massive red banners and waved red flags as troops goose-stepped past them.

Honecker admitted to Gorbachev his country did have difficulties but said they had been brought in from outside, recalls Soviet diplomat Valentin Falin. Gorbachev told Honecker, "He who hesitates is lost." Gorbachev added, "However, you are a sovereign state. The SED is an independent party, and you will decide yourself what now happens."[10]

In the Alexanderplatz, the atmosphere was relaxed during the afternoon, as people braved intermittent showers and ate barbecued spare ribs at birthday party stalls. The sea change came as the crowd swelled. By 5:30 p.m., the crowd was heading toward the Palast der Republik where Honecker, Gorbachev & Company were gathering. An array of East Bloc guests were listening to Honecker speak as, just a few yards away outside, international television teams filmed the protesters. The Stasi held back. For a while.

Night fell. Stasi plainclothes men moved in. At first they acted in sudden nervous outbursts, isolating single demonstrators, applying half-Nelsons, and marching them off like troublemakers at a football match. As scuffles broke out and more arrests were made, the concerted cries came louder and louder: "Stasi raus! Stasi raus!" ("Stasi out! Stasi out!") The catcalls and whistling were steady, drawn out. More scuffles and the calls of "Gorby! Gorby!" floated up to the guests behind the glass.

Mikhail and Raisa Gorbachev were seated next to Erich and Margot Honecker at the main table in the banquet hall. Honecker delivered his birthday address, saying, "Our friends in all the world can remain reassured that socialism on German soil, in the home of Marx and Engels, remains on unshakable foundations." Gorbachev was grim-faced.

On the streets around the Palast der Republik, uniformed police arrived by the truckload and encircled the crowd. Truncheon attacks broke up the demonstrators. Far away, birthday skyrockets burst in the night sky. The jeans-and-training-shoes army broke ranks, gathered its wounded, dispersed and ran and limped away along the damp streets to the dark, tumbledown ravines of Prenzlauerberg. The injury toll was over 100.

The "Gorby, Gorby" calls were the ones that really got under Honecker's skin. He refused to believe the demonstrators were not Western-inspired agitators. He was so annoyed that, according to Gorbachev, Honecker later told Krenz:

'You organized that demonstration. I'm not letting you get away with it.' And Margot was really sour. Yes, she complained to Honecker that it was all a conspiracy.[11]

On the streets, people were confident that, with Gorbachev in charge of the Soviet Union, no Soviet tanks would be ordered onto the streets to put down any insurrection, as had happened in 1953. They were right. Gorbachev remarked before departing for Moscow in frustration with Honecker's inflexibility, "Do we have to prepare for the worst? We have done all we can. What they want, support for Honecker from our position of strength, will not happen."[12] The tanks would not be sent in.

There was a coolness between the two men as Gorbachev prepared to leave for the airport that night. Honecker accepted with relief a suggestion that he remain with the other guests instead of accompanying the Soviet party to the airport. There was nothing more for him and Gorbachev to talk about.

Members of a band brought from Dresden to play during the evening had just arrived, and, as they stood at the foot of the stairs leading up to the banquet hall, were amazed to see Mikhail and Raisa Gorbachev come down on their own, wish them a good evening, and disappear into the night.[13]

Falin himself made no secret of his feelings, which were the same as Gorbachev's, "Soviet armed forces would not intervene, regardless of the pattern of events, as long as they had an internal character."[14]

Meanwhile, the tension was rising further south in Leipzig, as protesters gathered. The security forces were acting with increasing aggression. The "Chinese Solution"—a reference to the massacre of students in Beijing just a few months before in June—was everybody's fear.

Leipzig was to be the turning point of the revolt.

Saturday, October 7: Superintendent Friedrich Magirius, minister at the St. Nikolai church in Leipzig, saw events unfold from the vicarage window:

> Between 11:00 a.m. and 7:00 p.m., the city was turned into a military base. I could see police with helmets, shields and truncheons drive into demonstrators. Hour after hour, replacement units were brought in.
>
> The police did not discriminate between people who just happened to be passing by…they continued using force and carted people away in trucks. In front of our church…an older man was speaking to a group of people. The police suddenly drew up. The man was attacked. He lay bleeding on the ground…it was terrible …I even saw one man, already unconscious, get hit again.
>
> That night…the police appeared again. People disappeared into the police vehicles. They vanished like ghosts. The candles continued burning.[15]

On Monday, October 9, the Leipzig marchers turned out in the biggest demonstration in the country since the revolt in 1953. An official announcement said that a "protective operation" was to be made to defend the post office and the Hauptbahnhof. People were warned to leave the city before 4:00 p.m. Shops were told to shut early. Rumors swept the city that extra blood plasma had been brought in.

Everybody's thoughts were concentrated by the student massacre in Tienanmen Square in Beijing where the death toll was put at between 1,000 and 3,000. In East Berlin, the massacre was officially welcomed. The party paper, *Neues Deutschland*, said it had been a reply to "a counterrevolutionary revolt by an extremist minority." Some leading members of the party favored the "Chinese solution" and one insider recalled that neither

Honecker himself nor Stasi chief Mielke ruled out gunning down the protesters.[16]

Video cameras fixed to buildings around the city carried the scenes to Stasi headquarters. All afternoon, officers clustered round television monitors. Four churches held services. The conductor of the Gewandhaus Orchestra, Kurt Masur, passed a message—without party permission—to a radio station urging demonstrators not to give police or troops reason to open fire. Masur, Manfred Stolpe, the consistorial president of the Protestant church, spoke with both military and local party officials and appealed for the day to proceed peacefully.

The Karl Marx Platz is a broad concrete expanse between the glass-and-concrete Neues Gewandhaus and the clean lines of the Opera House. As the area began to fill up shortly before 6 p.m., Masur himself opened the doors of the Gewandhaus in case a bolthole were needed.

A chanting crowd of almost 100,000 moved off towards the Hauptbahnhof through a menacing alleyway of armed police and troops massed rows deep on either side.

Then the tension slowly eased. The march took place without a shot being fired.

The decisive factor was the sheer mass of people. The video cameras delivered an unambiguous message: this was not the work of troublemakers but something far greater.

The end of the incarceration, the end of the Berlin Wall, and the end of the regime were in sight.

NOTES

1. "The silence...," Guenter Schabowski in *Das Politbuero* (Reinbek bei Hamburg: Rowohlt Taschenbuch Verlag GmbH, 1990), 62-63.

2. Tommy spoke to the author in 1997. His girlfriend and daughter followed him a few weeks later when the borders were opened. All three now live in Hamburg.

3. Hungary was duly rewarded on November 17, when Horn was hosted by European statesmen at Strasbourg in a high-profile ceremony and the country's formal application for the Council of Europe was handed over and accepted. It thus became a front-runner among East Bloc states seeking to join the clubs of Western Europe.

4. "While the people...," Guenter Schabowski in *Der Absturz* (Reinbek bei Hamburg: Rowohlt Taschenbuch Verlag, 1992), 225.

5. For a first-hand account of the embassy announcement and the preceding negotiations with Shevardnadze and Fischer, see *Erinnerungen*, by Hans-Dietrich Genscher, (Berlin: Wolf Jobst Verlag, 1995).

6. "This was the hour…," Genscher, 21.

7. "Because of the…, " Wolfgang Berghofer in *Meine Dresdner Jahre,* (Berlin: Das Neue Berlin Verlagsgesellschaft, 2001) 155.

8. "We felt only…," Thoughts were in a letter to a clergyman that originally appeared anonymously in the Dresden-based *Die Union* newspaper on October 28, 1989. The author was later identified as Thomas Gloes.

9. Michael Sobotta had applied for an exit permit at the time he was arrested, but he remained in the East. Andreas and Gabriele Schulz went on to Switzerland. Both men now live and work near Dresden.

10. "He who hesitates…," Gorbachev quoted by Soviet diplomat Valentin Falin, who was with Gorbachev and Honecker, in *Politische Erinnerungen* (Munich: Knaur Verlag, 1995), 486. Falin's version of Gorbachev's departure, 484-87.

11. "You organized…," Gorbachev quoted in "Schoen, ich gab die DDR weg—Michail Gorbatschow ueber seine Rolle bei den deutschen Vereinigung," *Der Spiegel,* October 2, 1995.

12. "Do we have to…," Gorbachev quoted by Falin, 487.

13. Episode related by Michael Sobotta, who personally knew members of the band.

14. "Soviet armed forces…," Falin, 487.

15. "Between 11:00 a.m. and…," Text of Magirius's diary was published widely.

16. Some leading members favored the "Chinese solution," according to Peter Przybylski, in *Tatort Politbuero,* vol. 2 (Berlin: Rowohlt Berlin Verlag GmbH, 1992), 123. Przybylski was an East German public prosecutor.

EPILOGUE—THE FUTURE

EASTERN GERMANY'S PROSPECTS of emerging soon from its economic and psychological wilderness remain remote. Few of the omens are good. Attitudes on both sides of the divide remain far apart. Most Westerners can't be bothered even thinking about Easterners' problems. They merely see money being poured into a barrel without a bottom and a lot of ingrates voting for politicians associated with a dark past. Too many Easterners are caught in a trap in which they can't escape their own selective memory and continue to vote for The Left.PDS, even though few believe it has any answers to the major problems of the day. Although most Easterners do not support The Left.PDS, the issue does involve a a large minority. In the 2002 election, this minority did pull itself out of the soup of introverted misery but afterwards just let go and fell back into it.

A scintilla of political innovation might have been expected during the election campaign three years later, in September 2005 as the political parties competed for Eastern votes. But no party came up with a convincing Plan East.

Worse, some politicians seemed hell-bent on rubbing salt into the wounds. The main offender was Edmund Stoiber, a member of the Christian Democrats' sister party, the Bavarian-based Christian Social Union. While he was on the campaign trail, opinion polls reported a surge of support for The Left.PDS. Stoiber said, "The fact that in the former East Germany those great political failures, Gysi and (Oskar) Lafontaine, can win about thirty-five percent of the vote is for me unfathomable. I don't accept that the East decides once again who will be Germany's chancellor. The frustrated must not decide Germany's future."

The next day, Stoiber pointed out that Left.PDS election posters showed a photograph of Lafontaine, and he pointed out that Lafontaine, as a member of the SPD, had opposed unification. Stoiber added that Lafontaine had wanted to prevent Easterners from joining the social security system. And then he said, in reference to Eastern backing for The Left.PDS, "Only the dumbest of calves choose their own slaughterer."

The reaction was vicious. CDU/CSU party officials bent over to pick up the bits and to explain that what he meant was this and not that. But Stoiber was not finished. Later, in a reference to the voting habits of Easterners, he told a cheering audience in his conservative political heartland of Bavaria that "if everywhere were like Bavaria, we would have no problem. But, ladies and gentlemen, unfortunately, people everywhere are not as clever as those in Bavaria."[1]

Former German President Richard von Weizsaecker reacted quickly and acidly by saying Stoiber "has relatively little knowledge of Eastern Germany. He is always concerned with approval in Bavaria, whose people also know too little about Eastern Germany."[2]

Stoiber was not just another politician. He was also prime minister of Bavaria, a state that has been governed by the CSU for longer than most people care to remember. That he was prepared to sound like the mayor of a two-horse hick town to exploit the deep-seated mistrust of a predominantly Catholic and conservative region for a predominantly protestant and once-communist East, shows the depth of the East-West divide in some places.

However, with the sounds of Stoiber's grubby little *Schauspiel* still echoing, hopes for a more united future were raised when an Easterner, Matthias Platzeck, was elected national chairman of the Social Democrats. With the Christian Democrats led by the new chancellor, Angela Merkel, Germany two major parties were headed by former East Germans. *Der Spiegel* news magazine marked the occasion by featuring both on a front cover, standing side-by-side staring resolutely into the future in an artist's parody of a 1953 East German socialist realism propaganda poster.

The magazine prefaced its story by asking, "Will a 'take-off East' now lead Germany out of the crisis?"[3]

The answer was "no." After 146 days, Platzeck quit because of ill health.

NOTES

1. The Stoiber controversy was a major running news stories. See, for example, "Vom Gegner Belauert," "Verdirbt Stoiber Merkel die Wahl?" and "Stoiber und die Union: Mit Feuereifer Eigentore," *Hamburger Abendblatt*, August 12, 2005; "Haerter, Emotionaler," "Die Duemmsten Kaelber," *Der Spiegel*, August 15, 2005; "Der Osten Kann Eine Vorreiterrolle Spielen—FDP Vizechefin Pieper ueber den Aufbau Ost, zu viel Buerokratie und den Solizuschlag," *Berliner Zeitung*, August 17, 2005; "Schoenbohm vor dem Ruhestand," *Berliner Zeitung*, August 18, 2005.
2. "Has relatively little...," Richard von Weizsaecker in "Es ist Wunderbar, von Bamberg nach Naumberg zu Fahren...," *Wirtschaft & Markt*, October, 2005.
3. "Will a 'take-off'...," in "Hausmitteilung," *Der Spiegel*, November 7, 2005.

GLOSSARY

EAST GERMANY is the name commonly used to refer to the German Democratic Republic (GDR), which was established in 1949 in the Soviet zone of occupation. In the united Germany, this geographical entity is now referred to as EASTERN GERMANY.

EAST BERLIN, the eastern part of Berlin, was the capital city of East Germany. In the united Germany, it is now known as EASTERN BERLIN.

WEST BERLIN was the capitalist (noncommunist) part of the city of Berlin.

SED are the German initials of the Socialist Unity Party, which ruled East Germany for forty years. It was formed in 1946 when the communist party, realizing that the Social Democrats (SPD) had far greater popular support in the Soviet zone of occupation, forced the zone SPD to merge with it. The new party eliminated all SPD influence and remained communist in all but name.

PDS are the initials of the Party of Democratic Socialism, which directly succeeded the disgraced SED when East Germany was collapsing in 1989.

THE STASI was the East German secret police. Stasi is an acronym formed from *STAatsSIcherheit*, (Ministry for State Security).

FDY was the Free German Youth, the mass East German youth movement whose members, dressed in blue-and-white uniforms, were prominent at public events.

COMMUNISM is the most widely accepted term indicating the economic and political systems of, among others, those East Bloc countries under Soviet dominance during the Cold War.

STALINISM is the use of systematic terror to enforce compliance with state rule in a communist state.

Currency Note: All dollar equivalents shown are U.S. dollars at the rate applying at the time. East marks have not been converted because there is no meaningful way of converting a non-convertible currency. West marks (often known as deutsche marks) before 1971 have been left unconverted. So have some smaller sums.

SELECT BIBLIOGRAPHY

Allen, Bruce. *Germany East—Dissent and Opposition*. Montreal: Black Rose Books, 1991.

Arnold, Karl-Heinz. *Schild und Schwert*. Berlin: edition-Ost, 1995.

Bayer, Wolfgang; Berteit, Herbert; Busch, Ulrich; Ehrenberg, Herbert; Hickel, Rudolf; Mai, Karl; Nolle, Karl; Priewe, Jan; Richter, Edelbert; Steinitz, Klaus. *Ostdeutschland—Eine Abgehaengte Region?* Dresden: Junius Verlag, 2001.

Bennewitz, Inge and Potratz, Rainer. *Zwangsaussiedlungen an der inner deutschen Grenze*. Berlin:Ch. Links Verlag, 1994.

Borchers, Andreas. *Neue Nazis im Osten*. Munich: Wilhelm Heyne Verlag, 1992.

Brinkschulte, Wolfgang; Gerlach, Hans Joergen; and Heise, Thomas. *Freikaufgewinnler*. Berlin: Ullstein, 1993.

Christ, Peter; and Neubauer, Ralf. *Kolonie im eigenen Land*. Reinbek bei Hamburg: Rowohlt Taschenbuch Verlag, 1993.

Ditfurth, Christian v. *Ostalgie oder linke Alternative*. Cologne; Verlag Kiepenheuer & Witsch, 1998.

Eppelmann, Rainer. *Fremd im Eigenen Haus*. Cologne: Kiepenheuer & Witsch, 1993.

Falin, Valentin. *Politische Erinnerungen*. Munich: Knauer, 1995.

George, Klaus; and Uhlmann, Steffen. *Zur Sache Ost*. Berlin: W & M Verlagsgesellschaft, Edition klageo, 2000.

Gill, David; and Schroeter, Ulrich. *Das Ministerium fuer Staatssicherheit, Anatomie des Mielke-Imperiums*. Berlin: Rowohlt Berlin GmbH, 1991.

Grix, Jonathan; and Cooke, Paul, eds. *East German Distinctiveness in a Unified Germany*. Birmingham: University of Birmingham Press, 2002.

Hasselbach, Ingo; and Bonengel, Winfried. *Die Abrechnung—Ein NeoNazi steigt aus*. Berlin: Aufbau Taschenbuch Verlag, 1993.

Havemann, Robert. *Ein deutscher Kommunist: Rueckblicke und Perspektiven aus der Isolation*, Rowohlt Verlag GmbH, Reinbek bei Hamburg, 1978.

Herms, Michael. *Heinz Lippmann—Portraet eines Stellvertreters*. Berlin: Dietz Verlag, 1996.

Herrnstadt, Rudolf. *Das Herrnstadt-Dokument*. edited by Nadja Stulz-Herrnstadt. Reinbek bei Hamburg: Rowohlt Taschenbuch Verlag, 1990.

Hertle, Hans-Hermann. *Der Fall der Mauer—die unabsichtigte selbstaufloesung des SED-Staates*. Opladen: Westdeutscher Verlag, 1996.

Hough, Dan. *The Fall and Rise of the PDS in eastern Germany*. Birmingham: University of Birmingham Press, 2001.

Janka, Walter. *Schwierigkeiten mit der Wahrheit*. Reinbek bei Hamburg: Rowohlt Taschenbuch Verlag, 1989.

Janson, Carl-Heinz. *Totengraeber der DDR—wie Guenter Mittag den SED-Staat ruinierte*. Duesseldorf: Econ Verlag, 1991.

Ketman, Per and Wissmach, Andreas. *DDR*. Anders Reisen series. Reinbek bei Hamburg: Rowohlt Taschenbuch Verlag, 1986.

Koehler, John O. *Stasi—The Untold Story of the East German Secret Police*. Boulder, Colorado: Westview Press, 1999.

Lang, Jochen von. *Erich Mielke, Eine deutsche Karriere*. Reinbek bei Hamburg: Rowohlt Taschenbuch Verlag, 1991.

Lengsfeld, Vera. *Von Nun an Ging's Bergauf...Mein Weg zur Freiheit*. Munich: Langen Mueller, 2002.

Leonhard, Wolfgang. *Das Kurze Leben der DDR—Berichte und Kommentare aus vier Jahrzehnte*. Stuttgart: Deutsche Verlags-Anstalt, 1990.

———. *Die Revolution entlaesst ihre Kinder*. Cologne: Kiepenheuer & Witsch, 1992.

———. *Spuren Suche*. Cologne: Kiepenheuer & Witsch, 1994.

Lienicke, Lothar; and Bludau, Franx. *Todesautomatik*. Kiel: Stamp Media, 2001.

Lippmann, Heinz. *Honecker—Portraet eines Nachfolgers*. Cologne: Verlag Wissenschaft und Politik, 1971.

Maaz, Hans-Joachim. *Der Gefuehlstau—ein Psychogramm der DDR*. Munich: Droemersche Verlagsanstalt—Th. Knauer Nachf., 1992.

Martin, Ernst. *Zwischenbilanz: Deutschland politik der 80er Jahre*. Stuttgart: Verlag Bonn Aktuell GmbH, 1986.

Modrow, Hans; with Schuett, Hans-Dieter. *Ich wollte ein neues Deutschland*. Munich: Econ & List Taschenbuch Verlag, 1999.

Mueller, Uwe. *Supergau Deutsche Einheit*. Berlin: Rowohlt Berlin Verlag, 2005.

Nirumand, Bahman, ed. *Angst vor den Deutschen*. Reinbek bei Hamburg: Rowohlt Taschenbuch Verlag, 1992.

Nollau, Guenther. *Das Amt*. Munich: C.Bertelsman Verlag, 1978.

Przybylski, Peter. *Tatort Politbuero—die Akte Honecker*. Reinbek bei Hamburg: Rowohlt Taschenbuch Verlag, 1991.

Rehlinger, Ludwig A. *Freikauf. Die Geschaefte der DDR mit politisch Verfolgten 1963-1989*. Berlin: Ullstein, 1991.

Riehl, Hans. *Die Mark—Die aufregende Geschichte einer Weltwaehrung*. Hanover: Faeckeltraeger-Verlag Schmidt-Kuester GmbH, 1978.

Sauer, Heiner; and Plumeyer, Hans-Otto. *Der Salzgitter Report*. Berlin: Verlag Ullstein GmbH, 1993.

Schabowski, Guenter. *Das Politbuero*. Reinbek bei Hamburg: Rowohlt Taschenbuch Verlag, 1990.

———. *Der Absturz*. Reinbek bei Hamburg: Rowohl Taschenbuch Verlag, 1991.

Schaeuble, Wolfgang. *Der Vertrag*. Munich: Droemersche Verlagsanstalt—Th. Knauer Nachf., 1993.

Schmidt, Helmut. *Auf dem Weg zur deutschen Einheit*. Reinbek bei Hamburg: Rowohlt Verlag, 2005.

Schulz, Torsten. *Der Boxermacher—Manfred Wolke und Seine Champions*. Leipzig: Gustav Kiepenhauer Verlag, 2002.

Steingart, Gabor. *Deutschland: Der Abstieg eines Superstars*. Munich: Piper Verlag, 2005.

Thuermer, Mary; and Goetting, Markus. *Henry Maske—Der Gentleman Boxer*. Munich: Wilhelm Heyne Verlag, 1995.

Wawrzyn, Lienhard. *Die Blaue: das Spitzelsystem der DDR*. Berlin: Verlag Klaus Wagenbach, 1990.

Weber, Hermann. *Aufbau und Fall Einer Diktatur—Kritische Beitraege zur Geschichte der DDR*. Cologne: Bund-Verlag, 1991.

Weise, Klaus. *Henry Maske—Auf eigene Faust—Der Weg Zum Champion*. Berlin: Verlag Sport und Gesundheit, 1995.

Wollenberger, Vera. *Virus der Heuchler*. Berlin: Elefanten Press, 1992.

INDEX

CHILE AND THE NAZIS: FROM HITLER TO PINOCHET
Graeme S. Mount

Based on documentary evidence from the archives of the Chilean Foreign Office, and from U.S., British, German, and, intercepted, Japanese documents, Mount is one of the first authors to provide evidence of the events and circumstances surrounding Chile's reluctance to sever diplomatic ties with Nazi Germany allowing it to maximize its opportunities there, influencing Chilean politicians, military operations, and the popular media.

> "Mount reveals the conflict, the espionage, and the difficulty with policy which resulted from widespread Nazi influence...all issues that continue to be of importance even now, after the return of democracy to Chile."
> —Professor Florentino Rodao, Asóciacion de Estudios del Pacífico

> "A most impressive book, based on a variety of archival and oral historical sources from three continents...about a hitherto little-known, but fascinating aspect of twentieth-century history."
> —Stan Hordes, University of New Mexico

2001: 204 pages, paper 1-55164-192-5 $19.99 ✳ cloth 1-55164-193-3 $48.99

PURE SOLDIERS OR SINISTER LEGION: THE UKRAINIAN 14TH WAFFEN-SS DIVISION
Sol Littman

Traces the 14th Waffen-SS Division's fortunes from its formation in 1943, to its surrender in 1946, their subsequent stay as prisoners-of-war in Italy, and their eventual transfer as agricultural workers in Britain. In 1950 they began their immigration to Canada and the United States. Along the way they were recruited by the British as anti-Soviet spies and by the CIA as political assassins. In spelling out the Division's history, the author attempts to shed light on its true nature.

> "A well-researched, carefully documented forcefully-presented exposé."
> —Dov Bert Levy, former consultant to the U.S. Justice Department

> "[Littman] has been able to piece together this sorry but powerful tale on the basis of meticulous reference to all key archives."
> —Gerald Fleming, Emeritus Reader in German, University of Surrey

> "There have been few detailed studies of Nazi war criminals who came to Canada after WWII. Littman's book makes a welcome, if chilling, addition."
> —Francis Henry, Emeritus, York University, Toronto

2003: 264 pages, paper 1-55164-218-2 $26.99 ✳ cloth 1-55164-219-0 $55.99

OF RELATED INTEREST

EUROPE: CENTRAL AND EAST
Marguerite Mendell, Klaus Nielsen, editors

Situates changes in the former USSR and the eastern bloc into a larger historical and sociological perspective. Contributors to this volume consider the social complexity which surrounds any political and economic system, which establishes itself very slowly and over many years. Seen in this light, it is easier to understand why the free market has not been readily accepted without some turbulent rejection. Contributors include: John Campbell, Mihailo Crnobrnja, Agnes Czako, Endre Sik, Jerzy Hausner, Bob Jessop, Tadeusz Kowalik, Domenico Mario Nuti, Birgit Muller, Yakov M. Rabkin, Hilary Wainwright, and Claire Wallace.

1995: 300 pages, paper 1-895431-90-5 $19.99 ✕ cloth 1-895431-91-3 $48.99

GERMANY EAST: DISSENT AND OPPOSITION
Bruce Allen

This work on the scope of dissent in East Germany integrates the post World War II uprising and the birth of the opposition forces with the 1980s social change movements. Discuss some developments since the destruction of the Berlin Wall.

"The book is documented thoroughly enough to satisfy the professional researcher, and is readable enough to allow general readers to see dissent for what it is: the inevitable uprising of a suffering people." —*Books in Canada*

"A useful brief survey of dissent in East Germany." —*Small Press*

"Well written...designed to inform and encourage solidarity among political activists in the west." —*Choice Magazine*

1989: 191 pages, paper 0-921689-96-9 $18.99 ✕ cloth 0-921689-97-7 $47.99

SHOCK WAVES: EASTERN EUROPE AFTER THE REVOLUTIONS
John Feffer

This book paints a vivid picture of political and economic conflicts that are dramatically reshaping daily life in today's Eastern Europe.

"At a time when the predominant Western stereotypes of the East are of unbridled 19th century entrepreneurialism or medieval ethnic barbarism, this is very welcome....an ideal introduction for those wishing to get to grips with past and present developments." —*New Economics*

"...great book for readers needing a quick, and thoughtful introduction to conditions in Eastern Europe." —*International Affairs*

1992: 366 pages, paper 1-895431-46-8 $19.99 ✕ cloth 1-895431-47-6 $48.99

OF RELATED INTEREST

POLITICS OF EUROCOMMUNISM
Carl Boggs, David Plotke, editors

In the last years of the 1970s, determined to escape from political irrelevance, the Communist Parties of France, Spain and Italy rode the waves of Eurocommunism to the gates of governmental power. While there has been general agreement that Eurocommunism was an important and significant phenomenon, there has been less of a consensus about what it represents. In this volume, the contributors consider the origins of Eurocommunism in the post-war politics of Mediterranean Europe and the continuing process of de-Stalinization and its effects on relations between the Communists Parties and other social movements. A concluding section reviews its historical significance and assesses its prospects in the 1980s.

1980: 479 pages, paper 0-919618-31-6 $14.99 ✕ cloth 0-919618-32-4 $43.99

PEOPLE AS ENEMY: THE LEADERS' HIDDEN AGENDA IN WORLD WAR II
John Spritzler

The official view of WWII was that it was "the good war," but presented here is a very different, and disturbing view that argues that the aims of the national leaders were not democracy and self-determination, but opportunities to suppress and intimidate working people everywhere from rising up against elite power.

"The research is impressive...excellent in unearthing the instances of class conflict, and internal opposition during the 'good war.' You make a strong argument, well-documented...your point of view needs to be considered seriously." —Howard Zinn, *A People's History of the United States*

2003: 216 pages, paper 1-55164-216-6 $24.99 ✕ cloth 1-55164-217-4 $53.99

POLITICS OF SORROW: THE DISINTEGRATION OF YUGOSLAVIA
Davorka Ljubisic

Written in memory to a lost homeland, to the people who died, and to the people who survived, this book is a powerful commentary on war that provides insight into the roles that history, nationalism, ethnic conflict, and religion can play.

"Finely crafted historical dialectics." —Greg M. Nielsen, *Norms of Answerability*

"Essential reading for anyone who wishes to understand the recent history of the Balkan region." —Neil Gerlach, *The Genetic Imaginary*

2003: 224 pages, paper 1-55164-232-8 $24.99 ✕ cloth 1-55164-233-6 $53.99